Customer Loyalty

How to Earn It, How to Keep It
New and Revised Edition

Jill Griffin

Foreword by
General Robert T. Herres, USAF (Ret.)
Chairman, USAA

JOSSEY-BASS
A Wiley Imprint
www.josseybass.com

Published by Jossey-Bass
A Wiley Imprint
989 Market Street, San Francisco, CA 94103-1741   www.josseybass.com

Jossey-Bass books and products are available through most bookstores. To contact Jossey-Bass directly call our Customer Care Department within the U.S. at 800-956-7739, outside the U.S. at 317-572-3986 or fax 317-572-4002.

Jossey-Bass also publishes its books in a variety of electronic formats. Some content that appears in print may not be available in electronic books.

Library of Congress Cataloging-in-Publication Data

Griffin, Jill.
Customer loyalty : how to earn it, how to keep it / Jill Griffin ;
foreword by General Robert T. Herres.—New and rev. ed.
p. cm.—(The Jossey-Bass business & management series)
Includes bibliographical references and indexes.
ISBN 0-7879-6388-7 (alk. paper)
1. Customer loyalty. 2. Customer services. 3. Customer relations.
I. Title. II. Series.
HF5415.5 .G75 2002
658.8'12—dc21

2002008566

Printed in the United States of America
SECOND EDITION
PB Printing
10 9 8 7 6 5 4 3

The Jossey-Bass
Business & Management Series

Contents

Foreword

Years ago I read a comment by George Washington on the "essential characteristics or traits of the general officers of the Continental Army: character, professional ability, integrity, prudence and loyalty." Many times since, I have thought how timeless and relevant this formula is—not just for military people, but for people in the business world and, in fact, in any professional endeavor. In the language of his day, General Washington spoke of the importance of competence *(professional ability)*, good judgment *(prudence)*, and the enduring virtues of character, integrity, and *loyalty.* Reflecting on these qualities, it seems to me that the first four attributes when acquired and sustained will ultimately inspire the latter: the precious but elusive presence of *loyalty.*

Over the course of my military career, I learned a lot about this thing we call loyalty. I learned that it is intangible, sometimes unpredictable, and a two-dimensional attribute; an individual or an institution can engender loyalty within others, or loyalty may manifest an innate commitment to an individual or institution—which is what General Washington sought. In the business context, loyalty is delivered when properly inspired, and it is received when properly earned—a two-way street. The traits that can make that exchange happen were important to Washington's generals and are equally important in the world that surrounds us, including the business world.

In practical terms, I find it hard to imagine that consumers might want to buy insurance, automobiles, appliances, or airline tickets, for example, from companies whose professional competence, good judgment, ethical behavior, and dependable performance are questionable. Some might deviate from applying these standards as they choose products and services, but few will do so by choice. Yes, companies do have personalities and can manifest the same traits that define individuals. Great companies have *character* and *integrity,* and they have leaders and employees with good judgment and professional ability; they know their business. With that knowledge, customer loyalty is virtually assured and sustainability is inevitable. George Washington demanded no more of his generals than he himself demonstrated—and there can be no doubt that he engendered not only their loyalty, but that of many colonial leaders who would serve and support him as he led our nation in the years to follow. Today's great companies do these things as well.

In this book, Jill Griffin tells the stories of companies that have successfully nurtured loyalty by creating strong customer attachment and cultivating repeat patronage; companies with character, integrity, and competence. Let me share with you a recent story of customer attachment from our own company's experience. It happened on September 11, 2001, just two hours after the first attack on the twin towers in Manhattan. A customer service representative answered the phone and heard a frantic request for help from a young woman.

"I was at the World Trade Center!" she said. "The phone lines are down! Can you please get a message out for me?"

Desperately trying to find a way to let her family in Georgia know she was safe, this woman discovered that outbound calls could still be made on 1–800 lines, so she quickly called a company she trusted and knew would help—our company, USAA. The responding service representative immediately connected the woman with her family to personally share that she was alive and safe. Such attachment between consumer and organization is indicative of the loyalty our company has inspired and enjoys.

USAA has been a pioneer when it comes to treating customers as loyal family members. Trust has been essential to USAA's success since its founding in 1922. The company's early practices were rooted in its military founders' ideals— service, loyalty, honesty, and integrity. Upon that foundation the loyalty of generations of USAA members was built and the character of the company was formed. Today USAA's 22,000 employees still embody those same values as they sustain a powerful attachment with its almost five million members.

Whether or not your organization already enjoys a strong bond with the employees and customers who are its lifeblood, I urge you to consider and then pursue the concepts revealed in this book. Then remember that true loyalty is earned and endures only when built upon a foundation of trust. And if the standards George Washington set for his generals can be met, enduring loyalty is assured.

August 2002   GENERAL ROBERT T. HERRES, USAF (RET.)
San Antonio, Texas   CHAIRMAN OF THE BOARD, USAA

About the Author

Jill Griffin is an internationally published author, business consultant, and dynamic professional speaker. In her early career, she served as senior brand manager for RJR/Nabisco's largest brand and distinguished herself as one of the youngest flagship brand managers in the corporation's history. From RJR/Nabisco, she joined AmeriSuites Hotels, where, as national director of sales and marketing, she was responsible for the chain's nationwide launch. In 1988, she founded the Griffin Group in Austin, Texas, specializing in customer and staff loyalty research, CRM program development, and management training for such firms as Dell Computer, Advanced Micro Devices, Cendant, Hewlett-Packard, Sprint, Raytheon Aircraft, Ford, and the U.S. Navy.

Griffin is the coauthor of *Customer WinBack*: *How to Recapture Lost Customers and Keep Them Loyal* (Jossey-Bass, 2001), which is recognized as one of the thirty best business books of 2002 by Soundview Executive Book Summaries.

She is the customer care columnist for *iQ,* the Cisco Systems customer magazine, focusing on technology-driven loyalty strategies. She has served on the marketing faculty at the University of Texas McCombs School of Business. Her two books are the adopted texts for the MBA-level and undergraduate courses on customer relationship management offered at the University of Texas.

Griffin is routinely among the highest-rated speakers at national and international conferences. She addresses corporate and professional audiences on such topics as customer loyalty, customer service, branding, performance measurement, customer relationship management, and market trends. She and her husband make their home in Austin. She can be reached by way of www.loyaltysolutions.com.

To my grandmother, Ada Faircloth Marsh,
who first introduced me to writing and its possibilities

To my husband, J. Mack Nunn, whose endless love and belief in me
have brought a whole new dimension to the word "loyalty"

Preface

A few months before the first edition of *Customer Loyalty* was published, an acquaintance (and fellow author) cautioned me that little would likely change for me with the publication of my book. He couldn't have been more wrong. It turned out to be a wonderful milestone in my professional life (oh heck: in my life overall!). Here are some of the highlights:

- The book has been translated into numerous languages worldwide.
- It became a Money Book Club selection.
- The U.S. Postal Service bought twenty-four thousand copies to distribute to businesses as part of a nationwide promotion.
- Such companies as Hyatt Hotels and Ford purchased hundreds of copies to hand out to their employees and channel partners.
- It was adopted as the textbook for the MBA-level and undergraduate courses on customer relationships taught at the University of Texas.

Along the way, the book has enabled me to meet journalists and editors, professional colleagues, and (most important) readers, who have reached out to share their customer loyalty experiences and insights. So, why revise the book? After all, if it ain't broke, don't fix it, right? Wrong. As Bob Dylan says, "the times they are a-changin'." To earn customer loyalty, a business must change with them.

In the preface to that earlier edition, I wrote about growing up in the 1950s in Marshville, North Carolina, where, as in many small towns, a merchant's livelihood depended on his ability to create a personalized experience for his customers. Want a fountain drink? Our pharmacist, Mr. Guion, knew to make mine a cherry Coke and offer the newest *Archie* comic book in the process. New spring dresses just arrived? Dress shop owner Audrey knew to put aside a yellow one for my mother to try on. These businesses succeeded by relying on knowledge of past customer preference and, in turn, putting that information to work to make the business relationship ever more relevant, productive, and hassle-free.

The first edition examined how to create a similar corner-store experience. But the marketplace has changed dramatically since the initial publication. Today, widespread use of the Internet (at this writing, the Commerce Department reports more than half of U.S. households are using the Net) and knowledge-management breakthroughs have created even more demanding customers who expect to buy when, where, and how they want to. Customers of this new breed demand value, and when they don't get it, they don't hesitate to take their business elsewhere. Sadly, lots of customers are jumping ship and committing "serial defection." In fact, the average company today is losing 20–40 percent of its customers annually. Why? Because many companies are delivering an "underwhelming" customer experience that falls well below the new empowered customer's expectations. As a result, today's buyer unhappily migrates from one vendor to the next in search of better value.

New challenges call for new solutions. This is why the second edition of *Customer Loyalty* offers a number of new loyalty tools and techniques (many technology-based, some not) that help create a strong bond with the customer. For example, you'll discover:

- How the Internet is changing the customer's perception of responsiveness, and which technology tools are proving critical for companies as they address this increasingly demanding buyer

- Research findings indicating that customers who engage with a firm through multiple channels (Web, phone, fax, and so forth) exhibit deeper loyalty than single-channel customers do

- Why the converged call center is the new front line for many companies, and which skills these customer service reps need if they are to serve customers well

- How channel partner collaboration drives customer value delivery, and ultimately customer loyalty

- Why establishing trust is a critical first step in growing a loyal customer, and how team selling can help

- The biggest obstacle to being sure an online newsletter is read, and tips for making your customer newsletter (online or offline) an eagerly anticipated must-read

- Why establishing an online customer community helps create loyalty, and guidelines for successfully developing and managing your community

- Why lost customers are not a lost cause (and, as an illustration, how the Toronto Raptors have used affordable voice mail technology to win back inactive fans)

- How staff feedback surveys can help build staff loyalty, and ultimately customer loyalty

- Why loyalty is ultimately earned by responding to your customer's changing value definition (and which national food brand has a track record of more than twenty years of doing this exceptionally well)

But don't be fooled into thinking that new tools rewrite the Laws of Loyalty (which you will find following Chapter Ten). They don't. The more things change, the more they stay the same. Making sure all your tools and techniques support strong loyalty principles and, in turn, propel your customers to an increasingly higher level of loyalty is the only road to lasting loyalty.

So, use this second edition in *conjunction* with the evolving new technologies and strategies influencing selling and customer service. Consider it your master blueprint for turning noncustomers into loyal advocates. After all, moving the customer to ever higher stages of loyalty is what, in the end, really counts. Welcome aboard!

Austin, Texas   JILL GRIFFIN
August 2002   www.loyaltysolutions.com

Acknowledgments

Special thanks to Carol Parenzan Smalley, Scott Campbell, and Judy Barrett, who offered critical input to the manuscript in the second edition development process.

Acknowledgments are also owed, along with gratitude, to my first-edition editor, Beth Anderson; my second-edition editor, Kathe Sweeney; and my literary agent, Jeff Herman. I also wish to thank Professor Robert Peterson (University of Texas), Skip King (American Skiing), Judy Bayer and Mary Gros (Teradata), Katy Hartrich (Build-a-Bear Workshop), J. R. Rodrigues (askasalespro.com), Jim Hoogendam (SmartPrice.com), Ann Machado (Creative Staffing), Dianna Booher (Booher Communications), David Travers and Tom Honeycutt (United Services Automobile Association), Mike Burnett (Allied Waste), Chris Rapetto (Intuit), and Walter Janowski (Gartner Group). For their research contributions, a big thank you to Professor Linda Golden and her ace team of marketing interns, including Kara Eaton, from the University of Texas McCombs School of Business.

Finally, I give thanks to my Griffin Group consulting colleagues, Michael Lowenstein (my coauthor on *Customer WinBack*), Jennifer Reed, John Fava, and Cheryl Rae, always there to shine the loyalty light for clients that are ready to uncover and understand their customer loyalty drivers.

J.G.

Customer Loyalty

CHAPTER ONE

Customer Loyalty

The Way to Many Happy Returns

I'm often asked, "Does customer loyalty still exist?" Many think it has forever vanished and that lowest price is the only thing that keeps a customer returning. But, take heart. Customer loyalty is alive and well. Look no further than computer systems manufacturer Dell Computer, affinity credit card issuer MBNA, or home improvement retailer Home Depot and you'll find companies that are consistently earning customer loyalty while their competitors struggle. But each of these companies would also tell you that in today's unforgiving marketplace, creating and maintaining customer loyalty is more complex than ever. Here's why.

Two dovetailing events have dramatically expanded *how* companies pursue customer loyalty. First, widespread use of the Internet has changed how customers expect relationship-building to work. No longer is marketing and sales information simply pushed toward the customer. Now, a company must also allow customers to pull the marketing information they want, when they want it, and complete the purchase process on their terms.

Second, technology breakthroughs, particularly in the area of knowledge management, offer new and innovative ways to nurture customer relationships. Now a company's ability to thrive depends on capturing appropriate customer data from multiple points of customer contact: a Website click stream, e-mail, telephone, fax, a call center, a kiosk or store, a reseller, or a direct sales force. When used correctly, this data enables the company to individualize its response to each customer interaction in what's often referred to as "mass customization."

1

These two dovetailing advances have created customers of a new breed, with one distinguishing quality: they want to buy the way they want to buy. Yet most companies have not caught up with this newly empowered customer, and the customer experience has suffered. Consequently, the customer feels underwhelmed, overpromised, and underdelivered. Little wonder, then, that the level of customer loyalty is so low!

In a period of unprecedented marketing innovation like what we've experienced since the mid-1990s, it's tempting to dismiss many of the true principles for building customer loyalty and instead rely solely on a perceived panacea or silver bullet. We've seen plenty. From loyalty card schemes and point programs to CRM (customer relationship management) software to massive data warehousing efforts, firms have plowed millions of dollars into such areas in search of a quick fix. But not surprisingly, many firms report disappointing results. Headlines such as "The Truth about CRM: What You Need to Fight the Hype"[1] and "Delusions of Loyalty: Where Loyalty Programs Go Wrong"[2] are increasingly appearing in industry publications, reflecting confusion, concern, and an urgent search for a better way.

Your best insurance for building a strong loyalty strategy in the new millennium is to make sure your programs are built around the tried-and-true principles of loyalty. Without a doubt, more and more breakthrough technologies will evolve. The best way to leverage these exciting new tools is to ensure that they are applied to plans and programs that embrace strong loyalty principles. Otherwise, your probability of real success is limited. As Willie Nelson croons, "It's time to get back to the basics of life"; that's what this book is all about. Let's get started.

THE WAY TO MANY HAPPY RETURNS

Although customer satisfaction is necessary to any successful business, we are learning that satisfaction alone is not enough to build a loyal customer base. In the 1980s and 1990s, customer satisfaction was the watchword for business. Everyone was rushing around to find a way to make customers happy by meeting and even exceeding their expectations. The theory was that if customers are satisfied, they buy more and do so more often. Books, articles, and seminars touted such buzzwords as *customer service, service quality,* and *service excellence.* Behind all this was the belief that customer satisfaction produces positive financial results, especially in repeat purchase. Yet the latest research findings suggest otherwise: a high level of customer satisfaction does not necessarily translate into repeat purchases and increased sales. Consider these findings:

- Forum Corporation reports that up to 40 percent of the customers in its study who claimed to be satisfied switched suppliers without hesitation.[3]

• *Harvard Business Review* reports that between 65 and 85 percent of customers who chose a new supplier say they were satisfied or very satisfied with the former one.[4]

• Peter ZanDan, whose company Intelliquest conducts market research studies for computer manufacturers worldwide, reports that in more than thirty thousand interviews, his company has never found a high level of customer satisfaction to be a reliable predictor of repeat purchase.

• Research conducted by the Juran Institute reveals that in excess of 90 percent of top managers from more than two hundred of America's largest companies agree with the statement "maximizing customer satisfaction will maximize profitability and market share." Yet, fewer than 2 percent of the two-hundred-plus respondents were able to measure a bottom-line improvement from a documented increase in the level of customer satisfaction.[5]

Most managers assume that a positive correlation exists between customer satisfaction scores and customer buying behavior. The general belief is that increasingly higher satisfaction scores from a customer are followed by an increase in the customer's share of spending, rate of referral, and willingness to pay a premium price. Yet, as the findings I've cited illustrate, this correlation is unreliable. Satisfaction level does not necessarily translate into higher sales and profits.

What accounts for this disparity? Why would customers indicate one thing, yet do another? A number of factors contribute to the problem. At the time customers are queried about their satisfaction, they are unaware of future decisions and actions. For example, a software company analyzed the satisfaction ratings of a group of customers taken a short time before they defected to a competitor and found the ratings virtually identical to those of an equally large group of customers who remained with the company. Yet these reportedly satisfied customers went to a competitor once they became aware of greater value.

Another reason satisfaction scores are unreliable is that people often use these surveys as a way to communicate desires beyond the norm of sufficiency. This is often the case with price. The Juran Institute reported that for more than 70 percent of businesses studied, price scored first or second as the feature with which customers were least satisfied. Even so, when nearly all of the customers who had shifted spending to competing suppliers were interviewed, in no case were more than 10 percent of the lost customers motivated to switch because of price. In addition, a representative sample of customers who had exhibited the most loyalty in terms of buying behavior were as likely to report the same level of dissatisfaction with price as the lost customers.[6]

Perhaps the biggest reason for the disparity between satisfaction rating and repeat purchase is the measurement of satisfaction itself. Recent studies confirm that current satisfaction measurement systems are not a reliable predictor of repeat purchase. Some of the most convincing evidence is found in the research of Professor Robert Peterson of the University of Texas, who found that in most surveys of customer satisfaction, a substantial 85 percent of an organization's customers claim to be "satisfied" but still show willingness to wander away to another provider.[7]

This lack of correlation between customer satisfaction and repeat purchase may be partly due to the difficulty of accurately and reliably measuring customer satisfaction. Satisfaction measures are largely self-reported, which means that a customer answers a series of questions, usually in the form of a written survey. A number of factors can inflate a self-reported satisfaction rating[8]:

- *Question formation.* A question posed in positive terms ("How satisfied are you?" versus "How dissatisfied are you?") gets a more favorable response. The majority of satisfaction survey questions are posed in positive terms.
- *Measurement timing.* Measurements taken immediately after purchase are likely to yield more favorable responses than measurements taken later.
- *Mood of respondent.* A respondent's overall mood at the time of the survey can affect response.

An additional factor contributing to an overstated customer satisfaction rating is customer reluctance to admit having made a bad purchase. They feel a low satisfaction rating reflects badly on their purchase behavior or judgment. Therefore, they compensate by distorting their satisfaction with a higher-than-deserved rating.

Given the many problems with satisfaction measurement, it is little wonder that many companies are failing to find a strong relationship between customer satisfaction measures and economic performance. For example, the CEO of a manufacturing company that produces industrial equipment was feeling intense frustration with the lack of results from his firm's satisfaction program when he remarked, "It gives me a warm feeling to know that the customer satisfaction score is up again for the fourth straight year. Now, can someone tell me why profitability and market share are down again?"[9]

From the customer's inclination to overstate satisfaction to questionable extrapolation of data into sales and profit projections, one thing is certain: current satisfaction measurement systems cannot be used as a reliable predictor of repeat purchase.

THE TRUE MEASUREMENT: CUSTOMER LOYALTY

If customer satisfaction is unreliable, then what measurement is tied to repeat purchase? The measurement is *customer loyalty.* In the past, efforts to gain customer satisfaction have attempted to influence the attitude of the customer. The concept of customer loyalty is geared more to *behavior* than to attitude. When a customer is loyal, she exhibits purchase behavior defined as nonrandom purchase expressed over time by some decision-making unit. The term *nonrandom* is the key. A loyal customer has a specific bias about what to buy and from whom. Her purchase is not a random event. In addition, *loyalty* connotes a condition of some duration and requires that the act of purchase occur no less than twice. Finally, *decision-making unit* indicates that the decision to purchase may be made by more than one person. In such a case, a purchase decision can represent a compromise by an individual in the unit and can explain why he is sometimes not loyal to his most preferred product or service.

Two important conditions associated with loyalty are customer retention and total share of customer. *Customer retention* describes the length of relationship with a customer. A customer retention rate is the percentage of customers who have met a specified number of repurchases over a finite period of time. Many companies operate under the false impression that a "retained" customer is automatically a loyal customer. For example, the CEO of a burgeoning computer hardware company boasted, "We haven't got a loyalty problem; we've retained virtually every customer we've ever sold to." But on closer inspection, the executive discovered that at least 50 percent of retained customers (those who made a minimum of one purchase annually after the initial sale) were buying add-on systems and services from competitive vendors.[10] Retention was not the problem, but share of customer was.

A firm's *share of customer* denotes the percentage of a customer's budget spent with the firm. For example, a firm captures 100 percent, or total, share of a customer if the customer spends the entire budget for the firm's products or services with that firm. Whenever a firm's competitor captures a percentage of the customer's budget, then the firm has lost that portion, or share, of the customer.

Ideally, both customer retention and total share of customer are essential to loyalty. There are, however, some situations (government accounts, for instance) where the customer is restricted from purchasing from just one vendor. In such a case, earning a 50 percent share of the customer may be the most a firm can accomplish. Likewise, in many packaged goods categories, the buyer can be and frequently is multibrand-loyal. For example, a customer may be equally loyal to two beers, Michelob and Amstel, buying one this week and the other the next. In such circumstances, market conditions and product usage can dictate the limits of loyalty.

If customer retention and total share of customer are essential for loyalty, how are these buying behaviors achieved? An important first step is to notice how a number of well-established business strategies actually work against developing customer loyalty. The most frequently used of these strategies is market share.

WHY A MARKET STRATEGY CAN LIMIT LOYALTY

Since the 1970s, American companies have waged a fierce battle to win market share. In short, building market share by attracting new customers was considered *the* way to maximize profits. The belief was so popular that over the last two decades most leading U.S. firms pursued a market share strategy with the expectation that it was the surest way to the greatest profit. Pursuing market share has made many companies more concerned with finding new customers than with holding on to old ones. Statistics show that on average, American businesses spend seven times more money attracting new customers than trying to keep existing ones. Says Bain and Co. consultant Frederick F. Reichheld, "Ask a bank manager how many new accounts he signed up last month and he will probably know off the top of his head. Ask the same person how many accounts he has lost in the past month, and you will most likely draw a blank stare."

Table 1.1 compares the strategy of building market share with that of building loyalty. Note that although both strategies are used under the same market conditions (low-growth, saturated market), this is where the similarity ends. Success and failure in a market share strategy are evaluated in regard to competitors, while success and failure in a loyalty strategy are evaluated in terms of retention and share of customer.

ATTRACTING PRICE SHOPPERS, NOT LOYALTY SEEKERS

Because more effort is required to create customer switching than to maintain the status quo, costs are generally higher for the market share strategy than for the loyalty strategy. For example, in the market share strategy, a company often

Table 1.1. Increasing Market Share Versus Building Loyalty.

	Market Share Strategy	Loyalty Strategy
Goal	Buyer switching	Buyer loyalty
Market condition	Low-growth or saturated markets	Low-growth or saturated markets
Focal point	Competition	Customers
Measures of success	Share of market relative to competition	Share of customer; customer retention rate

uses a host of short-term marketing tools (a coupon, sales promotion, discounted price, and so forth) to woo the customer from a competitor. Though often creating a short-term boost in sales, these actions alone rarely create lasting value for customers, many of whom eventually leave for a competitor.

Consider the outcome of the "coffee wars." In the 1980s, three major brands—Folgers, Maxwell House, and Hills Brothers—dominated the ground coffee market. Each had roughly a third of the market and equally loyal consumer franchises. At one of the companies, a decision was made to implement an aggressive promotional plan to stimulate trial purchase among drinkers of competitive brands. The plan included heavy use of coupons to stimulate switching. The strategy worked so well that the other brands initiated similar programs. As a result, a massive war over market share began and heavy promotional activity became the industry standard. The results were disastrous for coffee manufacturers. By the early 1990s, brand loyalty had been severely eroded and many buyers had come to view coffee as a commodity rather than a preferred brand.

In the never-ending quest to build market share, these coffee manufacturers traded their brand-loyal customers for those who were price-sensitive and eroded their profits in the process.

But the damage didn't stop there. By turning the industry into a commodity market, the manufacturers unwittingly created a nearly perfect environment in which a little-known Seattle coffee retailer named Starbucks could develop a coffee bar empire. Under the leadership of CEO Howard Schultz, Starbucks looked closely at what was missing for coffee enthusiasts and created a unique way to address those wants. The company stopped thinking about coffee as simply a product that was bagged and sent home with the groceries and instead started selling coffee by the cup through Starbucks coffee bars.

Modeled after coffee houses in Italy, the Starbucks coffee bar was carefully designed to appeal to a coffee lover's five senses. The store's rich coffee aroma, married with flavorful coffee (at a premium price), browser-friendly product displays, beautiful music, and relaxing tables and chairs, were an instant hit with consumers who soon made a visit to Starbucks part of their daily routine. Today, the average Starbucks customer visits eighteen times a month and spends an average of $3.50 a visit. With close to three thousand stores and still growing, the company experienced 50 percent sales and profit growth through much of the 1990s. Starbucks is proof positive that real value, not price promotion, wins customer loyalty.

As the coffee industry illustrates, misused sales promotion can turn a loyal customer into a price-sensitive buyer. Research shows that such short-term marketing tools can increase the price sensitivity of all consumers. As a result, a company finds itself in a dilemma whereby it has little choice but to offer coupons and discounted prices because of continuous competitive promotion and strong customer conditioning. In this market, customers feel cheated when they don't have a coupon, rather than feeling rewarded when they do.

Home delivery pizza is another industry that has created a situation in which the customer is always searching for the lowest price. Customers who respond only to price cutting may churn orders, but they seldom become loyal customers. They buy from whichever vendor offers the lowest price.

WHEN HETEROGENEOUS CUSTOMERS MEET HOMOGENEOUS PRODUCTS

The problems with a market share strategy go even further. Pursuing market share can actually work against developing loyalty. Why? Because a substantial gain in market share can increase the diversity of the company's customer base. As a result, the company is forced to serve an increasingly heterogeneous base of customers with a homogeneous set of products and services. This disparity can create a dangerous dynamic within the company: the service and attention once available to high-potential customers are undercut and diluted to cater to an increasing assortment of less-promising customers. To make matters worse, the high-potential customers are undoubtedly receiving exceptional care and service from other companies in other industries. This positive experience with other companies makes them increasingly sensitive to and often intolerant of a company delivering anything less. It also makes them ripe for a competitor that can offer a more specialized product or service tailored specifically for the customer's particular needs.

Serving heterogeneous customers with homogeneous products has been the downfall of innumerable retailers, from department stores and variety stores to supermarkets, drugstores, and hardware stores. Caught in the middle and challenged on either side by specialty stores and volume discounters, many of these "all things to all people" stores have been forced to close their doors.

Those retailers that have successfully remained in the middle have changed their operations drastically. They have centralized management and downsized departments where they are unable to offer the customer a clear advantage. Many have remodeled their stores to resemble a series of specialty stores under one roof. In fact, such stores as Nordstrom and Lord and Taylor are no longer considered department stores but rather departmentalized specialty stores. Relationship building with customers is a priority. In many of these stores, a computer program linked to the cash register records the customer's address as well as purchase. The store uses the data to alert shoppers of sales and new merchandise shipments that match their buying profiles.

Today's companies must manage a strange paradox: in the race to win market share and its promise of profit, a company risks (and often loses) the highest-margin customers and in doing so worsens profitability rather than improving it. A company interested in building a solid, loyal customer base uses an approach different from that of a company interested in simply building market share. Loyalty building requires the company to emphasize the value of its products or services and to show that it is interested in building a relationship with the customer. The company recognizes that its business is to build a stable customer base rather than make a single sale. This shift in emphasis is sometimes subtle, but it is necessary to create loyalty among customers and an understanding of the importance of loyal customers to the company.

When Leslie Otten purchased Sunday River Skiway in Bethel, Maine, in 1980, he had a plan.[11] He intended to use all the well-established marketing techniques he'd learned to grab a share of the market for the largely unknown resort. By offering lower prices, longer hours, and more services, Otten expected to win his new customers by wooing them away from neighboring ski resorts. He knew that his resort was comfortable, attractive, and well managed, so there would be no reason for these new customers to be dissatisfied.

To Otten's dismay, he discovered that after five years of hard work, price cutting, creating customer incentives, sales, discounts, coupons, bonuses—doing whatever it took to get skiers to patronize his Skiway—results were less than satisfying. Sure, people came to his resort, just as they did to others in the area, but profits were not growing and his marketing tactics were not paying off.

This was when Otten sat down and took a long hard look at what he'd been doing. What he found when he examined his five-year company history surprised him. With the major emphasis on tracking sales and profits from new customers, old customers were going unappreciated and dropping by the wayside. Otten found that his staff was taking existing customers for granted. The staff assumed that Skiway didn't need to worry about losing those customers to the competition.

It was clear to Otten that he had to make a new plan to develop economic security for his business. The strategy he adopted flew in the face of standard procedures. Rather than striving for market share, engaging in a competitive discounting war, or luring new customers through short-term incentives, he decided to launch a campaign of "growing" customers.

The new plan paid off big. Instead of focusing only on increased services, price breaks, or longer hours, he and his staff began doing everything possible to turn first-time skiers—those who have never been "on the boards" before—into loyal customers. Otten's plan included making first-time visitors enjoy skiing at his resort so much that they would want to repeat the experience again and again.

Before Otten started courting first-time customers back in the winter of 1984–85, only 40 percent of the people who visited Sunday River ever returned. But thanks to Otten's retention programs, more than 75 percent now returned for more ski adventures. Those repeat enthusiasts were a major reason gross revenues increased from $6 million to $18.3 million. Pretax income climbed almost fourfold, to $4 million a year.

Otten explained his strategy: "If I can turn a first-time customer into someone who skis five times a year, that's $165 in revenue. Given that, I want to make the experience—especially the first experience—of dealing with us as pleasant as possible."[12]

For people just learning to ski, the process can be particularly frightening. Otten set out to minimize their anxiety. As visitors approached the resort, signs instructed them to turn their radios to Sunday River's low-power transmitter. A friendly, soothing voice welcomed them and explained where various slopes and services could be found. To make the transition to a snowy world even more pleasant, Often stationed helpers at every step along the way. His most experienced instructors were assigned to new skiers. Staff members helped new skiers select clothing, boots, skis, and accessories.

Unlike many business people who try to make their profit the first time the customer comes through the door, Otten barely broke even on skiers new to his resort. Instead, he offered incentives for customers to come back—again and again and again. On their first visit, novices paid for their first lesson, but equipment (skis, poles, and boots) and lift ticket were all free. The student was also given the chance to sign up for two additional lessons, which included the freebies. If students completed all three lessons, they were given a coupon for a fourth day of free skiing. Furthermore, Otten sold student poles, skis, boots, and bindings at cost.

The result of all this "nonprofit" activity was surprising. By the time skiers had finished the three lessons and free day at Sunday River Skiway, they were more than likely to become loyal customers. They were familiar with the resort, the ski areas, the equipment, and the service. Not only were customers satisfied; they were virtually sold on the resort as the place to ski. Return skiers guaranteed increasing profit and a stable growth rate.

It's been more than twenty years since Otten purchased Sunday River. A lot has changed. He's grown the company from a single small ski area in Maine into American Skiing, one of the country's leading operators with nine world-class ski resorts in both the eastern and western United States. Maintaining a keen eye on customer loyalty, the company resorts are increasingly embracing the Internet to help stay close to customers. As Skip King, vice president of communications, reports, "Our research shows that skiers and snow boarders, as a group, are strong users of the Web. Because they are well educated and affluent, they have early adopter tendencies, which makes the Internet and e-mail effective vehicles for communicating with them."

From e-mailing real-time trail condition maps to offering ticket sales online, and monitoring chat rooms and bulletin boards for ideas on better ways to serve customers, American Skiing recognizes the potential of online customer communication and is working hard to put these technologies to good use. King says that "for example, we're seeing significant year-to-year increases in online ticket sales, which is one indicator that we're moving in the right direction."[13]

The average American company loses 20–40 percent of its customers each year. Recognizing this pattern and its severe impact on corporate competitiveness and profitability, a business must move away from the long-accepted market share strategy to a radically different, more long-term approach to business: building customer loyalty. This reorientation produces significant results. Through increasing the rate of customer retention by as little as a few percentage points, banks, retailers, insurance brokers, distributors, health care providers, and software manufacturers can increase their profits by 25–100 percent.

THE LONGER THE LOYALTY, THE BIGGER THE REWARDS

The rewards of loyalty are long-term and cumulative. The longer a customer remains loyal, the more profit a business can reap from this single customer. Research shows that over a cross-section of industries (credit cards, industrial

Figure 1.1. Reducing Defections 5 Percent Boosts Profits 25–85 Percent.

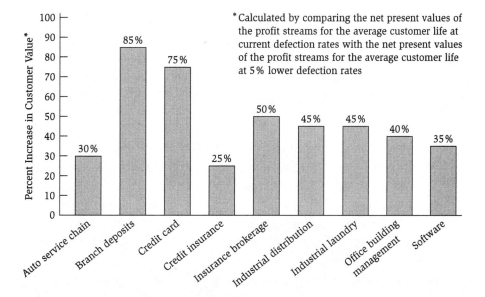

laundry, auto servicing, industrial distribution), the longer a company retains a loyal customer, the more profit that customer generates. For example, the expected profits from a fourth-year customer of an auto service company are more than triple those generated by the same customer in the first year. A company can boost profits 25–85 percent through increasing retention by as little as 5 percent[14] (see Figure 1.1).

If you find these profitability improvements too good to be true, consider a couple of factors. Increased loyalty can bring cost savings to a company in at least six areas: (1) reduced marketing costs (customer acquisition costs require more dollars); (2) lower transaction costs, such as contract negotiation and order processing; (3) reduced customer turnover expenses (fewer lost customers to replace); (4) increased cross-selling success, leading to larger share of customer; (5) more positive word of mouth; and, assuming loyal customers are also satisfied, (6) reduced failure costs (reduction in rework, warranty claims, and so forth).[15]

But the benefits of loyalty and its effect on profitability go well beyond cost savings. As usage increases, so does profit margin. For example, credit card companies spend an average of $51 to recruit a new customer. The person uses the card slowly at first, and the profit ratio is minimal. But a second-year customer is a different matter. Provided he has encountered no major problems with the company, he begins to use the card regularly and more often. The balance, and therefore the profit, grows. In the following years, he purchases even more and profits rise again. In comparison to acquisition spending, there is less expense involved in keeping this customer, and so the original $51 investment really begins to pay off.

This trend is true across industries. For one industrial distributor, profits grew steadily the longer a customer remained with the company. At some point, profits level off, but even after eighteen years with one customer the distributor found that profits from that customer were still going up. Otten, of American Skiing, said the motivating factor for his pursuit of lifetime customers was "greed"; he offered five reasons for wooing a first-time customer into becoming a lifetime buyer:

1. Sales go up because the customer is buying more from you.

2. You strengthen your position in the marketplace when customers are buying from you instead of your competition.

3. Marketing costs go down when you don't have to spend money to attract a repeat customer, since you already have her. In addition, as a satisfied customer she tells her friends, thereby decreasing your need to advertise.

4. You're better insulated from price competition because a loyal customer is less likely to be lured away by a discount of a few dollars.

5. Finally, a happy customer is likely to sample your other product lines, thus helping you achieve a larger share of customer.[16]

Regarding other product lines, Otten sells and rents lodging at his resort. Once he started building a loyal customer base, real estate income went up 52 percent, to $5.8 million, with pretax earning up 440 percent, to $1.3 million.

In addition to these five factors, one other element also supports retention. When a company is spending less on acquiring new customers, it can also spend money to continuously improve its product or service. This in turn can also help make customers more loyal.

THE LOYAL-CUSTOMER, LOYAL-EMPLOYEE CONNECTION

When a company is spending less to acquire new customers, it can afford to pay employees better. Better pay prompts a chain reaction, with a host of benefits. Describing this chain reaction, Frederick Reichheld says, "Increased pay helps boost employee morale and commitment; as employees stay longer, their productivity rises and training costs fall; employees' overall job satisfaction, combined with knowledge and experience, leads to better service to customers; customers are then more inclined to stay loyal to the company; and as the best customers and employees become part of the loyalty-based system, competitors are inevitably left to survive with less desirable customers and less talented employees."[17]

As a rule, customers are apt to become loyal if they develop a personal relationship with salespeople. A customer who regularly buys from the same person comes to rely on that person's help in making the next purchasing decision. Salespeople also find it easier to deal with the same customer again and again rather than having to establish a new relationship. This symbiotic relationship is beneficial both to the business and to the customer. In general, a repeat customer is likely to be satisfied, and an employee who is dealing with content customers is likely to enjoy the job more, do a better job, and remain with the company. A national automotive service chain implemented a customer retention program. Within a year, the company increased its retention rate by seven percentage points and reduced mechanic turnover to a fraction of the former level.

All businesspeople recognize that training a new employee costs both time and money, and that during the training period and for a time following, the employee is not functioning at maximum efficiency. If a company is able to retain good employees, loyalty both inside and outside the company improves.

THE COST OF LOSING A CUSTOMER

Just as customer retention has a positive impact on profitability, customer defection can have a negative impact. The very reasons a loyal customer is so profitable are the same reasons a lost customer is so detrimental. Simply stated, it costs less to sell and service a loyal customer. New customers are more costly. Therefore, defection by a long-term customer can cause a dramatic loss and affect the bottom line much more quickly than defection by a new customer does. It is difficult for a business to realize how expensive it is to lose a customer. (I analyze those losses in detail in Chapter Nine.) Today's accounting systems are designed to show short-term gains and losses and do not help track the benefits of maintaining a relationship with a customer over a long period of time. Expected cash flows over a loyal customer's lifetime cannot be evaluated using current systems. Yet it is clear that a satisfied, loyal customer can contribute a great deal to the financial bottom line of any company.

Consider the experience of Charles Cawley, president of MBNA America, a Delaware-based credit card company. Cawley recognized that customer defection could be an indicator of areas where the company needed improvement. In 1982, Cawley called a meeting of all three hundred MBNA employees and reported that he had had many letters from unhappy customers. He declared that from this point on, the company was going to work hard to keep these people happy and retain them as customers. To accomplish the goal, the company began asking questions of customers who were defecting: Why were they leaving? What were their problems? What did they want in a credit card company? Once the information was gathered, the company put together a plan of action and went to work. Products and processes were regularly adjusted to reflect the changing needs of the customer base.

As a result, fewer customers left the company. Eight years later, MBNA enjoyed one of the lowest customer defection rates in the industry. Some 5 percent of its customers left every year—half the rate for the remainder of the industry. Although the difference between 5 and 10 percent may seem insignificant, it reflected a huge difference in profitability. Without any acquisitions, MBNA's industry ranking moved from thirty-eight to number four. Profit soared sixteenfold.[18]

The company's loyalty legacy continues. Today, MBNA retains 97 percent of its profitable customers. In fact, the company is so committed to customer loyalty that it's the only credit card company reporting loyalty statistics in its annual report. This phenomenal customer loyalty rate drives the company's profitability. MBNA enjoys the best five-year annualized return of any bank in the S&P 500. In 2001, the company earned its fourth consecutive best-in-industry rank and inclusion in the Business Week 50, an annual ranking of America's best-performing companies.[19] MBNA is proof positive that customer loyalty drives company profits and long-term success.

The best alternative to expensive, short-term marketing tactics is a strategy that encourages customer loyalty. To begin this strategy formulation, let's take a close look at the dynamics of loyalty, covered in Chapter Two.

SUMMARY

- Contrary to popular opinion, you *can* earn loyalty from today's demanding customers.
- The Internet and other technological advancements offer new and innovative ways to nurture the customer relationship. But to be successful, these new strategies must be built around tried-and-true principles of loyalty.
- A high level of customer satisfaction does not necessarily translate into repeat purchases and increased sales.
- Question formation, measurement timing, and mood of respondent inflate a customer satisfaction rating and make it a poor predictor of purchase behavior.
- Unlike customer satisfaction, which is geared more toward attitude, customer loyalty is behavior-based; it is defined as nonrandom purchase expressed over time by some decision-making unit.
- Two important conditions associated with loyalty are customer retention and total share of customer. In the ideal, a loyal customer's purchase behavior reflects both of these conditions. The quest for market share can erode a firm's profitability and draw the focus away from its most profitable customers. Loyalty is the result of paying attention to what it takes to keep a customer and then constantly providing it. Increased customer loyalty leads to higher profitability, higher employee retention, and a more stable financial base.

GETTING STARTED

- At your next staff meeting, put this question to everyone: "Think about a company you most enjoy buying from. What is it about the experience that makes it pleasurable and keeps you coming back?" Compare those findings with your own company. What are some ways you can improve your company's customer experience?
- Look for ways to make customer loyalty an integral part of the company culture. For example, review the company's mission statement and the like, and insert the word *loyalty* in place of *satisfaction*. If customer loyalty is not part of the mission statement, consider adding it.

- Start immediately to educate employees about the reasons loyalty, not satisfaction, is the company's true goal. Use staff meetings, the employee newsletter, the employee Website, and so on, to get the message out.

- To better appreciate the financial rewards of customer loyalty, analyze two customers, a longtime one and a relatively new one. Create a side-by side comparison of marketing costs, transaction costs, cross-selling success, word of mouth, incidence of returns, and so forth between these two customers. The contrasts are likely to surprise you.

CHAPTER TWO

A Closer Look at Loyalty

Customers are more discerning than they used to be. In the 1990s, people were eager to spend and acquire, to base their buying decisions on a whim or an impulse, but the new millennium has changed all that. Consider these buyers:

When Dennis Knox, a forty-five-year-old marketing executive in Seattle, woke up one morning to discover his coffee maker had died, he went to Williams-Sonoma, the upscale kitchenware retailer, for a replacement. But he left the store without buying, figuring he could get a better deal by surfing the Internet. "Last year or the year before, I probably would have just bought it here," Knox reported outside the store. "I could still spend $120 on a coffee pot, but I am a lot more willing now to see if I can find one for $80 with some footwork. It's hard to watch your 401(k) retirement plan go down and not wonder about the economy, wonder when it's going to catch up with you."[1]

At Intel, employees using a new online booking program linked to its corporate travel department have turned into bargain hunters. As travelers scroll down a computer screen and see they can often save several hundred dollars by shifting to an earlier or later flight, many have become more willing to do so. The big chipmaker slashed travel spending 25 percent in the second quarter from a year earlier with such measures. Intel also began handling more meetings by phone and videoconferencing. "Anybody who has a modicum of Internet capability and wants to take what is now a modest amount of time can very rapidly find out and comparison shop," says Leo F. Mullin, chairman and chief executive of Delta Airlines. "There is almost perfect information out there."[2]

Marcie Everett, whose young family moved to Philadelphia from New York, is changing her buying patterns as well: "I figured out that we really didn't need the very latest electronic gadgets or the most up-to-the-minute wardrobes. I shop much more carefully now. All of a sudden, we realized that we have to look toward the future, and spending everything we have right now is foolish."

This new kind of buyer is not only limiting spending; buyers are also spending more wisely. They want real value for their money, and they are representative of hundreds of thousands of individuals and businesspeople in the market today.

How do we win the loyalty of these discerning consumers? Rewards are enormous for the company that can successfully develop, maintain, and enhance the loyalty of these savvy buyers. Managing customer loyalty begins with understanding how and why it develops. We begin this process by dissecting the customer purchase cycle.

LOYALTY AND THE PURCHASE CYCLE

Each time a customer buys, he or she progresses through a buying cycle. A first-time buyer goes through five steps: First, becoming aware of a product, and second, making an initial purchase. Next, the buyer moves through two attitude formation phases, one called "postpurchase evaluation" and the other termed "decision to repurchase." If the decision to repurchase is affirmative, the fifth step, repurchase, ultimately follows. The sequence of purchase, postpurchase evaluation, and decision to repurchase then forms a repurchase loop that is repeated a few times, or a few hundred times, during a customer's relationship with a company and its products and services (see Figure 2.1).

Figure 2.1. The Purchase Cycle.

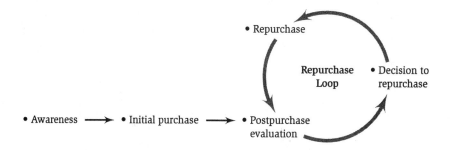

For example, a residential real estate agent may sell homes to a family once, twice, or maybe three times in the life cycle of the relationship. Following initial purchase, the repeat purchase cycle would be repeated two or three times. At the other extreme, a dry cleaner may repeat the cycle more than forty-five times annually for a family. With each revolution of the repurchase loop, the potential exists to either strengthen or weaken the bond with the customer. The stronger the bond, the greater the loyalty and the more benefit to you as a marketer. Let's take a close look at each step.

Step One: Awareness

The first step toward loyalty begins with the customer's becoming aware of your product. It is at this stage that you begin to establish the all-important "share of mind" required to move your product or service ahead of your competitor's in the mind of the prospective customer. Awareness can come about in a variety of ways: conventional advertising (radio, TV, newspaper, billboards), Web advertising, direct mail, e-mail, trade press, word-of-mouth communication (online and offline), and marketing activities such as in-store display and Web broadcast. At the awareness stage, a potential customer knows that you exist, but there is little bond between you. At this point, another company's advertising or marketing ploy can steal the customer away before you even get started.

Step Two: Initial Purchase

The first-time purchase is a crucial step in nurturing loyalty. Whether made online or offline, the first one is a trial purchase; the company can impress the customer positively or negatively with the product or service delivered, the ease of the actual purchase transaction, the encounter with employees, a store's physical surroundings, and even the company Website's page loading time or ease of navigation. Once this first purchase is made, you then have the opportunity to truly begin nurturing a loyal customer.

Step Three: Postpurchase Evaluation

After the purchase is made, the customer consciously or subconsciously evaluates the transaction. If the buyer is satisfied, or at least not dissatisfied enough to consider switching to a competitor, step four (decision to repurchase) is a possibility. As discussed earlier, most customers rate themselves as being at least satisfied with the product they are using. But satisfaction alone does not give a company a strategic advantage. Auto analyst J. D. Power agrees: "A satisfied buyer is a repeat buyer—maybe." For example, data show that the Acura automobile has an outstanding customer service rating (147, while the industry average is 118). Nevertheless, only half the owners of that car said they intended to purchase an Acura again.

Step Four: Decision to Repurchase

The commitment to repurchase is the most crucial attitude for loyalty—even more essential than satisfaction. Simply stated, without repeat patronage, loyalty does not exist. The motivation to repurchase comes from a favorable attitude toward the product or service that is high in comparison to the attitude toward potential alternatives. Decision to repurchase is often a natural next step when a customer feels a strong emotional bond with the product. Airstream recreational vehicles, certain cigarette brands, and Macintosh computers have successfully created an emotional bond with customers.

As we explore in later chapters, not every company offers a product that creates an emotional bond. Another powerful way to motivate a customer to repurchase is to establish the idea in the customer's mind that switching to a competitor will cost the customer, in terms of time, money, or performance. For example, Volvo emphasizes safety, certain photo processors offer the convenience of sixty-minute film developing, and Timex watches offer durability—qualities the customer might have to give up were she to choose a competitor's product.

Step Five: Repurchase

The final step in the cycle is the actual repurchase. To be considered genuinely loyal, the customer must buy again and again from the same business, repeating steps three through five (the repurchase loop) many times. Barriers to switching can support customer repurchase. The truly loyal customer rejects the competition and repurchases from the same company whenever an item is needed. This is the kind of customer that a business must court, serve, and nurture.

Remember Sunday River Skiway's Leslie Otten, discussed in Chapter One? Once he had created a frequent buyer, he fought to keep her. Otten understood that constantly cycling the skier through the repurchase loop was essential to building loyalty. He employed both emotional-bonding and cost-saving appeals to strengthen repurchase. New skiers were sent a certificate celebrating their completion of the learn-to-ski program. He created a frequent-skier program, modeled after airline frequent-flyer programs, that rewarded customers with a free day of skiing after as few as five visits, and customers received mailings describing special promotions. "We want to stay top-of-mind," said Otten. "We've worked too hard to have people forget us."[3]

ATTACHMENT: A PREREQUISITE TO LOYALTY

As demonstrated by the five-step purchase cycle, two factors are critical if loyalty is to flourish: an attachment to the product or service that is high compared with that of potential alternatives, and repeat purchase. Let's look at each factor closely, beginning with an examination of how a buyer forms a favorable attachment.[4]

The attachment a customer feels toward a product or service is shaped by two dimensions: the degree of preference (the extent of the customer's conviction about the product or service) and the degree of perceived product differentiation (how significantly the customer distinguishes the product or service from alternatives.) If these two factors are cross-classified, four attachment possibilities emerge, as shown in Figure 2.2.

Attachment is highest when the customer has a strong preference for a product or service and clearly differentiates it from competitive products. It is this highest attachment toward a Manhattan hair salon and its staff that prompts a friend of mine, who lives in New Jersey, to drive two hours round-trip into the city every six weeks for hair color services. Each trip costs her in excess of $90 for hair services and $22 for city parking. Though less expensive and more convenient hair care services are readily available closer to home, she feels strongly about getting the right hair color service and perceives the Manhattan salon as clearly superior to other service providers.

An attitude that is weak toward a company's product or service but differentiates it from competitors' offerings translates to high attachment and may in turn contribute to loyalty. An individual's attitude toward his auto mechanic may be mildly positive but much more so compared with that toward other mechanics. Therefore, these circumstances contribute to loyalty.

In contrast, a strong preference combined with little perceived differentiation may lead to multiproduct loyalty. This is particularly true in fast-moving consumer food goods. Sometimes a consumer chooses Ragù spaghetti sauce; other times, Prego. Sometimes the choice is Coke; other times, Pepsi. The customer has a set of two or three favorites, and situational factors such as shelf positioning and in-store promotion drive a particular purchase.

Figure 2.2. Four Relative Attachments.

Product Differentiation

Buyer Preference		No	Yes
	Strong	Low attachment	Highest attachment
	Weak	Lowest attachment	High attachment

Finally, a positive but weak preference associated with no perceived differentiation leads to lowest attachment, with repeat purchase less frequent and varying from one occasion to the next. For example, a homeowner who has her carpets cleaned sporadically may consult the telephone directory and call a different carpet cleaning service each time.

FOUR TYPES OF LOYALTY

After attachment, the second factor that determines a customer's loyalty toward a product or service is repeat patronage. Four distinct types of loyalty emerge if low and high attachments are cross-classified with high and low repeat purchase patterns (see Figure 2.3).

No Loyalty

For varying reasons, some customers do not develop loyalty to certain products or services. For example, I know a manager of a travel agency who goes anywhere in town to get a haircut, so long as it costs him $10 or less and he doesn't have to wait. He rarely goes to the same place two consecutive times. To him, a haircut is a haircut regardless of where he receives it. (The fact that he is almost bald may have something to do with it!) His low attachment toward hair services combined with low repeat patronage signifies an absence of loyalty. Generally speaking, businesses should avoid targeting no-loyalty buyers because they will never be loyal customers; they add little to the financial strength of the business. The challenge is to avoid targeting as many of these people as possible in favor of customers whose loyalty can be developed.

Inertia Loyalty

A low level of attachment coupled with high repeat purchase produces inertia loyalty. This customer buys out of habit. It's the "because we've always used it" or "because it's convenient" type of purchase. In other words, nonattitudinal, situational factors are the primary reason for buying. This buyer feels some de-

Figure 2.3. Four Types of Loyalty.

		Repeat Purchase	
		High	Low
Relative Attachment	High	Premium loyalty	Latent loyalty
	Low	Inertia loyalty	No loyalty

gree of satisfaction with the company, or at least no real dissatisfaction. This loyalty is most typical for frequently bought products. It's exemplified by the customer who buys gas at the station down the street, dry cleaning from the store down the block, and shoe repair from the nearby cobbler. This buyer is ripe for a competitor's product that can demonstrate a visible benefit to switching. It is possible to turn inertia loyalty into a higher form of loyalty by actively courting the customer and increasing the positive differentiation he or she perceives about your product or service compared to others available. For example, a dry cleaner that offers home delivery or extended hours could make its customers aware of this fact as a way to differentiate its service quality from that of competitors.

Latent Loyalty

A high relative attitude combined with low repeat purchase signifies latent loyalty. If a customer has latent loyalty, situational effects rather than attitudinal influences determine repeat purchase. I am a big fan of Chinese food and have a favorite Chinese restaurant in my neighborhood. My husband, however, is less fond of Oriental food, and so despite my loyalty I patronize the Chinese restaurant only on occasion and we go instead to restaurants that we both enjoy. By understanding situational factors that contribute to latent loyalty, a business can devise a strategy to combat them. The Chinese restaurant might consider adding a few all-American dishes to its menu to pacify reluctant patrons like my husband.

Premium Loyalty

Premium loyalty, the most leverageable of the four types, prevails when a high level of attachment and repeat patronage coexist. This is the preferred type of loyalty for all customers of any business. At the highest level of preference, people are proud of discovering and using the product and take pleasure in sharing their knowledge with peers and family. Loyal Swiss Army Knife users are constantly telling friends and neighbors how valuable the knife is; how many handy uses it has; and how often they have used it in a day, a week, or a month. These customers become vocal advocates for the product or service and constantly refer others to it. When I was starting my business, a friend was newly inspired by the Quicken software program, which automates one's checkbook. He insisted on bringing his program over and demonstrating it to me on my computer. He was displaying premium loyalty.

LOYALTY MANAGEMENT: HOW IT CAN WORK

Premium loyalty, or the lack of it, was a major reason for stagnant sales for Leegin Creative Products, a belt manufacturing company in City of Industry, California.[5] Company owner Jerry Kohl had watched with frustration as sales remained in the $9 million range for almost a decade. The $10 million barrier seemed impossible to break. Then, in the summer of 1986, Kohl went off to Harvard Business School for the first of three annual sessions in the Owner/President Management program. In the course of the seminar, Kohl realized the crux of his company's problem: Leegin was a belt manufacturer just like every other belt manufacturer. In the minds of Leegin customers (that is, stores that stocked Leegin products), there was no real penalty or substantial trade-off for buying from a competitor. In other words, Leegin had created no attachment through customer preference or product differentiation. As a result, many Leegin retailers had either no loyalty or, at best, inertia loyalty for the company's leather products.

Kohl set out to serve his customers in a way that none of his competitors did. He looked for ways to distinguish Leegin by helping his customers sell more belts and make more money.

Kohl hit upon the idea of the computer as a sales aid. What if all Leegin salespeople carried a laptop computer on all sales calls? What if their computer system allowed them to tell customers which belts were selling in other regions and which ones were not? What if, on the screen of the laptop, the customer could see an analysis of this year's sales compared with last year's or the number of belts sold by individual style, category, or color? Such a system, Kohl reasoned, could help both the buyer and the seller make an informed decision and give the customer a reason to be a loyal retailer of Leegin products.

Such a system was implemented at Leegin, and as a result profits rose steadily. In the year following the computer implementation, the company hit $10.8 million; in year two, $15 million; and $20 million the year after that. At the end of year four, Leegin recorded revenues of $47 million, and in year five $64 million.

Using computers has made life easier for both the employee and the customer. Salespeople do not have to put on a big sales pitch or try to twist an arm to make a sale; the information makes the sale. It also allows customers to select their inventory and maximize their own profit by buying belts that are selling well in their particular store. One men's store owner that deals with Leegin says, "Thanks to them, we make a lot of money in the small space we use for belts. It's probably one of the most profitable centers in the store."[6] The customer is able to trust the veracity of the information Leegin salespeople present, and loyalty grows as the system works. The intent to repurchase is there because it would be foolish for the customer to give up the service being received.

GOING MULTICHANNEL TO WIN MORE LOYALTY

"Doctoring" the inertia, latent, or no-loyalty conditions of your current customers and finding a way to upgrade them to premium loyalty are two aspects of loyalty management. An even more proactive approach is to start from the earliest stages of customer development and devise ways to nurture and enhance loyalty throughout the customer's history with your company. This way, you can better manage development of loyalty and minimize, or in some cases even avoid, such conditions as inertia or latent loyalty.

One way to proactively engage your customer and have a positive effect on loyalty is to consider going multichannel. Adding an Internet site or a catalogue operation, for example, can help deepen relationships with customers, says Judy Bayer, vice president of Teradata CRM Division. Bayer's research team tracked a group of retail customers who bought only in stores in 1998. At the start of 1999, the retailer added a call center and Internet channel. Analysis found that by the end of 1999, 40 percent of customers remained store-only buyers, and 20 percent were no longer store customers. Ten percent still shopped in the stores, but they were also now shopping on the retailer's Internet site. Twenty-five percent still shopped in the store but used the call center as well. Five percent of customers used all three channels (store, call center, Internet).

Here's where the findings get really exciting:

- Customer value (defined in this case as profit generated from the customer's actual spending) tended to stay the same for the 40 percent of customers who remained single-channel, store-only shoppers.
- For the segment who migrated to two channels, individual customer value increased between 20 percent and 60 percent.
- For those customers who migrated to all three channels, customer value increased between 60 percent and 125 percent.
- The attrition rate was also lower for customers who began using two or more channels.
- The type of product purchased by customers who shopped in more than one channel increased in breadth and variety.

But Bayer is quick to point out there is more to learn: "We still need to understand what exactly caused customers to change shopping behavior. For example, is it because they sought a deeper relationship with the retailer? Or was it because the retailer simply made it easier and more convenient to shop more frequently?"[7]

In any event, the Teradata team observed that when a store-only customer became a multichannel customer, the loyalty behavior increased: the rate of attrition decreased, the buyer was more likely to continue or increase shopping activity, and the customer increased the variety and quantity of products bought.

Staples, the office products giant, is also leveraging the benefits of going multichannel. Says Kelley Mahoney, chief marketing officer at Staples.com, "one of our mottoes is 1 + 1 = 5. That means that if you have more than twelve hundred retail stores, a catalogue business, kiosks, and a Website, then when you migrate a customer from shopping through a single channel to shopping through two channels, the person will actually spend two-and-a-half times as much as a single channel shopper would spend. When he shops three channels or more, he spends four-and-a-half times as much."[8]

These are impressive statistics. But keep in mind that simply opening additional sales and communication channels is not enough. Customer service standards within these new channels must be at least on par with the service customers have come to expect from you. Whether they call, e-mail, use your Website, or walk into your store, customers expect to receive consistent service no matter how they engage your company. If service standards are inconsistent, these additional channels will work against you, not for you, in growing customer loyalty.

THE NORDSTROM MULTICHANNEL CHALLENGE

Perhaps no one can relate more to the risks and rewards of bringing a century-old tradition of personal service to a whole new channel than Dan Nordstrom, who led the launch of NordstromShoes.com in November 1999. The name of the Seattle-based retailer with 111 stores in twenty-three states has become the gold standard by which customers, industry experts, and competitors evaluate other retailers. Translating that reputation for high customer service standards to online retailing was a huge undertaking. But by focusing first on shoes, a segment of retailing where the company has strong market leadership, Dan and his team were able to test new strategies and online processes in the quest to become the world's largest online shoe store.

The launch team included a cross-functional group of stakeholders: corporate officers, manufacturers, buyers, consultants, and contact and fulfillment center employees, who pulled together to ensure that by the time of the launch, thirty million pairs of shoes were available online. From setting up a state-of-the-art order fulfillment center in Cedar Rapids, Iowa, to sharing the around-the-clock call center with Nordstrom's existing mail order catalogue operations, Nordstromshoes.com served as the retailer's successful entry point to the Web.

Building upon this knowledge base, the company moved quickly to expand beyond the shoe segment and take all the retailer's 330,000 individual products online. The first task was to create the system that would help Nordstrom.com visitors navigate through such a large product catalogue. Organizing product around brands that the customer already knows proved successful. This online brand boutique system mirrors the retailer's in-store merchandising strategy, allowing the customer's shopping experience to be similar online and offline.

Recognizing the high customer service expectations of the Nordstrom customer, Nordstrom.com has built its site around three online service principles:

offer products customers want, make it quick and easy to locate products, and make sure that help is always available when the customer needs it. "Our Live Help function is a good tool," reports Julie Bornstein, general manager of the Internet at Nordstrom.com. "We have twenty personal shoppers, online and available with the click of the mouse, who are trained in all Nordstrom products. They help people navigate to make their purchases. A visitor to our site would click on 'Live Help,' type in the question, and click on 'Go.' If you were to type 'I need something to wear to a wedding,' rather than just to point you to the formal dresses section, the personal shopper would send a message back to ask you whether it is day or a night wedding and how formal it is."[9] Nordstrom's goal is to enable customers to ask any question and feel as though a salesperson is right there to assist them. To ensure that the personal shopper has helpful information about products, every item offered in the online catalogue hangs on a rack in the call center within easy reach of the staff so that they can see and touch the products while answering customer questions.

Nordstrom relies on customer feedback as a key way to improve online service. The more than eight thousand customer e-mails per month are read, analyzed, and categorized. New technologies such as color swatching (shows the online customer a swatch so they can see the precise color of what they are buying) were added to the site on the basis of customer requests. Each week, Bornstein hosts a weekly meeting at which a team of technical staff, personal shoppers, and manufacturers review e-mail tracking results, focus group findings, and other research. This information is used by the group to direct Nordstrom.com's work plan and priorities. With more than three hundred thousand site visitors a month, Nordstrom is constantly in search of ways to improve customer service. "Individualization, trying to make recommendations or accurate predictions for our customers, will be very important," says Bornstein.[10]

Indeed, Nordstrom recognizes that increasingly sophisticated data gathering and data mining software is creating a loyalty building opportunity online that offline channels may struggle to match. Walk in the door at Nordstrom, and the retailer has no easy way to identify who you are. But log on to the Nordstrom.com Website and the capability to personalize is much greater. Imagine what might happen if Nordstrom follows in the footsteps of the Amazon.com site. The Nordstrom site could e-greet you by name, recommend a customized selection of products on the basis of past purchases, give you a battery of candid customer reviews for every product of interest, and as you leave the site even request permission to e-mail you about upcoming offers custom-tailored to your interests.

This kind of individualization could be where Nordstrom.com is heading as the retailer increasingly uses a multichannel strategy to deliver the loyalty mandate: *create* what customers want, *remember* what customers want, *anticipate* what customers want. Early results are encouraging. Nordstrom.com's sales for the 2000 holiday season increased 300 percent over 1999, the first holiday season for the site. Combined, the Internet and catalogue divisions reaped $310 million in sales for 2000, of which 30 percent came from online sales.[11]

Beginning in Chapter Three and continuing throughout the book, we trace the evolution of loyalty over the life cycle of the customer and present strategies for anchoring a high level of loyalty at each stage of customer development.

SUMMARY

- Every time a customer buys, she advances through a buying cycle. Each step of the buying cycle is an opportunity to seed loyalty.
- Depending on the nature of the product or service, a customer may repurchase a few times or a few hundred times in the course of the relationship. With each repurchase there is an opportunity to strengthen or weaken the bond with the customer.
- A customer's level of attachment coupled with the level of repeat purchase defines the condition of loyalty.
- There are four types of loyalty: none, latent, inertia, and premium loyalty. The goal is to upgrade as many of your customers as possible into premium loyalty by converting them from the other types.
- "Doctoring" the inertia, latent, or no-loyalty conditions of your current customers and finding a way to upgrade them to premium loyalty is one vital aspect of loyalty management.
- A proactive approach to loyalty management is to start from the earliest stages of customer development and devise a way to nurture and enhance loyalty throughout the customer's history with your company.
- New research suggests that a customer who engages with a firm using multiple channels (Internet, call center, and so on) exhibits deeper loyalty than a single-channel customer.

GETTING STARTED

- Consider your firm's most popular product or service. Think through the five steps in the purchase cycle (awareness, initial purchase, . . .) and the decision process your customer goes through. What is your weakest link (or links) in this process, and how can you strengthen it (or them)?
- Using your current customer list, identify several customers who can be classified has having no loyalty. Develop a profile of the customer who typically shows no loyalty. What distinguishes this customer from others on your list? Are there elements in your current marketing program that attract this type of customer, and if so, how can they be altered?

- Using your current customer list, identify several customers who have latent loyalty. Think carefully about each one. What do you know about his or her needs and wants that could help you cultivate premium loyalty?

- Using your current customer list, identify several customers who can be classified as having premium loyalty. Develop a customer profile (age, sex, purchase habits, and so on). What distinguishes these customers from others on your list? Are there elements in your current marketing program that attract this type of customer, and if so, how can you attract more like them?

CHAPTER THREE

Growing a Loyal Customer

The Seven Key Stages

For most shoppers, produce is a generic product. Tomatoes are tomatoes, mushrooms are mushrooms, lettuce is lettuce. Most of us don't have a favorite brand of lettuce, but Frieda Caplan, chairman and founder of Frieda's Finest, has created a well-known and thriving company on the basis of selling produce with a difference. Buyers look for Frieda's name because she realized years ago that she was really in the business of serving her customers rather than selling produce.

Frieda first tested this philosophy in 1957, when for two weeks she was left on her own to watch over Giumarra Brothers, a Los Angeles produce supplier. Only a clerk at the time, Frieda promised a buyer for a major grocery store chain that she could furnish enough mushrooms for the store's major advertising campaign at Thanksgiving time. Frieda was unaware that demand for fresh mushrooms peaks at Thanksgiving—the same time supplies are also most limited.

In the produce industry, there is little time for a written contract or paper verification. Verbal commitment is how business is done, and once Frieda had committed to providing the mushrooms, she had to provide them. How did she honor her commitment? She hustled. She coaxed. When necessary, she pleaded. In some cases, she even packed her new baby into her station wagon and drove out to the mushroom farms and helped pack the mushrooms herself. Then she delivered them to her client.

Frieda realized that pleasing customers and keeping them buying were the tasks facing anyone interested in building a successful business. Today, she and her two daughters run a business that concentrates on building loyalty within their customer base. To do that, they add value through extras that make their produce stand out from everyone else's. Seminars, advertising assistance, and product selection assistance are a few of the tools the company uses to help retailers maximize sales of Frieda's produce. She gives the retailers what they need and also helps them sell to their customers. For example, she offers explanatory labels that describe how the product can be used and publishes a free newsletter for any customer who wants to receive it.

Typically, the produce supplier puts the tomatoes, lettuce, or kiwi fruit on the shelf and it's up to the retailer to sell it. Frieda realized that she would be building her own business and that of her customers, the retailers, if she helped market the produce. Instead of offering unusual fruits such as kiwi and hoping someone would want them, Frieda made available information on the fruits, and she encouraged chefs and restaurants to use them and develop recipes. In short, she developed the market that then created customer demand for the product. She proved that being proactive in winning loyalty brings big rewards.[1]

CUSTOMER DEFINED

The definition of the word *customer* offers an important insight into why a business must develop and nurture the customer rather than simply attract a buyer. It is derived from the root word *custom,* defined as "to render a thing customary or usual" and "to practice habitually."

A customer is a person who becomes accustomed to buying from you. This custom is established through purchase and interaction on frequent occasions over a period of time. Without a strong track record of contact and repeat purchase, this person is not your customer; he is a buyer. A true customer is grown over time.

THE LOYAL CUSTOMER: A WORKING DEFINITION

As we discussed in Chapter One, many companies have counted on customer satisfaction as a guarantee of future success but were disappointed to find that satisfied customers might shop elsewhere without a moment's hesitation. Customer loyalty, on the other hand, seems to be a much more reliable measure for predicting sales and financial growth. Unlike satisfaction, which is an attitude, loyalty can be defined in terms of buying behavior. A loyal customer is one who:

- Makes regular repeat purchases
- Purchases across product and service lines

- Refers others
- Demonstrates immunity to the pull of the competition[2]

There is a common denominator that runs through all these behaviors and helps explain why loyalty and profitability are so inextricably linked: each behavior, either directly or indirectly, contributes to sales.

Let's look at each of these behaviors in the context of Harley Davidson, a company with perhaps the most loyal customer base in the United States.

HARLEY-DAVIDSON: AN AMERICAN LOYALTY CLASSIC

Harley Davidson will celebrate its hundredth birthday in 2003, and it will no doubt be a big bash, if its other birthday celebrations are any indication. HD's ninety-fifth birthday celebration in June, 1998, was a four-day blowout of concerts, parties, and parades led by celebrity Harley owners Jay Leno, Peter Fonda, and Larry Hagman. Boasting a 48 percent U.S. market share and steady growth, the company had plenty to celebrate along with the one hundred thousand Harley owners and enthusiasts who flowed into Milwaukee, the company's ancestral home. One biker group attending the festivities had just covered 1,350 miles on their Harleys from York, Pennsylvania; over the course of the five-day drive to Milwaukee they were cheered by thousands of well-wishers lining the roads, honked at by congenial truckers, and welcomed at every stop by Harley dealers.

But Harleys weren't always this popular. At the start of the 1980s, few people gave Harley-Davidson much chance of surviving, and certainly no one predicted that the company would come back with such remarkable vigor. Harley was the last surviving U.S. motorcycle maker, and the company was being run out of business by Japanese manufacturers. HD realized that without some major changes, it was on the verge of extinction and thus went to work to correct a host of quality problems in its product line. By 1987, thanks in part to greatly improved products, Harley regained its market momentum. Since that time, the HD motorcycle has continued to grow in popularity and loyalty among older Americans who can afford a bike that averages $10,000.

Was the turnaround simply a matter of better manufacturing? Hardly. Although the Harleys are now better-made bikes, the major boon to business came from developing a loyal customer base. The company identified the "typical" Harley-Davidson owner and began to meet that person's needs. Although the media often present Harley owners as bearded, tattooed, and scary, most customers are ordinary middle-class or upper-middle-class citizens who work for a living—the man or woman next door. These people enjoy their motorcycles as a hobby or sport. The bikes are fun; they are exciting; they are a grown-up's toy that enhances everyday life. And Harley-Davidson customers are loyal. Once they become HOGs (Harley Owners Group members), they stay HOGs. Look at Harley owners in the context of our four-pronged definition of the loyal customer.

Makes Regular Repeat Purchases

Richard Inzerillo, a lawyer, and his wife, Deborah, went from zero to five Harleys in just fifteen months; with each purchase, they're trading up. The West Islip couple started with an Electra Glide in August 1991, bought a Sportster that September, traded in the Sportster with thirty-three miles on it a month later, bought two Softails, then replaced the Electra Glide with an Ultra Classic Electra Glide, purchased a custom Softail, and most recently bought a Nostalgia.

One segment of the Harley customer base is referred to as RUBs (rich urban bikers). These people enjoy having new bikes, having a bunch of bikes, and dressing up their bikes. They buy new models as they are offered, then they spend additional money customizing them. New seats, new exhaust pipes, and new headlights are just a few of the options that keep the customers coming back again and again. The HOG-wild Inzerillos, for example, spent $4,000 apiece on accessories for their Softails. But it's not just the RUBs who pamper their Harleys. Working-class men and women are spending big dollars to retool the bikes too.

Purchases Across Product and Service Lines

Not only do customers buy one Harley after another, but they are constantly buying accessories for their bikes. Some customers take a $10,000 bike and add additional items that raise their investment in the machine dramatically. One customer has $28,000 invested in his bike. Whenever something new comes out, the loyal customers are waiting in line to buy it.

Since the mid-1990s, the company's line of branded merchandise—available only at Harley dealers and promoted through a glossy catalogue—has taken off. These products, which are only peripherally related to the bikes themselves, are an important growth area for the company. The goods range from $500 Harley black leather jackets down to $65 fringed bras and even $12 shot glasses.

Marty Altholtz sold bikes for twenty-five years, but he finds that now a big part of his business involves selling accessories for bikers and others who just enjoy the Harley image. "We've turned into a miniature Macy's," says Altholtz.[3] Harley-Davidson offers key chains, mugs, pins, belt buckles, pen and pencil sets, shot glasses, knives, sunglasses, cuff links, piggy banks, playing cards, wallets, caps, T-shirts, sneakers, snow globes, paperweights, and ashtrays. There are HD sweatshirts, coats, and, of course, leather jackets.

Harley wants to increase the opportunity for dealers like Marty to sell to accessory-hungry prospects. Just recently, the company began selling branded apparel, collectibles, and accessories through dealer Web pages set up in its Harley RoadStore section of Harley-Davidson.com. Consumers can choose dealers on the basis of preference or proximity. A key feature of the store will be a wish list that consumers can e-mail to friends or family as gift suggestions. But don't expect to see bikes sold online. Says Ken Ostermann, Harley's interactive communications manager, "Our e-commerce initiative is designed to take customers from the online world into the physical world. . . . For motorcycle sales, those products need to be set up and delivered, and we believe that the relationship needs to be established between the dealer and that motorcycle purchaser within the physical dealership."[4]

Refers Others

Michelle Russo, a twenty-five-year-old secretary with the Long Island Railroad, had a boyfriend. He had a Harley. Before long, she had a Harley too. Although Michelle began with little interest in owning a motorcycle, her boyfriend constantly reminded her what a great machine his Harley was and what fun they would have if she rode too. Michelle's boyfriend convinced her to buy not a motorcycle, but a Harley. She began with a Sportster, considered a starter bike by Harley owners. Now she is moving up to another model, a Low Rider. Harley people say there is no known cure for Harley fever, and it seems to be spreading. Membership in HOG numbers nearly five hundred thousand.

Demonstrates Immunity to the Pull of the Competition

Harley owners refuse to admit that other kinds of bike even exist. They are sure that if someone owns another kind of motorcycle, he or she must secretly be miserable. It isn't because Harleys are the fastest or leanest bikes on the road. They aren't; many Japanese models are faster, sleeker, and perhaps more economical. But Harleys are classics. Their owners consider them beautiful machines that deliver a sort of transcendental riding experience. Getting there faster is not the point; getting there on a Harley is.

The Harley is a bike over which grown men have been known to weep, a bike commanding such love and loyalty that as many as 10 percent of its owners are said to have the name tattooed somewhere on their person.

GROWING A LOYAL CUSTOMER

How can other companies engender the same loyalty that Harley Davidson has developed? To understand the process, consider nature and the lessons it offers. In my seminars, I sometimes show a slide of an acorn and ask my participants what an acorn becomes over time (an oak tree, of course). This doesn't happen in a day, a week, a month, or even a year; it's a long, step-by-step progression.

People grow into loyal customers by stages as well. The process is accomplished over time, with nurturing, and with attention to each stage of growth. Each stage has a specific need. By recognizing each stage and meeting those specific needs, a company has a greater chance of converting a buyer into a loyal customer or client. Let's look at each stage one by one.

Stage one: suspect. A suspect is anyone who might possibly buy your product or service. We call them suspects because we believe, or "suspect," they might buy, but we don't know enough yet to be sure.

Stage two: prospect. A prospect is someone who has a need for your product or service and is able to buy. Although a prospect has not yet purchased from you, she may have heard about you, read about you, or had someone recommend you to her. Prospects may know who you are, where you are, and what you sell, but they still haven't bought from you.

Stage three: disqualified prospect. Disqualified prospects are those prospects about whom you have learned enough to know that they do not need, or do not have the ability to buy, your products.

Stage four: first-time customer. A first-time customer is one who has purchased from you one time. This person can be a customer of yours and a customer of your competitor as well.

Stage five: repeat customer. Repeat customers are people who have purchased from you two or more times. They may have bought the same product twice or bought two different products or services on two or more occasions.

Stage six: client. A client buys everything you have to sell that he can possibly use. This person purchases regularly. You have a strong, ongoing relationship that makes him immune to the pull of the competition.

Stage seven: advocate. Like a client, an advocate buys everything you have to sell that she can possibly use and purchases regularly. In addition, however, an advocate encourages others to buy from you. She talks about you, does your marketing for you, and brings customers to you.

Lost customer or client. A lost customer or client is someone who was once a customer or client but has not bought from you in at least one normal purchase cycle. When a lost customer or client becomes active again, she is considered a regained customer or client. A customer is considered to be at-risk if there is a high probability of defecting.

Online customers evolve through similar stages: surfer, first-time site visitor, repeat visitor, first-time customer, repeat customer, client, advocate, at-risk customer, lost customer, and regained customer.

THE PROFIT GENERATOR® SYSTEM AND THE CUSTOMER STAGES

The process of growing loyal customers—of shepherding them through the stages of development—can be accomplished by various methods. Choosing the most effective, most cost-efficient, and most direct methods is a challenge to every business.

How the Profit Generator System Works

In my marketing seminars, I use the image of the Profit Generator system to illustrate the marketing challenges every company must address to be profitable (see Figure 3.1).

The Profit Generator system works like this. An organization funnels suspects into its marketing system, and each is either qualified as a high-potential prospect

Figure 3.1. The Profit Generator System.

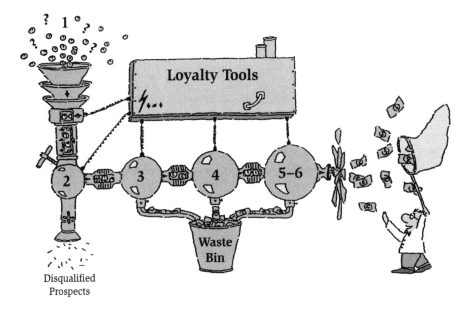

The Profit Generator System works like this: an organization funnels suspects (1) into its marketing system, and these people are either qualified as high potential prospects (2) or disqualified. Qualified prospects are then focused on with the goal of turning them into first-time customers (3), then repeat customers (4), and eventually clients (5) and advocates (6). Without proper care, first-time customers, repeat customers, clients, and advocates can become lost or inactive customers representing lost profits (characterized by the waste bin).

or disqualified. Disqualified prospects are filtered out of the system, while qualified prospects remain inside. The sooner a disqualified prospect is filtered out, the better for you. Wasting time and money on a suspect who will not buy or is unable to buy cuts dramatically into your profit, so you want to identify disqualified suspects as quickly as possible. You then focus on qualified prospects with the goal of turning them into first-time customers, then repeat customers, and eventually clients and advocates.

While moving them through the Profit Generator system into higher levels of loyalty, you also want to encourage the customer to buy regularly from you and stop buying from your competition. Without proper care, any first-time customer, repeat customer, client, or advocate can become inactive, causing the company substantial losses in sales and profit.

You'll notice that in the figure the globes representing each customer stage become progressively larger. This is because, despite the fact that the number of customers in each stage is smaller than that in the preceding stage, the further along in the system the customer goes, the more bottom-line profit the organization can enjoy.

Every business has customers and clients that fall into some if not all of these categories. A residential real estate company has homeowners as clients. A homeowner could transition through five stages: suspect, prospect, lister, seller, and advocate. A hotel chain catering to corporate travelers has the travel department of major corporations as clients. The customer stages could be suspect, prospect, first-time booker, repeat booker, client, and advocate. Although the actual name of the customer stage may be modified, most organizations have customers that evolve through a similar transition.

Other applications of the Profit Generator system vary as well. For example, in many industries buyer monogamy (whether the person is buying only from you or is also buying from a competitor) is the client-stage litmus test. In some sectors (such as state government) that cannot buy exclusively from one seller, this may not be a reasonable requirement. In this situation, the best a company can hope for is to be one of two or three sellers used exclusively by the buyer. Depending on the nature of your business, a stage can be modified to address the specifics of your own buying situation.

The rule of thumb in working within the Profit Generator system is that the goal for you within each stage of development is to grow the relationship into the next stage of development. The goal of interacting with a prospect is to turn a prospect into a first-time customer, a repeat customer into a client, a client into an advocate. Once you reach the advocate stage, your job is to keep the person buying and referring. As we saw earlier with the definition of loyalty, a company can enjoy real profits once the customer has evolved into the latter stages of the Profit Generator process. Failure to grow a customer to an advanced stage robs the company of profit and valuable referrals.

We devote a chapter to each of these stages later in the book, but here is an overview of the evolutionary process.

Suspects and Prospects: Attracting Those with Long-Term Potential

The first job of any marketer is to identify suspects and prospects, qualify them, and move them to the first-time customer stage in the Profit Generator system. This is the most challenging and most expensive part of marketing. The word *suspect* may sound harsh and contrary to an age of customer satisfaction, but it serves as a reminder that at this stage in the relationship we suspect that a person (or a company, in the case of business-to-business marketing) may have a need for our products and services, but without more information we cannot be sure.

The closer your suspect is in habit and need to your established clients, the better the chance of the suspect qualifying as a prospect and eventually becoming a customer. Careful qualification of a suspect into a prospect is essential to preventing waste of time and money.

To qualify as a prospect, someone must meet at least two key criteria: have the need for your product or service and have the ability to buy. In the thrill of the hunt, many a company has pursued a suspect with considerable marketing time and money, only to realize too late that the suspect never met the necessary criteria to begin with. Because marketing resources are in short supply, the sooner a suspect is identified as unqualified, the quicker the company can move on to those with long-term potential.

Turning a qualified prospect into a buyer is where the selling begins. Research has found that this is becoming an increasingly prolonged process. A 1991 study of industrial sales calls found that the number of calls needed to close a sale is up almost 50 percent, from 4.3 in 1979 to 6.3 in 1991. This finding makes the process of qualifying a prospect more critical than ever.

First-Time Customers: The Art of the Transaction

The sale is not the objective of the marketing process; it's the beginning of a lifetime customer relationship. It is a rare case when a customer can be sold something only once. Even items that may be bought only once (a swimming pool, a set of encyclopedias) can generate peripheral sales (pool equipment, annual update volumes).

The first-time customer stage is a crucial one and coincides with the trial purchase portion of the purchase cycle outlined in Chapter Two. As we discussed earlier, the first-time customer is essentially trying out your product or service. If a continuing relationship is going to be developed, it has to begin with the first purchase. If the first purchase does not satisfy the customer, there will probably not be a second purchase. Such a customer comes to the purchase with a set of expectations gathered from a variety of sources. From the buying experience, he forms a set of perceptions. If the perceptions meet or, even better, exceed expectations, there is a good likelihood he is open to repurchase. If his perceptions fall below expectation, the chance of repurchase is much less. A poor first-time buyer experience is a major handicap to further deepening of the relationship.

At the first-time customer stage, the buyer and seller are in a transaction phase, wherein the customer is likely to pay close attention to timeliness, accuracy, and other facets of the products and services provided. Being a dependable seller is critical to launching a long-term relationship.

The three early stages of the Profit Generator system (suspect, prospect, first-time customer) are the most expensive areas for a marketer. As you progress through the stages, your marketing efforts can become more efficient.

Repeat Customers: Providing Value with Each Interaction

It is critical to keep your customers in the Profit Generator system and expand the business relationship. It's the fastest and easiest way to higher profits.

Once at the customer or client stage, you have the greatest opportunity to recognize each of your customers as an individual and offer products, services, and information tailored to her unique needs. Every interaction should be seen as an opportunity to add value. It is important that your interaction with a repeat customer works to deepen the relationship. This customer in turn responds with more information about herself, becomes increasingly loyal, and continues to drive sales and profit upward.

To achieve this level of bonding, you must move away from mass advertising to a private dialogue, conducted directly with each customer. Depending on your business, this can be through a phone call, a newsletter, a letter, or salesperson. The customer wants to feel that the company knows her. Follow-up marketing that is personalized to this customer can deepen your relationship with her, not just make a sale. The highest levels of human need—those concerned with involvement and individualization—can be addressed as part of the seller-buyer relationship. These actions enable the repeat customer to view your business not just as a building at a particular address or a phone number in the Rolodex, but as a company of human beings with whom she has formed a relationship.

Client Stage: Shifting from Salesperson to Consultant

At the client stage of the relationship, the buyer feels a real commitment to buy from you and proves it by buying every product or service of yours he thinks he can reasonably use.

One of the benefits of the client stage is that the relationship has progressed in trust so that you can now be more proactive with the client. From the history that developed through the earlier customer stages, you have proved yourself dependable and accountable. You have now earned his confidence, and he increasingly seeks your input for ideas and services. With this level of contribution, you add more value.

As the customer goes out of his way to be served by you, even if doing so means paying more for your services, he ceases to see you as a salesperson; rather, he sees you as an ally and partner. When the relationship moves to this level, there is little a competitor can do to lure your customer away. You are perceived as being worth more than simply the product or service you sell.

Almost a year ago, I changed my long-distance carrier. I chose the new carrier because of its low rates. Over the next twelve months, I increasingly relied on my sales representative to give me input on a number of phone issues, including my office phone system, an outbound telemarketing setup, and a toll-free line. Her input helped me save valuable time and money. Now, when I have phone system questions, whether it involves long-distance or not, I usually consult her. Other long-distance carriers have approached me, some with even lower rates, but I stay with my current carrier. Why? Because I find the advisory aspect of the relationship so valuable.

Advocacy: Your Best Advertising

Once a customer becomes an advocate for your product or service, you have achieved a relationship of great closeness and trust. This is the most valued and sought-after level of bonding, where word-of-mouth advertising flourishes. The bond at this level is strong. But an element of risk has been added, because the original buyer's relationship with your company is now visible to others. Therefore, you must be prepared to follow through promptly and professionally and make the new customers feel as valued and important as the advocates who recommended them.

Inactive and Lost Customers and Clients: Your Unharvested Acre of Diamonds

From the moment a customer first buys from you, he is vulnerable to being wooed away by a competitor or stopping altogether. Generally, the further the customer has progressed in the system, the more you stand to lose if he becomes inactive. When inactivity strikes, it is imperative to find out why he fell out of the Profit Generator system and to win him back.

Winning back lost customers is frequently the most overlooked source for incremental profit. Research studies tell us that a business is twice as likely to successfully sell to a lost customer as to a brand new prospect.[5]

If you contact people who have discontinued a buying relationship, three great things happen. First, you have an excellent opportunity to renew the business relationship. Studies have shown that if an unhappy customer has an opportunity to talk to you about her problems—even if you don't do anything to fix them—she is twice as likely to buy from you again than if you never talk to her. The second benefit is that you have begun to stop the negative publicity. The customer knows that you care about her and tells others. Finally, as your last benefit, you'll identify what's wrong within your system so you can take immediate steps to correct the problem and prevent it from occurring with other customers.

The key questions that a company needs to address are "How many customers do we lose each year?" "What would it cost to keep these customers?" and "How does this cost compare with the cost of finding new customers?"

THE IMPORTANCE OF THE BIG PICTURE

The Profit Generator system can put the importance of customer conversion and loyalty into perspective for every employee in an organization. As we began to see in Chapter Two, the profitability of a loyal customer is significant. A loyal client for Domino's Pizza, for example, is worth approximately $5,000 in sales over the life of a ten-year franchise contract. Phil Bressler, coowner of five Domino's stores, discovered that it paid big dividends to explain to every order taker, delivery person, and store manager that a loyal customer was worth $5,000. For Phil, simply telling employees that customers were valuable was not nearly as effective as communicating the precise dollar amount: "It's so much more than they think that it really hits home."[6]

A similar philosophy is practiced by Ford Motor Company, which has found through research that the lifetime value of a single customer represents an asset worth about $142,000. Like Domino's Pizza, Ford finds that the benefit of communicating this fact to employees can help put day-to-day operations into perspective. An employee who is in charge of collecting overdue bills, for example, is less likely to view a customer as a delinquent deadbeat than as a valuable asset that must be nurtured.

Company employees are not the only ones with shortsighted vision. Until recent years, completing a sale was the end of the process for too many marketing strategists. Little or no time or money was allocated for creating a special relationship with the company's best customers. Most companies—whether selling goods or services—failed to grasp, must less calculate and record, the lifetime value of a customer. Most focused on making a sale rather than concentrating more marketing dollars on having that sale lead to a long-term profitable relationship.

An early pioneer of the concept of growing a customer is car salesman Joe Girrard. He has been in the *Guinness Book of World Records* twelve times for being the world's greatest salesman; each year for eleven years running, he sold more new cars and trucks than any other human being. Joe's success was based on his realization that the sale is only a brief encounter, and that without a commitment on his part to establishing an ongoing relationship with the buyer, the encounter can lead nowhere.

Joe says the whole process begins with attitude: "I look at a customer as a long-term investment. I'm not just going to sell him one car and then tell him to shove it when he is not satisfied with that car. I expect to sell him every car he is ever going to buy. And I want to sell his friends and his relatives. And when the time comes, I want to sell his children their cars too. So when somebody buys from me, he is going to love that experience and he is going to remember it and remember me and talk about it to everybody he runs into who needs a car. I look at every customer as if he is going to be like an annuity to me for the rest of my life."

Scott Hanson Galleries operates with a keen focus on repeat sales. Hanson's galleries are situated in such tourist spots as Sausalito, New Orleans, and Rodeo Drive in Beverly Hills. Visitors often browse and come away without buying any art, but it is unlikely that someone will buy from Hanson Galleries only once. The average Hanson customer makes seven purchases within the first three years, and the average Hanson invoice is a respectable $4,200. Who is the Hanson Galleries customer? A middle-class art buyer looking for a piece to hang over the couch or mantel. The galleries retail limited-edition graphics by popular artists such as Marc Chagall, Thomas McKnight, and Peter Max.

How does this company achieve such a remarkable repeat purchase record among such an unlikely target market? By encouraging its staff to focus on two key things: attitude and follow-up. After fifteen years in the business, founder Scott Hanson has learned that the salespeople—called art consultants—must view the walk-in visitors as a revenue stream, not as a one-shot sales possibility. With the right attitude on the part of the art consultant, the next goal is the prospect's attitude. To persuade a prospect to become a buyer, the art consultant must lead the prospect through the three attitude steps: first, that buying art is OK and not frivolous; second, that she is capable of making an intelligent art purchase; and third, that Hanson Galleries is a good place for her to buy art.

"Education is critical to our sales," says Hanson. "You buy a work and then everything that happens with that artist, you're notified. You now become knowledgeable about that artist and his work. You can talk about him with people at cocktail parties."[7]

"Our salespeople are not just selling a product," relates the director of the gallery in La Jolla (California), Joy Ortner: "They're finding out who you are, what you do, where you live, how big your home is, what color your walls are. That's the key to multiple acquisition." This customer information goes on cards kept on file and is the key to the art consultant's following up by telephone. All consultants are required to spend roughly 50 percent of their time on the phone and the other half on the floor.

Mailings go out announcing new works, and clients get called before and after the announcements are sent. Sales Director Jennifer Walker confirms that this constant contact makes a difference. "Lots of our clients are doctors, businessmen," she says. "We get right through to them. The secretary will say, 'It's your art consultant.' "[8]

Each Hanson Galleries art consultant generally brings in between $500,000 and $1 million in sales each year. The consultant succeeds by changing attitudes and purchasing habits, and by turning first-time buyers into loyal clients.

HOW A DATABASE CAN INCREASE CUSTOMER LOYALTY

R. H. Macy started his first dry goods store on New York City's Sixth Avenue in 1858. His business grew because he knew each of his regular customers so well that he could anticipate their needs and even make a personal call when one of them was sick. Times have changed since Mr. Macy started his business. Companies have hundreds or thousands of employees. It is impossible for the huge department store that bears Macy's name today to turn back to the 1858 form of micromarketing, but it can use modern technology to approximate it. One key way an organization can approximate this quality of relationship is with a customer database.

Thanks to the computer, the names and addresses of customers or potential customers, coupled with information about their purchasing habits and preferences, can now be stored electronically and searched for items corresponding to certain criteria. For example, a salesperson could manually go through dozens of files to determine which clients have not placed an order in the past six months. A computer, however, fed the right search criteria, can identify those customers in seconds, saving valuable time that can be spent with customers.

An up-to-date list of your current customers is the most valuable list you can own, because by definition it identifies people who have already made it into at least the second stage of the Profit Generator cycle. You can use the list to help motivate your current customers to buy more frequently and to spend more when they buy. In other words, your customer database moves you from a reactive realm in business building to a proactive one. You no longer have to wait for your customer to contact you.

A database gives a company the ability to segment names into the stages of the Profit Generator system and to personally address each subgroup member with attention to his or her particular situation. Letters, offers, inquiries, and phone calls can all be made with pinpoint accuracy to help your company build loyal customers. For example, a hair salon can isolate all repeat customers of the salon who are not users of perms or color services and send a special offer to them. A clothing store can identify repeat customers and clients that buy a particular line of clothing and, when the store sponsors a trunk show for that line, notify those particular customers. This addressability enables you to develop an ongoing relationship between your company and an individual customer, and by using the tools of data processing you can track the relationship's progress and long-term profitability.

A Database in Action

Robert Sidell started California Cosmetics in 1985 with a distinct product advantage. Sidell had been successful for twenty-seven years as a Hollywood makeup artist. He did the makeup for movies and TV series such as "The Waltons," *Body Heat,* and *E.T.* In the process, Sidell had developed specialized skin cleansers and toners for the stars he worked with. When he launched his retail cosmetics company in 1985, he found a ready market. In their first full year, Sidell and his partner, Paula Levey, generated $1.6 million in revenues. The second-year revenues reached $4 million, and the third year, $12 million, with net margin growing to 12 percent. Sidell discovered, however, that maintaining the aggressive growth and profits meant he had to constantly discover new customers. To support his increasing sales, his overhead continued to rise as a result of a growing advertising budget, additions to his product line, a larger payroll, and other expenses. Sidell called the vicious circle of increased sales leading to increased overhead his "treadmill."

So, how did Sidell get off the treadmill? By using his customer database to sell more to *existing* customers. Sidell discovered that selling more to customers who had already bought from him was much less costly than finding new customers. Before starting his new program, Sidell's average customer spent $30 a year. This meant he had to have 400,000 customers to produce $12 million in revenue. To hit $16 million with reliance on new customers, he would need 133,000 new customers. Simply by getting his existing customer base to spend an additional $10, however, he could reach his $16 million goal without the additional acquisition costs associated with new customers.

Sidell came upon his new strategy by accident. With sales typically down in the summer months, he instructed his service reps to call ten customers who had not placed an order in a while and find out why: "Eight placed an order right there. They had meant to give us a call but had been too busy or they had misplaced our catalog. But as soon as someone asked them to buy, they did. You don't have to kick me in the head for too long for me to realize something. We were missing a golden opportunity."[9]

Recognizing the gold mine he had in his existing client base, Sidell went further. His sales reps routinely asked for the birth date of each new customer. With this information, Sidell began to send his customers a birthday present: a set of three makeup brushes (each of which cost him 45 cents). Along with the gift, he enclosed a $5 gift certificate and a birthday card. A remarkable 40 percent of the people who received the present placed another order.

The lesson? Take steps to nurture and build your relationships with your customers. By motivating the customer to buy from you once, you have already taken a big step in creating share of mind with the customer. Your company is not a stranger; she knows who you are. Your next step is to begin to treat her in a personal, individual way. She will respond. A marketing database is the key tool for making that happen.

Share of mind is a term marketers use to describe the dominance a customer perceives in one product compared to alternatives. Commenting on the opportunity for combining database technology with the customer's share of mind, direct marketing veterans Stan Rapp and Tom Collins say:

> When you join these two forces together, the share of mind and the customer database, it is as if you have ignited a second-stage rocket to boost your company into higher orbit. Now you can go to customers who are already favorably disposed to your product and company and offer them other products, services or benefits especially selected to fit their individual tastes. This deepens the share of mind and their resulting loyalty. Then these responses feed additional personal information into the customer database. This makes possible more and better benefits and services, which in turn deepens the share of mind—in an endless feedback loop.[10]

Data Analysis in the B2B Space

Nowhere is building share of mind, and in turn customer loyalty, more complex than in the business-to-business (B2B) environment. In some cases, B2B transactions can involve six or more parties in a single endeavor. For example, a food manufacturer must build effective B2B relationships with those distributors and retailers that form the distribution channel to the ultimate customer. Multiply those parties by the many touch points in the life cycle of a B2B sale—initial transaction, ongoing support, account management, and so forth—and you've got thousands of interactions that must be monitored and coordinated. This is why solidifying a strong B2B relationship often starts with sophisticated database analysis.

Just ask Franciscan Winery, in California's Napa Valley, which is working to double its business over the next five years. In years past, Franciscan followed industry tradition and relied on haphazard selling, where lone-ranger sales people negotiated sales, closed deals, and in the process shared little information with others in the company. But the winery now realizes this approach kept the lid on a lot of valuable information the company needed to dramatically improve its marketing strategies.

Franciscan recently moved away from its lone-ranger sales model and into a customer relationship management model in which team selling is now practiced. The winery has begun using CRM software to collect and track data about interaction with distributors buying their products. This data collection and tracking is paying off. For example, the winery has discovered that distributors buying a greater range of Franciscan Wines typically recommend the Franciscan brand over competitive brands. Why? Because when it comes to wine, distributors know that restaurants and stores champion a brand name over a single product. What does this mean for Franciscan? Marketing efforts and selling incentives should be honed for distributors who buy multiple products of the same brand and not simply bulk orders of a single product. Moreover, the winery is working to constantly identify those distributors who most successfully sell Franciscan wines to bars, restaurants, and supermarket chains, which in turn sell to the ultimate customer. For the winery, identifying these high-value distributors is a crucial step in improving key B2B relationships and thereby in maximizing Franciscan brand loyalty throughout the distribution channel to the end consumer.[11]

Likewise, several years ago, Hewlett-Packard began using CRM data analysis to sharpen its marketing strategy in the Asia-Pacific region by identifying which resellers were doing a better job of selling specific HP products. Now, Hewlett-Packard is able to direct qualified leads generated from its customer-facing Website to those Asia Pacific resellers that have proven themselves most productive in driving HP product sales. CRM reseller analysis is also helping Hewlett-Packard manage the often-thorny issue of deciding which new products go to which resellers in which geographic areas. In essence, the manufacturing giant optimizes its Asia Pacific distribution network by knowing the reseller's selling strength and how quickly inventory is likely to turn over.

THE THRILL OF THE CHASE
AND OTHER MISCONCEPTIONS

The Profit Generator system is about focusing marketing and selling efforts on a company's most promising future customers: those it already has. A new idea? Not at all. But most organizations give it lip service at best.

There are essentially three ways to do more business:

1. Have more customers.
2. Have more purchases.
3. Have more expensive purchases.

The Profit Generator system focuses on leveraging items two and three. Currently, there seems to be a sense in marketing that landing new customers (acquisition program) is more rewarding and exciting than holding on to current customers (retention program) or increasing business volume among current customers. For some reason, the thrill of chasing new customers and of closing the first deal seems more challenging than keeping the customers you already have. Finding new customers often involves flashy advertising, new sales techniques, and innovative marketing approaches. This sometimes makes marketing people feel creative and aggressive, but in fact it is possible to be both creative and innovative in devising methods for keeping existing customers happy—and the financial returns are generally much greater for retention than for acquisition.

Market researchers Kevin J. Clancy and Robert S. Shulman call the constant search for new customers the "death wish paradox." A company expends ever more energy and money in a program that results in ever less value. Even if the program is successful in finding new customers, the cost is excessively high.

A study by Marketing Metrics tell us that the probability of selling something to a prospect is only about 5–20 percent, while the probability or selling something to an existing customer is 60–70 percent. Given these odds, it is amazing that more companies are not focused on service and developing their existing customer base. Yet they aren't. For example, the international marketing research firm Yankelovich Clancy Shulman reported that an apparel maker was dissatisfied with its sales record. The results of Yankelovich's study showed that among the maker's best accounts, the company was receiving only 22 percent of the dollars these buyers spent on apparel. Furthermore, the study showed that among those who were once regular buyers, 12 percent had not purchased from the company in more than a year. When inquiring into the company's marketing strategy, Yankelovich found that a huge sum was being spent on finding new customers, but almost nothing on cultivating existing accounts. As a result, the company continued to see high turnover among customers, high marketing expenses, and low customer loyalty.[12]

BUILDING A LOYAL CLIENTELE
ONE STEP AT A TIME

Marketing consultant Murray Raphel conducts seminars that deal with marketing questions. On one occasion, he held a seminar for hockey team owners. One owner asked, "How do I sell ten thousand tickets to our next game?" Murray responded, "Sell them one at a time."

It is important to keep in mind that each transaction with an individual customer is significant. It is impossible to consider your market as one homogeneous package. If you consider small pieces, you can get a much better handle on what works and what doesn't. Concentrating on individual sales, individual customers, and customer groups leads to overall improvement in sales and increased income much more quickly than trying to come up with a grand scheme appealing to the whole universe.

The same philosophy of pieces can be applied to building customer loyalty. Frieda Caplan, Harley-Davidson, Scott Hanson Galleries, Robert Sidell, Franciscan Winery, and Hewlett-Packard all understand that loyalty doesn't happen overnight. Customer loyalty comes about gradually, over the course of stages of development. Each of these companies has a plan to develop loyalty, not just a plan to make sales.

SUMMARY

- An effective marketing strategy must include targeting new prospects and retaining current ones.
- A loyal customer displays four distinct purchase behaviors: makes repeat purchases, purchases across product and service lines, provides customer referrals, and demonstrates immunity to the pull of the competition.
- A customer's loyalty grows through seven stages: suspect, prospect, disqualified prospect, first-time customer, repeat customer, client, and advocate.
- Attitude and follow-up are essential to growing a loyal customer. If a customer becomes lost or inactive, measures should be taken to attempt to win back the business. Odds are in your favor that win-back efforts will pay off. Research finds that a business is twice as likely to successfully sell to a lost customer as to a brand new prospect.
- Computer databases are an important tool for building individual customer relationships.
- The ability to be flexible and adapt to the needs of the customer is essential in a loyalty-based marketing system.
- The customer must be thought of as an individual and treated as such if he is to remain loyal and help your business grow and prosper.
- Business-to-business relationships can be complex given the number of entities and factors involved. Solidifying a strong B2B relationship often starts with sophisticated database analysis to uncover hidden needs and the like.

GETTING STARTED

- Consider the four behaviors of a loyal customer: makes regular repeat purchases, purchases across product and service lines, refers others, and demonstrates immunity to the pull of competition. Look at your customer tracking capability to ensure you have the means for identifying and tracking these behaviors customer by customer. Make changes as needed.
- Using your customer list, identify which loyalty stage each customer is currently in (suspect, prospect, first-time customer, repeat customer, client, advo-

cate, lost or inactive customer). For your higher value customers, create a plan for moving them to the next loyalty stage (or if they are already at the advocate stage, develop a plan for sustaining and leveraging advocacy).

• Take a fresh look at your customer database and ask: (1) What are its biggest usability weaknesses? (2) What hidden insights exist that are currently going untapped? (3) What does each department most need to know about customers to add maximum value, and how can the customer database help supply it?

CHAPTER FOUR

Turning Suspects
into Qualified Prospects

In the 1950s, McGraw-Hill Business Publications developed a magazine advertisement that has become a classic. It shows a veteran buyer sitting solemnly in his chair facing the would-be salesperson and declaring:

> I don't know who you are.
> I don't know your company.
> I don't know your company's product.
> I don't know what your company stands for.
> I don't know your company's customers.
> I don't know your company's record.
> I don't know your company's reputation.
> Now, what was it you wanted to sell me?

The ad concludes:

> Moral: Sales start before your salesman calls—with business publication advertising.[1]

This award-winning advertisement, developed more than fifty years ago, still vividly illustrates the tasks and challenges a company faces today in turning suspects and prospects into loyal customers. Today the stakes are even higher, since consumers and business buyers are constantly surrounded by marketing messages at every turn. Empirical studies estimate that the average American sees about one million marketing messages per year—about three thousand messages per day.[2] With the advent of the Internet and e-mail, this daily message exposure is likely to escalate even further.

The main question facing any company is how to cut through this clutter and find high-value prospects to nurture into customers. Never have the stakes been higher. Consider the average cost of a business-to-business sales call. According to a recent survey by *Sales and Marketing Management,* the average cost of one B2B sales call is $239 for a company using a value-added selling approach.

But this is just part of the investment. Robert Davenport, who researches sales force effectiveness, says "companies that sell sophisticated products and services are investing in costly systems and processes to make sales people more effective because customers, especially those that are narrowing their pool of suppliers, demand it." The result is that "you have to get deeper into the organization and partner with the customer so they look at you as value-added," says Davenport.[3]

To lower sales costs and increase the closing rate, companies the likes of IBM are investing heavily in online technologies such as Web callback and instant chat. IBM reports that before implementing these features, IBM.com's average sale was closed after 7.2 calls. With Web callback and instant chat, the IBM goal is to slash that number to three calls per order; the company reports being close to achieving it. Technology advances help a company increase sales call efficiency and effectiveness, but selling to new customers remains a costly business, in part because you are trying to lure away someone else's loyal customer.

We all recognize that some investment must be made to find new customers and convert a suspect or prospect into a customer. To do this as efficiently as possible, it is important that your company focus on three key marketing questions at an early stage:

1. *Who* to target? How to identify those groups of people most likely to buy your products and services?

2. *How* to position your products and services? How to best position your product or service in the mind of your prospect to earn his dollars and loyalty?

3. *How* to qualify prospects? How to focus on high-potential prospects rather than mediocre suspects?

Each of these considerations supports the key function of marketing at this stage in the Profit Generator system: to create the right conditions and lay the right foundation in the mind of a well-chosen prospect so that the sale can be made easily.

WHO TO TARGET

Developing loyal customers and clients begins by searching out the type of customer to whom a company can provide superior value and determining how best to reach that prospect. Many companies, particularly start-ups, suffer early defeat when they fail to discover how big their market is and how to approach it. With limited financial capability, they often shy away from the hefty price tag of research designed to help answer these crucial questions. Instead, they try a scattershot approach that in the long run wastes money and still doesn't produce a good customer base.

Biosite Diagnostics took another approach. This biotechnology firm, founded in 1990 and headquartered in San Diego, was started by four former employees of Hybritech, a biotech unit of Eli Lilly. Although resources were tight, the four men spent $150,000 for two market surveys to ascertain whether their new product had a market. In reality, the surveys did much more than simply tell them that. The research played a significant role in helping the fledgling company attract investors, redefine the target market, and redirect its business strategy.

Triage, Biosite's first product, is a small, disposable diagnostic device that tests urine for the presence of drugs in just ten minutes. Before market research was done, it appeared that emergency rooms were the company's best initial market for the product. This market, however, was relatively small; moreover, there were already two large companies competing in the field. These facts tended to discourage potential investors.

The research firm surveyed potential users, including four hundred physicians and laboratory technicians. In addition, focus groups were conducted among approximately one hundred possible users of the device. As a result of the research, the company learned that although there were competitors in the market, the Biosite product had definite advantages. It was confirmed that emergency room physicians needed drug analysis in order to select treatment, but it was also discovered that they needed the information quickly. Biosite could produce the results several hours faster than its competitors. Biosite's device cut the testing time dramatically.

The surveys also indicated that although doctors ordered the tests, the laboratory technicians chose the test to be administered. This information led to a two-pronged marketing thrust, directed at doctors and laboratory staff.

In addition, the research showed that the company's proposed target market was larger than the young company could easily handle. Instead of stretching its resources to the breaking point, the company decided to find distributors to help fulfill the orders for the product. "We could have sold it ourselves, but it would have taken much more money and much more time," one of the partners explained.[4]

As a result of early testing, Biosite successfully introduced its first diagnostic product, with a second soon to follow. The company saw profits leap from $3 million to $8 million in a year's time. The information gained from the market research helped the company make cost-cutting, effective decisions while planning its marketing program. Instead of guessing, management made choices on the basis of reliable information that gave them specific targets for their sales force. They learned who needed the product, why it was needed, and the most cost-efficient way of getting it to the customer.

Not all research studies have such a profound effect on a company, but one thing is certain: a careful study of potential markets can save a business unnecessary cost and product delay.

Hitting the Bull's-Eye with Your Target Marketing

With marketing expenses forever on the rise, it is clear that the successful business is going to have to spend its money wisely. The problem is how to do so. The potential market for many products and services is huge; there are all sorts of people and organizations that might want to buy what you have to sell, but you can't possibly try to sell to everyone in that amorphous mass.

This is why target marketing is so important. When you think about the potential market, you realize some of your prospects can't afford your product, some want to shop locally, and others already have a supplier to whom they are loyal. There are many reasons a suspect doesn't qualify as a good prospect. Target marketing lets you identify, within that broad market of all logically possible buyers, those prospects most likely to purchase your product and offering the greatest return for your investment.

Why *target* marketing? Picture a target. The bull's-eye is small but valuable, the first ring is somewhat larger but not quite as valuable as the bull's-eye, the second ring is larger and less valuable, the third ring is still larger and less valuable, and so on, until the target area is complete. Off the target, there is no value. Using this same analogy, think in terms of your business. Your bull's-eye contains the greatest concentration of qualified prospects of any circle on the target. But every ring thereafter contains fewer and fewer of the individuals or organizations most likely to buy from you.

Suppose you need $100 in sales to break even and you have $15 to spend on marketing. Think of each dollar as an arrow. Every bull's-eye brings in $10. The first ring is worth $6, the next ring $3, and the outer ring $1. Clearly, the more bull's-eyes you hit, the better off you are. You *have* to have some bull's-eyes just to break even.

Obviously, you don't just start flinging arrows every which way (though a lot of sales and marketing efforts do resemble a scattershot approach). As with archery, you do better by taking careful aim than randomly firing flights of arrows. Furthermore, your marksmanship improves with practice.

Hitting the bull's-eye with target marketing is something Jeff Hoogendam and Jim McKinley focus on every day as cofounders of SmartPrice, an online services agent that helps residential customers and small businesses compare, select, purchase, and manage long-distance services.

In their 1999 start-up phase, SmartPrice commissioned market research that discovered the majority of residential customers and small businesses believe they are overpaying for long-distance services. Moreover, this research confirmed that more than 70 percent of Internet users search online for long-distance supplier and plan options. But there was one big challenge. The research also showed that shopping for long-distance service is not a high priority for most.

This makes leveraging those key trigger events when people are most interested in changing carriers critical. Hoogendam, the president and CEO, explains: "Getting an unexpectedly high phone bill or having a bad experience with a customer service rep are some typical catalysts for switching. Our job is to find those people online who are looking for us." To connect with potential switchers, Smart-Price uses pay-for-performance online marketing. This means the company carefully tracks the source of its prospects and pays those online portals and sites only for prospects successfully converting to SmartPrice buyers. Says Hoogendam, "We can track our prospecting results as often as every ten minutes if we want to"; but he's quick to add that SmartPrice resists making a lot of knee-jerk changes to the approximately seventy-five campaigns the company has running on the Internet at any given time and instead lets "sufficient data" help point the way.[5]

Once the prospect gets to the SmartPrice site, a second round of bull's-eye qualifying begins. The site's proprietary profiling model quickly collects enough information to create a profile regarding the prospect's calling habit and current long-distance spending. This profile is run through a comprehensive decision engine that quickly shops it against 140 plans from dozens of carriers (MCI, Sprint, AT&T, and so on). The site then presents a solution back to the prospect in an objective, apples-to-apples comparison format, with an estimation of the actual monthly bill under the new recommended plan. The prospect can then elect to switch immediately to the new plan online. (This entire process of analyzing and switching takes a quick five minutes.)

After plan selection, with the customer's permission, SmartPrice monitors usage along with market rates for ongoing verification of the customer's savings and notifies the customer about a newer plan when further savings are possible.

The two-pronged bull's-eye prospecting plan is bearing fruit for the fledging company. SmartPrice reports a sevenfold increase in customers from January to December 2001 and a level of customer defection 33 percent below the industry average for long-distance services. A twenty-fourfold increase in revenue for twelve months ended December 2001, along with a just-announced major marketing partnership with Yahoo!Finance, put the firm on track to reach cash flow breakeven by January 2003.

Uncovering Your Natural Target Market

Like Biosite and SmartPrice, Steve Tran understood the importance of identifying his target market. When he wasn't selling enough cars at Mac Haik Chevrolet/Subaru in Houston, Texas, he knew why: "The market is far too competitive to simply wait for customers to show up and buy from you. You have to bring them in."[6]

As a first-generation immigrant from Vietnam, Steve, a former teacher, knew what it is was like to struggle with the language and cultural differences in the United States. He reasoned that other Vietnamese in the Houston area felt the same pressure and might appreciate buying a car from someone who spoke their language and had a similar background.

Steve got the Houston phone book and compiled a list, by hand, of residents with Vietnamese surnames. He sent these folks a letter, in Vietnamese, with his picture on it. Included in his letter was the statement "I am Vietnamese and a former teacher. Like you, I always believe that no one can understand the needs and the taste of Vietnamese people better than a Vietnamese."[7]

Within four months after beginning his targeting strategy, Steve Tran was leading the dealership in sales, with almost half of his sales attributed to the business generated from his Vietnamese target market.

Targeting Loyalty-Based Customers

Establishing a successful Profit Generator system depends on attracting the type of customer who can buy again and again over a long period of time. Sam Walton, founder of Wal-Mart, the largest retailer in the world, asserted in his autobiography, *Made in America,* that "[customer loyalty] is where the real profits in this business lie, not in trying to drag strangers into your stores for a one-time purchase based on splashy sales or expensive advertising. Satisfied, loyal repeat customers are at the heart of Wal-Mart's spectacular profit margins."

As you begin targeting your market, you narrow down the universe in which you try to sell your product or service. You want to discover the right customers, those who are likely to do business with you again and again. These are not necessarily the easiest customers to reach, or even the most profitable in the short run.

Writing in the "Manager's Journal" column of the *Wall Street Journal,* business innovation specialist Michael Schrage says, "Contrary to popular belief, customer service doesn't begin with the customer's expectations of the business—it begins with the business's vision of the customer. Smart businesses pick customers—and learn from them. While some customers consistently add value along several dimensions, other customers are value-subtracters: What they cost in time, money and morale outstrips the prices they pay."[8]

As we saw from discussing the conditions of loyalty in Chapter One, there are some customers who are just not loyal; no matter what you do to please them, they are ready to bolt at the drop of a hat. Your challenge as a marketer is to avoid targeting as many of these people as possible and instead concentrate your energy on those who can be developed into loyal customers.

Careful analysis of your existing customer base can suggest lots of direction in effectively targeting new prospects. This is what cofounders Judy Corson and Jeff Pope discovered in 1988 when they were gathered in a meeting room with their top managers to ferret out why their fourteen-year-old marketing research company, Custom Research, Inc. (CRI), was no longer growing. In an effort to get some answers, the group calculated a contribution margin for every CRI customer by subtracting all direct costs and selling expenses from the total revenues generated by the customer for the year. The result was an analysis that divided customers into four categories, according to the account's perceived value to the bottom line: (1) high-volume, low-margin; (2) high-volume, high-margin; (3) low-volume, low-margin; and (4) low-volume, high-margin.

The results were sobering. Only 10 of the 157 customers qualified for the most desirable category (those generating high dollar volume and high profit margin), while a shocking 101 customers delivered little to CRI's bottom or top line. "Many weren't profitable at all when you factored in the selling costs," Pope says.

The analysis showed clearly that CRI was spending too many employee resources and time on too many unprofitable customers. No doubt, bold changes were required to jump-start CRI's growth. The remedy was to systematically dismiss many existing customers, aggressively grow existing high-potential customers to greater profitability, and ruthlessly qualify prospective customers to ensure they passed muster. CRI did just that, completely overhauling its business development model. The results speak for themselves. In 1987, with 157 customers, CRI had $11 million in revenues. Ten years later, with a customer base of just 78, revenues topped $30 million, a boost of 175 percent.

CRI has invested years in crafting a one-to-one marketing strategy by which each customer is treated differently. When a carefully selected new customer comes aboard, CRI provides custom-tailored "surprise and delight" services, including special perks and regular reviews to grow the new account into increasingly higher volume and profitability. Through candid discussion with the new customer, CRI is clear about the expectation of earning additional business over time. CRI goes to great pains to surpass customer expectations and measure performance for the customer. But if these efforts aren't getting results, the customer can be "fired."

Learning to shrewdly screen for prospects with strong loyalty potential has been the key to CRI's solid growth. Experience has taught CRI to look for these qualities in evaluating a would-be customer: it must be a prospect (1) that comes referred from other users; (2) whose scope of work is more than simply a quick, one-time project; (3) whose project budgets are safely within CRI norms; (4) whose projects do not require blind bidding, a bidding war, or a drawn-out, committee-style decision; (5) that lists CRI's chief rivals as contenders for the work, as opposed to firms outside CRI's market space; and (6) that doesn't switch suppliers too easily.

The company's key gatekeeper, Beth Rounds, talks to most callers and estimates she rejects roughly 90 percent of all potential customer queries. Recognizing her delicate balancing act of both diplomacy and research, Beth admits that "when I explain CRI and how we do things, many take themselves out of the running. That makes it easy to make referrals." As such, Beth serves as a help desk of sorts for the industry by referring rejected prospects to a short list of respected competitors. Beth estimates that of the twenty to thirty callers she talks with each month, only two or three have real potential. Occasionally, a dejected caller will respond, "What's the matter; don't you need the business?" Says Beth, "But 99 percent understand what we're trying to do."[9]

Ten Steps to Effective Targeting

Consider these steps in identifying and selecting those markets with the greatest loyalty potential:

1. *Survey the total market.* Continually identify all types and categories of people, industry, and the like that might use your expertise or product.

2. *Segment your markets.* Break down your list of potential markets into groups that have common characteristics. You might list people by their profession, or industries by their product, for instance.

3. *Analyze your markets.* Discover as much as you can about the market groupings you have segmented. Find out what they need, what they want, what they fear, and who they buy similar services from. Find out everything you can that helps you evaluate how much potential they offer to you and how you can go about selling to them.

4. *Study the competition.* Find out how your successful competitors go about marketing and selling. Although you do not want to copy their approach, you need to know what works in your market. Knowing what your competitors do also helps you decide how to cut into and capture some of their market.

5. *Stratify the market.* Rank various market segments by priority. Your primary market should be the market segment you can reach most easily with the lowest investment and the greatest expectation of return. In the long run, return should be measured not simply on the basis of volume or sales but by profit. A number of factors can contribute to profitability, including the target group's proven responsiveness to marketing, its growth potential, readiness and ability to make a buying decision, and the ease with which the target group can be reached.

6. *Do an in-depth market analysis of your top markets.* Uncover as much information as you can about your most likely suspects, including what they read,

what trends they are concerned about, and how they think. Find out who in your field they consider to be best and why.

7. *Analyze which marketing vehicles are most effective.* The fewer resources a company wastes marketing to people who will never be prospects, the more it can invest in reaching and selling to its genuine prospects. Asking new buyers, "How did you hear about us?" can help you zero in on a way to reach new customers.

Frequency is typically the key to effective penetration. Studies have shown that once people hear about your company or product four or more times, they perceive you as credible. Choose marketing vehicles that enable you to afford and achieve such penetration. Carefully consider your marketing budget. If your funds allow you only a flash-in-the-pan approach, you are probably wasting your money and need to rethink your choice.

As a rule, the more focused and smaller the target market and the more clearly a company can identify individual prospects, the more cost-efficient marketing becomes. Such direct marketing techniques as mailings, e-mail, telephone calling, and personal selling can be very effective. (More and more companies are using e-mail to reach prospects as well as current customers. E-mail costs can be as little as a twentieth of regular mail and the response rate can range up to five times as great. Moreover, the anthrax scare has caused many firms to increasingly rely on e-mail. eMarketer reports that spending on e-mail ads was $496 million in 2000 and is projected to approach $4.6 billion in 2003.)[10] On the other hand, if the target group is large and homogeneous, then mass-marketing techniques such as television, newspapers, and radio can work efficiently.

8. *Test your markets.* To get a better idea of what really works, you have to contact a few prospects in each high-potential market. This tells you which ones are easiest to sell to, which approach works best, and how receptive the prospects are. You may find that what you thought was your best market is really not as good as your second-best market. By evaluating your sample in terms of cost, efficiency, and successful approach, you learn a great deal that can save you time and money later.

9. *Analyze what is doable.* For most businesses, a threshold number of calls is required for each sale. Anything less than this threshold requirement makes all previous activity a waste.

In the days before Web callback and instant chat, the average sale was closed after approximately seven calls. Now, many companies are finding they can reduce the number of calls per order to three or four. In establishing a sales projection or quota, consider such factors as how many contacts are required to reach threshold, the average number of calls per day a salesperson or call center agent can make, and the number of sales-days available per period. Considering these factors can help you realistically plan for sales results and help avoid the disappointment that accompanies an overstated projection and unrealistic expectations.

10. *Choose your markets.* Keep in mind that it's not how many target markets you can identify and open; it's how many you can profitably penetrate, market to, and serve. Treat your target market selection as an open-ended question, constantly identifying and investigating new markets of opportunity.

Some exciting technological advances enable a business to select a profitable market with keen precision. Sophisticated customer profiling and computer data modeling helps a firm identify high-potential prospects and pinpoint the marketing messages to which they are likely to respond. At the heart of the capability are computer models that enable a market to be viewed in terms of users and nonusers. Users are divided into those who are truly committed and loyal and those who are *convertible*, meaning they are declining in loyalty and susceptible to being pulled away by a competitor. Nonusers (prospects and former customers) are divided into two groups: potentially convertible, and unavailable (since they are committed to their current supplier).

When applied to the banking sector, one such model found that banks in the United States, for example, have a committed-customer score almost twice as high as do banks in the United Kingdom. This suggests that many UK bank customers are at high risk of defection and an easy target for new competitors. In addition to prospect identification, such modeling can be useful for a company in planning the amount of advertising and promotional activity required for prospects according to their commitment level and potential value.

Whether you are using sophisticated computer modeling or your own grassroots research, the importance of targeting can be summarized this way: before you do anything else, you need to find out *who* and *where* your best prospects are and *what* are the most efficient ways to reach them.

HOW TO POSITION YOUR PRODUCTS AND SERVICES

Once the target market has been identified, the next step is to create and communicate your message to the prospects throughout your market. Marketing is most effective when it imparts information to the target market about the availability of a product or service that addresses a want in the market.

Many people erroneously believe that the right advertising and marketing can be used to change people's minds about what they want. This belief is questionable regardless of budget, but for a small firm with limited resources the cost of such a task is out of the question. Most firms simply cannot advertise enough to change customers' attitudes. It is much more practical and profitable to find out what those attitudes are and then organize your business in accordance with them.

It's a lesson Maxine Clark knew well. As president of Payless ShoeSource, she had successfully developed the retail chain into the number one seller of children's licensed footwear in the world by paying close attention to customer needs. But four years later, she was bored and longed to create something truly unique. "I wanted to re-create the excitement and magic I felt as a child in certain stores," she said, "when going shopping was an event." She wanted to take the concept of children's interactive and entertainment retailing and turn it into "experience retailing" in a mall setting. "Little, if any, real opportunity exists in retailing for kids to get involved and participate, even in the best of the entertainment stores," explained Clark.[11]

Maxine examined what was available in children's retail and found a few unique concepts. One was a factory operation where, when she took the tour herself, she witnessed a special look in children's eyes that said they were enthralled with seeing products actually being made. Reflecting upon the factory experience, Maxine conceived her new business: create a place where children build and dress their own bears or bunnies or other stuffed animals.

Gathering all her best resources and favorite ideas from forty years of shopping experience, Maxine went straight to her prospective customers, and to her best source: kids. Their in-depth feedback formed the positioning and basis for Build-A-Bear Workshop mall stores. The first one opened in St. Louis in late 1997. Four short years later, Build-A-Bear numbered seventy stores nationwide, bringing in close to $100 million in revenue. Maxine confesses that "we expected to have this many stores. We didn't expect to have this much volume."[12]

Thirty years ago, as a young retail trainee, Maxine attended a presentation by Stanley Goodman, who was then CEO of May Company, where he talked about retailing as entertainment and the store as theater. "I remember vividly," Maxine says, "his statement, as if he were saying it to me alone: 'When customers have fun, they spend more money.'"[13] She took this lesson to heart and built a company culture around constantly monitoring children's definition of fun and tailoring the store offerings to match this feedback. With her Cub advisory board of children from five to fifteen years old and the thousands of e-mails from young Build-A-Bear fans, the company gets ongoing feedback daily. And the company listens. For example, when the Build-A-Bear kitty was originally produced in a light color, the Cub advisors complained, saying it "looks too much like macaroni and cheese." When shoes on the bears were a big hit, a young customer suggested . . . what else but socks!

This ongoing customer feedback ensures that the fun formula runs rampant throughout the store's eight hands-on stations. First up, "guest bear builders" (note that customers are referred to as guests) go to the Choose Me Station. They select a skin that will become a bear, dog, cat, elephant, or even a monkey. Next, they move to the Hear Me Station, where they choose sounds to put inside the animal. These can be prerecorded or personalized. Then there's Stuff Me, Stitch Me, Fluff Me, Name Me, Dress Me, and last, Take Me Home. By this time, each builder has invested time in creating a stuffed animal unlike anyone else's. They range in price from $10 to $25; clothes run $3 to $15 and accessories start at $2. From a back-to-school line complete with argyle sweaters to the Skechers for Bears line of athletic shoes, Halloween costumes for the furry friends, and roller blades and sunglasses, new clothing and accessory additions arrive regularly, many of which come from ideas contributed by guests.

Listening to her target market and responding accordingly is producing stellar results for Maxine and her company. In its few short years, Build-A-Bear is producing performance statistics that many retailers only dream about. The stores average more than $700 per square foot, compared to a national mall average of $350. The average store guest returns more than five times a year. Unlike toy stores that do 40–50 percent of sales and an even bigger percentage of profits during the holiday season, Build-A-Bear business is more evenly distributed. The stores are usually booked solid for parties throughout the year, celebrating occasions that range from a birthday to a corporate outing for employees and their families. The cash flow and schedule-planning advantages are obvious. Clark says "this is my first experience with guests making reservations to shop."[14]

Perhaps no company in history has done more to develop and advance the art and science of product positioning than Procter and Gamble, the $40 billion consumer-goods powerhouse and maker of such household brand names as Crest toothpaste, Dawn detergent, and Ivory soap. Founded in 1837 by partners William Procter and James Gamble, P&G has built a history of more than 165 years, successfully developing new products that carefully address existing consumer attitudes and wants. It follows, then, that the Cincinnati-based company would look closely at the Internet's possibilities for quickly and effectively testing consumer demand for new products.

Beginning with small initiatives in 1998, the company has increasingly embraced the Web as a powerful test marketing tool. Procter and Gamble invites online consumers to sample and give feedback on new prototype products, conducting 40 percent of its six thousand product tests and other studies online. If the new product gets great reviews, P&G may roll out the item to retail stores. If not, it's curtains.

Barbara Lindsey, director of the family care business unit at P&G, explains the quick turnaround advantage of online research: "Let's say you're introducing a new iteration of a product. . . . It used to be that you would have to conduct traditional focus groups and surveys and then wait more than two months for the results to be tabulated and interpreted. That's all changed. Now we can e-mail a concept test to our target audience on Thursday and have the results on Monday."[15]

Although her testing timetable was somewhat longer, the Web helped P&G brand manager Val Bogdan-Powers launch one of the most successful new products in Procter and Gamble history. Scheduled to launch Crest Whitestrips (a new home tooth bleaching kit) in August 2000, the brand team was still uncertain whether consumers would embrace the product's hefty $44 retail price. So Bogan-Powers turned to the Web to test market the product, using an eight-month campaign offering strips exclusively on P&G's Whitestrips.com. P&G ran TV spots and magazine ads in lifestyle publications such as *People* and *Good Housekeeping*. E-mails were sent to customers who had opted in to receive product updates on the P&G Website. "We wanted to pre-seed the marketplace so we could show retailers that there was a huge consumer demand for this product," says Bogdan-Powers. "Then when we introduced it at retail, we would be confident that the product and price point worked. We were willing to sell a little and learn a lot."[16]

Consumer response quickly proved that P&G had a winning product. A remarkable 144,000 whitening kits were sold online in eight months. An impressive 12 percent of visitors who registered for product information went on to purchase the new product. Armed with these sales data, Bogdan-Powers was able to make a convincing case to retailers to stock the product, despite the high price. Healthy sales soon followed. Three months after introduction, and backed by print and TV ad support, Crest Whitestrips had sold nearly $50 million worth of kits—a marked success for a new product by any standard.

The Internet is also proving useful in helping P&G refine existing products to match consumer preferences. At Reflect.com, the San Francisco-based beauty care dot com spun away from P&G in 1999, consumer feedback yields valuable input. Commenting on a recently revamped skin care moisturizer line, Vice President Richard Gerstein explains that "we heard our customers saying, 'I'd like to get even more specific benefits in a moisturizer.'" They also wanted more upscale packaging. When Reflect.com delivered on both a number of months later, sales "exploded," according to Gerstein, increasing 500 percent in just six weeks.[17]

Matching potential customers with their product preferences has been the key to the success of Build-A-Bear Workshops and Procter and Gamble. Roger Thompson has had less success trying to *change* market preferences. When he opened a hair salon in North Dallas, Thompson, who was formerly artistic director for Vidal Sassoon, refused to do "big hair" so popular in Texas, preferring the more natural look—straight, short, and styled without gels, sprays, or teasing combs.

Thompson's natural bent runs contrary to the regional trend for hair color. Hair color manufacturers such as L'Oréal report that Dallas is one of the biggest markets for bleach. Even former Texas Governor Ann Richards boasts big hair. (Commenting on the governor's widely recognized white hairdo, gubernatorial hairdresser Gail Huit proclaimed, "I rat the tar out of it. I spray the hell out of it. We get it up. We defy gravity."[18])

Not giving clients what they want has created a less-than-booming business for Thompson. Five months after the salon opened, three of the six stylists were let go. Prospects for repeat business are looking dim as well. Just ask Sue Eudaly, who, after being persuaded by a Thompson stylist to change from blond, found herself with brown hair she did not like and a $225 bill. "It was very depressing," said Eudaly, who showed her dissatisfaction by not leaving a tip. A few weeks later, Eudaly got another salon to bring back the blond. "The Roger Thompson Salon is very definitely New York," she said. "But they need to understand that this is Dallas, Texas."[19] Moral: find out what your customers want and then give it to them.

Is It Image, or Is It Character?

As I stated earlier, marketing creates an environment that convinces the prospect of the value of doing business with the company. The goal is to create a condition that makes a prospective customer want to do business with you. Although it may appear that you have sold a product, you have actually sold a perception of your company. You have planted an idea in your customer's mind about what doing business with you is like. To keep generating new customers, as every thriving business needs to do, you should project a clear, simple, powerful image to those with the desire and ability to buy what you are selling.

One of the earliest lessons on positioning and projecting the right image or character can be found in the late 1930s and early 1940s, when Packard was America's prime luxury car. The Packard was the standard by which all other cars were compared. In terms of today's market, it was like BMW and Mercedes-Benz combined into one car. Everyone aspired to own a Packard. Then the company began a new advertising and marketing campaign. It decided to introduce a much less expensive car with the slogan "Now everyone can drive a Packard." Within one year, the company was in deep trouble. The luxury car buyers were turning to Cadillac. The company did not realize that it was the exclusivity of its product that made it successful. As soon as "everyone" could drive a Packard, no one wanted to drive one.

Image-Driven Marketing: Friend or Foe?

For decades, large corporations have used image marketing to sell their wares. As a result, image-driven campaigns such as Nike's "Just Do It" and Chevrolet's "Like a Rock" have become familiar fixtures. When a company delivers customer value consistent with its image, customers respond in a positive way, as evidenced by the success of Carnival Cruise Lines.

Carnival's success stems from delivering a consistent message and travel product. Supporting its "fun ship" image, everything in the cruise ship's marketing message connotes fun. Traditional cruise advertising has promoted ports of call, but Carnival's TV spots hype the ships—where vacationers spend 80 percent of their time during a cruise—and the activities on them (dining, nighttime entertainment, exercise facilities, dancing, and more fun). Even the ships themselves support the image of gaiety, with such names as *Mardi Gras* and *Fantasy.*

"We're 'Happy Valley,' not 'Death Valley,' " says Bob Dickinson, senior vice president of sales and marketing for Carnival, referring to the cruise industry's history of being a vacation haven for retirees. "If you tell people you're the 'fun ships,' you're going to attract people disposed to having fun."

To maximize the company's consumer base, Dickinson says, Carnival sees itself in the vacation industry, where virtually everyone is a prospect, rather than in the cruise industry. Even though almost two-thirds of Carnival customers are new to cruising, repeat business has doubled in the past five years. "If you like fun," says Dickinson, "you don't graduate away from fun."

Carnival Cruise Lines delivers a travel service consistent with its image, but many companies using image marketing do not. As a result, the consumer's positive reception to image marketing is being replaced by increasing cynicism as the buyer continually encounters situations where a company does not deliver on the promises implied by its image.

Character-Driven Marketing: The New Generation

A number of companies have seized this opportunity to build credible relationships by expressing their character rather than simply an image. Commenting on the difference between the two approaches, Peter Laundy, principal of Laundy Rogers Design, a New York City communications firm, said, "Image positioners compete; their actions invite analogies involving sports or war. They focus on winning and therefore on the competitor. Character expressers, on the other hand, are aware of competitors but are not as focused on battle. They chart their own course, independent of their competitors and in tune with their customers and their values. A company that expresses character looks for situations that simultaneously build pride in the organization and loyalty in customers."[20]

Publix Supermarkets, Ben & Jerry's, the Body Shop, Smith and Hawken, and Starbucks Coffee are all character expressers. These companies have carved out an identity that attracts those prospects destined to become loyal. Says Laundy, "Instead of blowing up minor differences between themselves and their competitors, these companies have built real differences deep into their products and organizations."[21] Anita Roddick founded the Body Shop, a cosmetic company, to give customers products that supported their "well-being." In sharp contrast with long-standing cosmetic companies that stress sex appeal and instant rejuvenation, the company projects a deep sense of environmental responsibility and supports this character with herbal ingredients; a policy of no animal testing; and use of inexpensive, recyclable containers.

In regard to marketing communication, image expressers and character expressers are worlds apart. Laundy explains: "Image positioners see communications—in their catalogs, brochures, direct mail pieces, annual reports, advertisements, and so on—as a message they want to get across. Character expressers see communications as an opportunity to demonstrate that their companies do what they say they do."[22] For example, Ben & Jerry's has a highly visible program of social responsibility. Consider this passage from the "Social Performance Report" section of Ben & Jerry's 2000 annual report:

> Ben & Jerry's continues to struggle with diversity in the workplace. The number of people of color working for the company increased slightly in 2000, but Ben & Jerry's remains an overwhelmingly white company. Given Vermont's demographics—it is one of the whitest, most homogeneous states in the country—the racial composition of the workforce is unlikely to change much. . . .
>
> The company's safety record improved. Even so, the injury rate for the company's manufacturing workers, who comprise the majority of its employees and who do the hardest and most dangerous work at Ben & Jerry's, is higher than the industry average. This is an area in which the company still has much room for improvement.[23]

Yes, the content is negative, but the far bigger message about the company's behavior is entirely positive and reinforcing. Most annual reports are an expensive chronicle that shareholders read with some consider-the-source suspicion, but Ben & Jerry's annual report breaks new ground.

Another believer in character expression is Swatch founder Nicolas G. Hayek. His company single-handedly saved the Swiss watch industry by bucking traditional wisdom and keeping manufacturing of his inexpensive watch in high-wage Switzerland. This decision forced Hayek to find other ways to compete and was the genesis of his low-cost, unrepairable, flashy, and fun Swatch watch. In the ten years the company has been in business, one hundred million watches have been sold and annual profits have soared to $286 million.

Hayek attributes his success in part to character expression. Explaining why character and not image has worked for him, Hayek says, "An image is passive and can be interpreted in different ways. A message about a product is immediately clear and understandable to everyone. It also must be honest."

"I sent the first message about Swatch when I created a four-hundred-foot working Swatch and arranged to hand it over to one of the most prestigious banks in Frankfurt. The display was accompanied only by the words: Swiss. DM 60 [approximately $40]. The promotion sent the following message: high quality, because it was Swiss. Low price, because DM 60 was practically unheard of at the time. Provocative, because a four-hundred-foot plastic watch was hanging on a stuffy bank building. And joy of life."[24]

Reflecting on the synergy built by character expression, Laundy adds: "Character instills pride in the organization and teaches employees how to behave when no one is looking over their shoulders. It delights customers, who refer new business, and journalists, who write good things about the company. Together, employees, suppliers, customers, and journalists become an unpaid but highly credible sales force, reducing a company's expenses for promoting itself."[25]

Perhaps the biggest advantage of marketing through expression of character is that it can be a company's greatest asset in building a loyal customer base. Why? Because unique character is difficult, if not downright impossible, for your competitors to emulate.

The Awesome Power of Perception

Whether you choose to project an image or a character, one thing is certain: your efforts can succeed only if your products and services actually deliver what you communicate. Somebody once said that the ultimate definition of successful selling is "The Power to Persuade Plenty of Prospects to Purchase Your Product at a Profit." Marketing's role in this process is to zero in on those people who most need what you have to sell and then communicate a benefit-driven positioning that both differentiates it from the competition and answers for the prospect the "What's in it for me?" question.

When Big Isn't Better

In today's marketplace, many people are looking for a feeling of personal, intimate service rather than a large, assembly-line type of aura. This need is especially acute in the funeral industry, from which people in grief-stricken circumstances seek comfort, understanding, and fairness. Nobody understands and has leveraged the principle better than Robert L. Waltrip, founder, chairman, and chief executive of Service Corporation International (SCI), which handles one in every eleven funerals nationwide at its 662 homes in thirty-nine states. Approaching $1 billion in annual sales, SCI has succeeded by standing the chain concept—perfected by restaurants, retailers, and hotels—on its head. Instead of using a common name to vouch for consistency, its funeral homes keep the local names that promise distinction and personal service.

SCI recognizes that although hamburger chains might benefit from the customer's perception of quick-serve efficiency and standardization, such an assembly-line approach would offend most funeral home patrons. As one writer said, "Nobody wants a McFuneral."[26]

SCI has been successful by combining the local with the regional focus. It purchases a group of funeral homes with deep local roots in a particular area. Each home appears to be locally owned and operated, but the business structure allows centralized purchasing, training, finance, transportation, and embalming. Whereas in a local funeral home the vehicles sit idle waiting for a call, SCI uses hearses and other vehicles at more than one location, thus maximizing their value. By clustering homes in a region, SCI keeps staff and equipment consistently busy.

SCI as a corporate entity is essentially invisible. Instead, there are many local funeral homes that meet the needs of clients with efficiency and profitability. In New York City, where ethnic and economic groups all insist on their own funeral homes, SCI meets those needs by maintaining the local standards that established loyalty to the local company in the first place.

Campbell, the leading chiefly Christian funeral home, on Manhattan's East Side, and Riverside, the leading Jewish funeral home, on the West Side, proclaim their identity in bold lettering on sidewalk canopies and awnings. Plaques inside preserve the memory of their founders. At each home, SCI stays anonymous.

Your business may profit from positioning itself as a local supplier, as SCI has, or it may do better by declaring itself an exclusive market, as Packard initially did. Whatever the particulars of your own business, your image must be clear to both your clients and your staff. Decide who you are, and project that image clearly if you want to attract your target market.

IDENTIFYING HIGH-POTENTIAL PROSPECTS

At the beginning of this chapter, we identified three key marketing issues that must be addressed. We have examined the first two: targeting your market, and creating the right positioning in the mind of the potential customer. Let's consider the third of this marketing trilogy: identifying and separating out high-potential prospects for additional selling and marketing efforts in the future. This is an important step since establishing stringent qualifying criteria can greatly reduce the risk that you'll waste valuable time on a supposed opportunity that, with a bit of just-in-time analysis, you would otherwise no longer pursue.

Let's examine the all-important qualifying step in two circumstances: (1) when you contact the suspect, and (2) when the suspect contacts you.

When You Contact the Suspect

When you take the initiative and contact suspects over the phone or in person, your initial objective is to get these potential customers to give you their attention and time so that you can qualify them. In today's business environment, people are conditioned to say *no* much more quickly than yes to a new purchase opportunity, so a careful strategy to overcome this resistance is important. Your opener is critical to a successful first contact; there are three requirements for making this initial contact effective:

1. *Introduction.* Address the person by name and then pause for him to respond (say, "Mr. Jones?") if you are talking with this person live. The more formal "Mr. Jones" is preferred to "Bill" if you are contacting this person for the first time. The formality sends a signal of respect.

2. *Statement of benefit.* Immediately offer a statement that summarizes what you do and what makes you unique. This statement must be simple and to the point, with well-chosen benefits that the suspect finds appealing.

3. *Permission to continue.* Ask a question that seeks permission to pursue the discussion.

Applying the three-part approach in a telephone call, consider this:

[Introduction:] Mr. Nunn? [Wait for his response] This is Jill Griffin with the Griffin Group in Austin, Texas. [Benefit statement:] We're specialists in helping companies like yours attract profitable customers and keep them loyal. [Permission to continue:] Is now a good time to talk briefly?

Such an opener is designed to gain the suspect's permission for you to spend more time with him once you have initiated the contact.

Now let's look at the dynamics when the suspect contacts you. Remember, your first step is to qualify. You need cooperation to get the information you require.

When the Suspect Contacts You

Motivating the potential customer to take an action that then identifies the customer as a potential prospect is one strategy often used by marketers. For example, Renault, the automaker, sent watches with no movement in them to three hundred thousand German car buyers. Along with the watch was a note saying that the rest of the watch could be obtained by test-driving a Renault. One-third of the Germans, one hundred thousand people, took the bait. Of those, two thousand bought Renaults.

How was the program's ultimate success determined? By the number of watches given away? By the number of people who test-drove the Renault? No. The program's success was evaluated by the number of cars actually sold.[27]

For many companies, the problem is not how to get potential buyers to contact them but how to move them toward a sale once they call. In his newsletter to furniture retailers, publisher Jerry Fried addresses this issue in a feature article aptly titled "Prospects Are Expensive, So Give a Damn." Fried begins his article with these questions: "What possible good is there in getting people into your store if you don't sell them anything? Do you have any idea how much it costs to deliver a warm, breathing prospect into your store?"[28]

Many companies, regardless of industry, operate as if getting the potential customer to contact them is the real feat. They fail to develop a system for qualifying the suspect as a high-potential prospect and then converting the prospect into a buyer.

Consider this real-life example. It was the afternoon of day two of Wayne Morgan's three-day sales seminar for residential real estate agents on fulfilling classroom licensing training. Wayne brought a speakerphone into the training room and called, at random, homes listed for sale by realtors in the classified section of the newspaper. Wayne called six realtors. On each call, he identified himself as a possible buyer and asked three questions:

1. Will the house sell VA [loan for veterans]?
2. Does the house have a large lot?
3. What down payment is required?

In every case, the agent simply answered the question Wayne asked. Period. Finally, Wayne said, "Give me the address and I'll drive by. If I like it, I'll call you back."[29] Without any hesitation, all six agents gave him the address, but not one asked him for his telephone number. Only one even asked his name. "Wayne" was the answer; the agent did not probe further to get the last name!

This example points out a common problem with marketing and sales programs. Oftentimes, more thought and preparation goes into how to get the telephone to ring (strategy) than what to do once it rings (execution and implementation). A company must ensure that the staff members receiving these calls are appropriately trained to handle them. They must be trained to "shepherd" a suspect through the qualifying process and, once the suspect is qualified as a prospect, must have the sales skills for turning a qualified prospect into a first-time buyer. Otherwise, the effectiveness is greatly diminished.

In the case of these real estate ads, aside from making the home seller feel that his or her house is being marketed, the ads are basically used to create a pool of suspects that can be qualified as prospects and ultimately sold a home. If this principle is not understood, then you end up with agents only answering questions, not asking them. Their options for qualifying people and then ultimately making a sale to them are dismally lost.

How to Qualify a Suspect

Whether you contact a suspect or a suspect contacts you, the person must be qualified as a prospect. To do this, several key questions need to be answered. These questions may vary depending on your particular industry, but general concepts apply; does the suspect have:

- A problem you can help solve (does the person have a need)?
- The desire to solve the problem (what does the person want)?
- The authority to buy?
- The willingness and ability to pay for your products or services?
- The authority to make a decision within a certain time period?

A yes to these questions can "graduate" a suspect into a prospect. Let's revisit the question sequence from Wayne's training seminar and see how it could be changed.

Needs and Wants. To the question "Will the house sell VA?" the agent could have replied, "Yes. Is a VA loan important to you?" The realtor could use the same approach about the size of the lot: "Are you looking for a home with a large lot?" To the question "What down payment is required?" the agent could ask, "What size down payment would you be comfortable in making?"

This questioning approach enables the agent to stay in control of the qualifying process and seek answers to key questions. A little-known fact is that very few homes are ever sold through classified ads. The ads are designed to generate prospects that can be matched to other homes more in keeping with the prospect's buying needs. You cannot match if you cannot graduate the suspect into the prospect stage, however.

Let's look at the request for an address. Giving out the address loses the suspect. In addition, many homes do not have particularly good "curb appeal" but are "grabbers" only once the suspect is inside the front door. Wayne teaches this approach: tell the caller that the owner has asked that all prospective buyers be accompanied to the house and that the agency is bound to this commitment. The agent would then offer to accompany the caller to the home at the caller's convenience. Finally, Wayne coaches the agents to request the name and telephone number of the caller. Only then can they possibly follow up.

Yes, the agents will get some resistance and some negative answers. But those responses are a screening device as well. Ask yourself this: If you were really interested in the house, would you let an agent's request to show you the property keep you from moving ahead? Experience says no.

Authority to Buy. If you are not talking with the decision maker, you may be wasting your time. To determine if your suspect is the decision maker, pay close attention to how you ask the question. You do not want to ask, "Are you the decision maker?" since the question can bruise or insult. Instead, ask such questions as "Before making your final decision, who else will you want to consult with?" and "Whose name will appear on the contract?" If another party is identified, you should try to speak to the decision makers together. In some cases, however, you may have to work through the decision influencer to sell yourself to the ultimate decision maker.

Sometimes you are faced with a totally unpredictable set of circumstances. Mark McCormick, chairman of International Management Group, a sports marketing company, tells of an experience with an automobile company that was introducing a new model and wanted to be identified with a major sport. For months, McCormick's company had bombarded a senior vice president at the automaker's advertising agency with proposals, with no results. Yet the executive continued to encourage McCormick.

Just by chance, a friend at the auto company informed McCormick that this SVP was the wrong person to talk to. The automaker had moved sports promotion in-house. The advertising SVP, whose ego may have been bruised, did not have the nerve to tell McCormick.

Willingness and Ability to Pay. Business consultant Nido Quebein uses a qualifying technique that is also the first step in his relationship with a suspect. Nido has a set fee for conducting a needs assessment for a prospective client. He reasons that if the prospective client is unwilling to pay for the needs assessment, he or she is probably unlikely to agree to the larger fees for the consulting project. Nido tests the criterion of ability and willingness to pay early in discussion with the suspect.

Many professionals become uncomfortable and often apologetic when the conversation turns to fees. The best approach is to confidently state, "Our fee for that service is $4,000," and then follow up the statement with the question "Is that in your budget?" The question helps you uncover any price resistance; if it exists, you can deal with it then and there.

Time Period. Is your suspect in a position to make a decision within a certain period of time? Several years ago, I was at a "parade of homes," where community home builders showcase new homes in a subdivision over a two- or three-day period. Salespeople representing these builders are on hand to prospect for new business. It is imperative that the suspects be quickly separated from the prospects, and when the crowds are large, these salespeople must work smart, not just hard.

I heard a savvy salesperson ask a zinger of a qualifying question to a woman who expressed interest in buying a custom-built home. His first qualifying question to her was "Do you have your present home listed for sale?" I was struck by how profound this question was as a qualifier. In one single question, the salesperson could get a good gauge of the woman's seriousness in changing homes. A response such as "Yes, our home is for sale with a realtor and we've had a couple of calls" says a lot about the likelihood that that this person is a qualified prospect for a custom-built home.

On the other hand, a response like "My husband refuses to even let a realtor appraise our house; we moved in a year ago, and he says he wants to stay at least three more years" would make the woman a less likely prospect. Understanding your suspect's buying cycle is important to the qualifying process.

With these questions answered, you have now determined that the person you are talking to has the authority to make the decision to hire you, has a problem you can help solve, and has the resources to pay you. In essence, you have a qualified prospect. This person is truly deserving of additional investment of time and resources to convert her from a qualified prospect into a first-time customer.

Attracting plenty of high-potential prospects requires targeting, positioning, and qualifying. After you have gotten your own house in order by learning all you can about your market, defined your target market, created and refined your company's image, and qualified prospects, you are ready to move on to the next step. Each step is essential if your business is to be successful in the long haul.

Although making the first sale is not necessarily the most important part of the process, it is definitely the most exciting and the *sine qua non*; if you don't make the sale, you won't develop the buyer into a loyal customer.

SUMMARY

- A well-chosen target market dramatically increases your probability of successfully qualifying prospects and developing loyal customers.
- Market research, surveys, and segmentation are all vital tools in properly targeting your market.
- Customer service begins with the company's vision of the customer. A smart business carefully selects its customers and then learns from them.
- Allow customers to know who you are and what you stand for. It helps them identify with you and can enhance your position in the market.
- Two key positioning tools are image and character. It is vital to choose the vehicle that best supports your positioning in the marketplace.
- The bottom line is that you must deliver what you communicate.
- In qualifying a prospect, train your employees to ask the right questions. Too many marketing plans focus on strategy and fall short on execution.
- Customer profiling and computer data modeling can help you identify high-potential prospects and pinpoint the marketing messages to which they are likely to respond.
- The Internet is proving to be a valuable research tool for quickly testing consumer demand for new products and for refining existing products to match consumer preferences.

GETTING STARTED

- Diligently track where your best prospects originate. This understanding then helps you gauge the effectiveness of your marketing dollars. Adjust your marketing dollars to focus on those sources that prove most reliable in bringing in prospects that graduate to loyal buyers.

- Examine your firm's qualifying criteria for prospects. Are the criteria the same for every salesperson in your firm? Are the criteria in writing? If not, establish a written set of qualifying criteria and train your sales team accordingly. Update as needed.

- Compare the profitability of your current customer segments, and rank them from most profitable to least. Let this ranking guide you in targeting prospects.

CHAPTER FIVE

Turning Qualified Prospects
into First-Time Buyers

Turning qualified prospects into first-time customers requires a direct or indirect act of selling. Let's take a quick glance back at the history of selling in America.

Since before the beginning of recorded time, the art of salesmanship has been practiced, converting qualified prospects into first-time customers. Archaeological evidence supports the idea that Stone Age people traveled great distances to barter for goods unavailable in the area where they hunted and gathered food. In effect, "selling" has been taking place for thousands of years.

For a long time, there were no specialists who concentrated their efforts exclusively on selling. Generally, in those distant days, whoever had too much of one item and not enough of another simply took the leftovers and traded them for something else. In the early 1800s, all of that changed. It happened in Massachusetts, where some mill owners decided they wanted more business than they were getting. They found a man who would take samples of their work around the countryside and talk with potential customers about bringing their raw materials to the mill. He was, in fact, the first salesman. His only job was to get more orders. Although it is common practice today, in those days it was an innovative and revolutionary idea. But the idea took hold and worked for the mill. As a result, more and more manufacturers sent representatives out to find business. Selling has followed that pattern ever since.

For the past two hundred years, American business has focused primarily on the mission of getting new customers, and sales forces across America were diligently trained to maximize sales. The zeal of customer acquisition and of making the numbers has done much to make American industry strong. Unfortunately, in the process, the same drive for sales and profits caused some buyers to be misinformed, misled, and high-pressured into buying things they later wished they hadn't. That reality has left a negative perception about selling.

When I taught marketing at the University of Texas, I included in my class lectures a section on selling. I always began the lecture by asking my business students to make a list of adjectives that best describe a salesperson. Words like *manipulative, insincere, untrustworthy, opportunistic,* and *evasive* were frequently heard. The emphasis on hard selling and acquisition marketing has taken its toll.

Now, almost two hundred years after that early sales strategy was introduced in Massachusetts, a new breed of salesmanship is emerging. Today, "value-added selling" and "consultive selling" are the priority across many industries. This new generation of selling suggests that companies are beginning to understand that the strategy of "making the sale" is not always compatible with the strategy of developing a customer.

Alfred Zeinen made it clear how his conception of a customer differed from the norm soon after he became CEO of Gillette. When asked how his company's approach departed from his competitor's, Zeinen answered, "We capture customers. Remington sells shavers."[1]

The process of selling to a customer is an admirable, worthwhile pursuit. You will never have the loyal customer base you deserve without first mastering the principles of selling. This chapter examines how to use selling principles to help lay the groundwork for long-term customer development and retention, and in doing so how to turn a qualified prospect into a first-time customer.

THE INGREDIENTS OF A SUCCESSFUL SALE

A recent sales force productivity study sponsored by *Sales and Marketing Management* magazine surveyed 192 companies representing a total of nearly ten thousand sales representatives. Survey respondents reported that it took an average of seven calls to close a first sale, compared with only three calls to close a subsequent sale.[2]

Although recent statistics continue to prove the validity of the frequency of "seven," the concept has been recognized by some marketers for more than a half-century. The "rule of seven" can be traced back to the 1930s movie industry. The Great Depression made money scarce, and the studios quickly realized that despite the talents of film stars the likes of Charlie Chaplin, Gary Cooper, and Marlene Dietrich, a movie ticket was anything but a sought-after commodity. What's more, the movie marketers had a product with a short life span. The movie was viable only until the next feature film came to the theater. Movie marketers had to find a way to entice the most people in the shortest length of time to spend their hard-earned money on a movie.

The rule of seven offered the solution. The movie marketers found that a prospective moviegoer had to hear about a particular film at least seven times in a seventy-two-hour period in order to decide to buy a ticket.[3]

The objective here is to get a realistic picture of what it may take to turn your qualified prospect into a first-time buyer. Depending on your product or service, it may be unrealistic to expect to get a yes on your first, third, or even sixth visit with the prospect. You are building a relationship, and it takes time to grow a relationship.

Perseverance Pays

Jerel Walters is a sales representative for Union Carbide Specialty Powders, selling industrial powders for use in transportation systems. A year and a half ago, Jerel qualified American Airlines as a potential new customer. Over the next eighteen months, Jerel regularly called on the purchasing agent, discussing such benefits as price, quality, and service. The airline's purchasing agent was not particularly receptive. He had been in his position for a number of years and had strong loyalty to another company supplying specialty powder. Nevertheless, Jerel continued to contact the buyer regularly with updated proposals and new product information. With each contact, he learned more and more about his prospect's specialty powder needs.

Then something happened. Jerel received a call from American Airlines. The buyer had recently retired, and a new purchasing agent had replaced him. The new purchasing agent needed an emergency shipment of powder. Did Jerel have the quantity on hand? Could it be at American Airlines in twenty-four hours? Jerel and Union Carbide said yes to both.

Shortly after the shipment, the new purchasing agent contacted Jerel, ready to discuss a sizable contract with Union Carbide. He had reviewed his predecessor's files and was interested in exploring the cost-saving opportunities found in Jerel's proposals. How does the story end? The Jerel company got 27 percent of the American Airlines specialty powder business, representing $250,000 in annual sales.

How many contacts and follow-ups did Jerel invest in this first-time sale? Ninety-two completed telephone calls, thirteen onsite meetings, and eighteen letters over a twenty-four-month period, according to Jerel's computerized sales activity tracking system. The reward for his efforts was a $250,000 annual contract. It's a fact: 20 percent of the sales representatives sell 80 percent of the products. The ones who keep working to build a good relationship with a prospect reap the biggest rewards.

The Required Investment May Be Rising

Although the norm in closing has been seven contacts in the past, experience is suggesting that the number may be rising. Why? At least three things appear to be contributing to the amount of time and contact required to convert a prospect into a first-time buyer.

First, customers and suppliers are forming deeper alliances. Product quality, consistency of service, and trust are the key to the relationship. Price is frequently a secondary factor rather than a primary one. The relationship, once formed, can be hard to infiltrate.

Second, in a tough economy customers often change their mental outlook. They avoid salespeople, thinking it is time to save money rather than spend it.

Third, cultural differences in a global market make relationship building critical. Learning and adapting to different ways of doing business takes time.

Consider the experience of the Stern Organization, an investment real estate brokerage in New York that has sold more than two million square feet of real estate in the past two years. One of Stern's brokers may meet with a potential investor half a dozen times without presenting a property. It's a selling style that goes over well, particularly with the Japanese. "We talk about political views, social things, investment objectives. When we cease being strangers, then we may talk business," says Stern. "I believe in making long-term relationships instead of short-term, quick deals."[4]

Patience Is the New Watchword

The need to market internationally demands a new level of patience from American marketers, one not encountered before. "Global markets are the thing from now until the end of time," says Tom Peters. "That's true for small companies, many of which have extraordinary records overseas, as well as for the giant companies." Unlike the Western style of quick, overnight alliance and "let's make a deal," Peters summarizes the essence of a successful global marketing strategy in two statements: "Relationships are everything" and "We must learn to be patient."

Consider these statistics from Peters. It took ARCO three and a half years to negotiate a tiny offshore drilling contract with China. It took Rohm, the Silicon Valley telecommunications equipment maker, twenty visits over a multiyear period to land its first tiny order with a Japanese company. It took Coca-Cola ten years of investment and development of business in Japan before it first turned a profit. It takes time to develop a relationship.[5]

In his book *Thriving on Chaos*, Peters suggests that we'd be better off if we pretended that all our customers are foreigners who do not speak our language. He maintains that we carry around a crippling disadvantage in being overly concerned about our products and services. Our customers, whether international or here in the United States, see the product through an entirely different set of lenses. Peters tells us, "Education is not the answer; listening and adapting is."

IT'S A MATTER OF TRUST

Can the person and the company be trusted? That's the first thought most people have in considering dealing with someone they haven't done business with before. The issue of trust is translated into such thoughts as these:

- Is the person really knowledgeable?
- Can we trust his integrity?
- Is the salesperson concerned with our welfare, or just with making a sale?
- Will the company still be in business in two years?

Actions speak louder than words. When you think long-term, the willingness to invest in the relationship makes sense. Rich Barsalou, a financial planner with John Hancock, realized that breaking into a new market would be difficult. He began by seeking out a reputable, well-known accountant in the area from whom he might be able to get some referrals to prospective clients. Instead of just asking for referrals, Barsalou hired the accountant to prepare his income tax return for him. He began to establish a relationship. Barsalou got to know the accountant on a personal level, and as time passed he gained his respect and trust. Eventually, the accountant gave him some names of prospective clients.

One of the referrals was a man who had recently purchased a local business and was in need of an employee benefit plan. Barsalou traveled to the plant at his own expense. To his disappointment, he discovered that the forty employees were well satisfied with the service and low cost of their existing plan. Barsalou soon concluded that his company could not offer a more competitive price, and so he offered to act as the company's negotiator in renewing the contract. What did Barsalou receive in return? No money, but lots of goodwill.

Soon after, that same client hired Barsalou to develop and launch a pension plan valued at $125,000 a year. The pension plan covered the local plant and another group in a second state that had traditionally faced high worker's compensation costs because of the nature of the research work the group did. Barsalou was able to persuade his company to offer a lower rate if the members of the group passed a health examination.

To make sure the deal went through without any hitches, Barsalou wanted to close the sale quickly. He took an inspector and a nurse with him to the other state and quickly had all the workers examined, the applications completed, and the sale made. Within a day, he had eighteen new disability plan members (most of whom later bought life insurance) and a happy client. The man who owned the business was so pleased with Barsalou's quick and satisfactory action that he bought $2 million worth of life insurance.

But the new business kept coming. After talking to his clients about Barsalou's performance, the accountant became a customer. He replaced his company's disability plan with one from Barsalou and added $2 million in life insurance for his firm. "It started with my tax return," said Barsalou, "and I had no idea where it would take me."[6]

Barsalou's experience illustrates an important lesson: trust is like credit. If you are reliable, pay your bills on time, and have a good work history and income, you can usually get credit. On the other hand, if you have a record of unpaid bills and a spotty work history, credit is hard to get. In some circumstances, it takes only one mistake to permanently tarnish your record. We may not keep a running audit on each other's trustworthiness, but we do learn over time who we can count on and who's more likely to disappoint us. Whether we know it or not, we do have a trust account. When we show that we are trustworthy, our trust account builds.

In deciding whether or not to trust another person or situation, we know the most important information we have in helping us make our decision is history. How has this person (or company) performed in the past? What's the record of trustworthiness? To gain and keep any prospect's confidence and trust, you must first deserve it. Let's outline five key trust builders.

1. Appeal to a Prospect's Recognition Filter

A study on credibility found that when people hear about you, your company, or your product four or more times, they tend to perceive you as credible. This principle is what led sales management expert Rick Barrera to his cardinal rule of prospecting: before you appeal to someone's need, first become familiar and recognizable. Barrera sends a prospect three or four letters, a week apart, before making his first sales call. This way, he avoids making a totally cold call.

Barrera explains, "Rather than having my prospects read the content of my direct mail to decide whether my product or service fits their current need, I want them to recognize my name, and my company name, because of my direct mail. I don't care if they read it; I just want them to see it and recognize it."[7]

Experience has taught Barrera that a typical prospect reads mail as follows. The first letter is glanced at and thrown away. On receiving the second letter, the prospect says to himself, *Didn't I get something from this person before?* With the third letter, the receiver wonders, *I know I got something else from this person, but what did I decide?* By the fourth letter, the prospect thinks, *I've heard lots about them; maybe I should give them a call.*

When Barrera makes his first personal call on the prospect, he comes as a somewhat known quantity, and he usually gets an appointment right away. Through using direct mail, he has established a certain amount of credibility. His prospects have heard his name and his company name and are willing to consider what he has to say. Using these mail contacts, Barrera has taken the first step to opening the door to a relationship.

Studies show that, on average, one out of every ten interactions with a prospect or buyer is a transaction. This means the remaining nine interactions are marketing or service-related contacts. Rick Barrera found direct mail an effective trust builder for his business, but sometimes a potential purchaser is turned off by unsolicited marketing. Fortunately, the Internet environment presents an alternative: permission or opt-in marketing, whereby prospects and customers allow a firm to market to them specific products and services about which they have expressed interest. For example, prospective buyers typically opt in when searching a Website for information ("Check this box to receive a monthly e-mail newsletter about our latest widget news") or purchasing online ("Check here to receive online notification of our next sale").

First evangelized by business author Seth Godin in his book *Permission Marketing,* the concept is based on the premise that because these prospects have given their permission for your communication, they are willing and ready to listen to what your company offers. Over time and with ongoing dialogue, your can learn more and more about their specific needs, enabling you to further customize your e-mail messages to them. The payoff can be substantial. Permission marketing advocates report that relevant and personalized communications can boost the response rate to the range of 30 percent, a big improvement over the 3 percent of printed direct mail. (It's important to note that Barrera followed his direct mail communication with a face-to-face sales call, thereby boosting his conversion rate above what it would have been if he relied on direct mail alone.) What's more, the price for permission marketing is extremely affordable. E-mail marketing can cost a firm from one to twenty-five cents per message, compared to one to two dollars per piece of direct mail.

But Nick Usborne offers an important caution about this technique: "Permission marketing isn't just about getting permission. It's not just a box with a check in it. When a person checks a box or says 'Yes', it doesn't mean that you now own the customer and the customer's constant attention. You have that customer for just a very brief moment. The key to success is how you use that moment. Help people find what they want; be trustworthy, and obsess over service."[8]

2. Put the Customer's Interest Ahead of Your Own

Although your goal in business is to make your own enterprise successful, the best way you can accomplish the goal is to make your customers happy and successful themselves. One way to ensure that both you and your customers are successful is by giving them the information they need to make comfortable and informed decisions.

Sharon Story learned this during her first experience as a salesperson. Story was selling industrial filter bags. During her visit to her new territory, she found that the client, a large steel company, was having a great many problems with its bags. The client asked many questions, and Story answered as well as she could, but both ended the meeting feeling dissatisfied.

A few weeks later, Story arranged for the general manager of her company to visit the executive and present him with the technical information he needed. By that time, however, an order had already been placed with another company.

Story was convinced that she had mishandled the account and that it was lost forever. But a few months later, the steel company executive called her. He was reviewing quotes for another bag order and realized Story's company was not on the bid list. At the executive's request, Story submitted a bid on another bag order. In this case, Story was successful. Her company got the $150,000 order. Story says, "If you go out of the way to try to help a prospect or customer, sooner or later one of them will go out of the way to help you."[9]

3. Use Only Honest Facts and Figures to Back Up Claims

Inexperienced salespeople (as well as veterans) can fall into the trap of telling customers what they want to hear in order to keep them happy. Since making the sale is the goal, there is an incredible tendency for salespeople to do everything possible to get the order. This is often the case in selling long-distance services, according to Lenora Hyche, a top sales producer for American Telco, a long-distance company. For the past two years, Hyche has earned the distinction of being her company's most productive salesperson; in one year she tripled the company average for individual sales by bringing in 596 new accounts, for close to $1 million in annual billings.

Hyche recalled a recent experience in which she and another long-distance carrier were in contention for a firm's business. Responding to the firm's request for specialized options, Hyche submitted a proposal that included purchase of some additional equipment. Without the new equipment, Hyche reported, the capabilities could not be provided. The competitor's sales representative insisted that his company could meet the firm's requirements without new equipment, and he submitted a much lower bid. The firm accepted the competitor's proposal.

Knowing the competitor had misrepresented the facts, Hyche graciously accepted the decision and took a wait-and-see attitude. Weeks later, the firm called Hyche with instructions to come and install the new equipment. The firm had dismissed the rival carrier. After misrepresentations and repeated delays, the sales representative conceded that he could not actually meet the firm's requirements without the purchase of new equipment. This unhappy experience resulted in the firm's staunch refusal to consider subsequent proposals from the competitive carrier as well as from its subsidiaries.

The tendency for salespeople to do everything to get the order can backfire, as evidenced by another story, told me by a friend.

My friend was looking for a new car. She lives in a small town and found a program car that she liked. This car had been driven for a short time by employees of the dealership. In discussing the car with the salesperson, she asked specifically about the warranty.

"Am I right in believing that the warranty is the same as on a new car?" she asked.

"Yes," the salesperson confirmed. "Just like a new car: three years or thirty thousand miles."

"And that includes everything?" she pressed.

"Everything except normal maintenance—gas, oil, that sort of thing."

So my friend bought the car. She was pleased that she could buy from a local dealer, and the car suited her needs. A week or so later, however, she took the car in to the repair shop to fix a couple of small things that she'd found didn't work right.

The shop told her those things were not covered by the warranty. She wanted to know why not.

"Well, they were covered up to three thousand miles, but since yours is a program car, it already has more miles on it than that. The salesperson should have made this clear."

The cost was minimal, but my friend had lost confidence in the dealership. A relationship that most likely would have lasted for years and through several automobile purchases was spoiled. She will not go back to buy her next car at that shop, simply because a salesperson was too eager to close the sale. Had she been told the facts to begin with, she probably would have bought the car anyway and expected to pay for minor repairs. But since that wasn't the case, she now has a bad feeling about the whole dealership.

Always tell the truth. False statements, or even the inference of falsity, can come back and haunt you, particularly when it's time to ask the customer to reorder.

4. Promise Only What You Can Deliver

There exists no more critical time to build trust than during the initial encounter between prospect and salesperson. With no prior history, the prospect is often anxious and earnestly searching for reasons to believe. Handled correctly, an early encounter can lay the foundation for a relationship and sale. Mishandled, these encounters can ruin any opportunity for business now or in the future.

Consider the letter in Exhibit 5.1, received by a travel agency that grossly mishandled the follow-up contact with a qualified prospect who had the potential to become a loyal, profitable corporate travel client.

Exhibit 5.1. A Lost Prospect Speaks Out.

Dear *(Name Withheld)*,

I received your business solicitation folder today—it is well done.

    As a new businessman in town in December, I had no travel agent. I met your owner at a Chamber or Boy Scout meeting—I can't recall which. I told him I was looking for a good travel agent. I later called him back to remind him of my need and to ask for information on Barcelona for the Olympics. I called again in April asking for a visit. At that point I went with another agency, since no one from your agency appeared interested (after my three calls).

    Since then: My son and I went to Barcelona, first class for the Olympics; my wife and I have visited Vancouver twice; I've been to meetings in Colorado Springs, first class; I took all 14 members of my family to Florida in May; I've taken three friends to Boston; and I've taken business trips to Phoenix, Washington, and Boca Raton.

    There have been various other trips to sundry locations. I've been wondering if I'd ever hear from your agency, and I guess this mass mailing is it! Put down in your book that I sure tried to do business with you. I'm not mad, just curious to know that you're still there! My current agency says I'm a real good customer—like to go places and complain rarely. I went there since I met the owner in a barber shop and she was in my office the next day.

    Why did I write this letter? Because I appreciate it when someone tells me how thoroughly we've screwed up a potential relationship.

Sincerely,

(Name Withheld)

As this prospect's words so vividly illustrate, trust is an all-important factor in converting a prospect into a first-time customer. At this stage, the prospect is looking for clues as to what he might expect as a customer and why he should trust this company. Nothing stifles trust more quickly with a prospect than poor follow-up. The travel agency demonstrated to the prospect by its actions (or lack of them) that it is not reliable. It flunked the prospect's first test of trust, confidence, and reliability.

5. Practice Team Selling

Team selling can help build prospect trust. That's what sixteen years of leadership has taught Ann Machado, CEO of Creative Staffing, a $13 million temporary services firm in Miami. When a big sale is on the line, a six-member sales team—comprising Machado, her chief financial officer, her sales director, the sales rep, the operations manager, and the staffer who would service the account—mobilize to make the call. Machado says, "When you explain what each person does, it helps quickly build the credibility." Customers agree. "It's nice to have access to all the players. You know who's going to carry out the service," concurs one.

In addition to building credibility, Machado says the team selling approach also reduces overall selling time and cost. "It used to take us three months or more to close a major deal," she relates, "but now it can take us as little as four weeks because the team gathers more and better information—faster." It's a divide-and-conquer approach. While the operations manager may be exploring worker training requirements, the CFO can tackle issues such as worker's comp and payment planning. This due diligence has enabled Machado and her team to make winning proposals to prospective clients and consequently earn sizeable contracts, worth $2–5 million. The benefits of team selling have gone beyond the initial sale. "Just recently, two of our $2 million accounts were under attack by a competitor. We applied the same team approach and saved the accounts," she says.[10]

LISTENING: AN IMPORTANT FACTOR IN BUILDNG TRUST AND RAPPORT

Golda Meir once said, "You cannot shake hands with a clenched fist." The secret to unlocking the clenched fist and developing a sense of trust and rapport with a new prospect is to learn to listen.

Listening is the key to building trust because of three important factors:

1. I am much more inclined to trust a person who shows respect for me and for what I say.

2. I am much more likely to trust you if you've listened carefully and helpfully to my problems than if you've tried to tell me what my problems are.

3. The more I've told you, the more I trust you.

The Key: Listen More and Talk Less

A recent survey of 432 corporate buyers found that 87 percent of the respondents said salespeople don't ask enough questions about their needs, and 49 percent reported salespeople just "talk too much." "Poor listening skills have a functional implication as well as a social implication," observes sales training executive Sean Carew. "You won't get the information, and you won't be able to relate to what your customer's needs are."[11]

Why Listening Is Hard Work

On the surface, listening seems simple. We all talk; we all listen. But it's not that simple. Why is listening hard? Why do so few people do it well? Basically, the problem is caused by the fact that we think much faster than we talk. For most Americans, the average rate of speech is around 125 words per minute.[12] This rate is slow for the human brain, which is made up of more than thirteen billion cells and operates in such a complicated manner that, in comparison, great modern digital computers seem slow. As a result, most people find that because of the slow rate of speech, they have time to think of things other than the words being spoken. Subconsciously, they decide to sandwich a few thoughts of their own between the auditory ones that are arriving so slowly.

But sooner or later, on one of the mental sidetracks, the listener is sure to stay away too long, and when she returns, the speaker is moving along ahead of her. At this point, it becomes harder for the listener to understand, simply because she has missed part of the oral message. The private mental sidetracks become more inviting than ever, and the listener slides off into several of them. Slowly, the listener misses more and more of what the speaker has to say.

Although the obvious solution is to slow thinking down to the speaking rate, it is almost impossible to do so. Listening creates spare time in the brain that is almost automatically filled up by our own thoughts.

A major task in helping people listen better is teaching them to use their spare thinking time well. An extensive study of people's listening habits found that good listeners regularly engage in four mental activities during listening. They tend to direct a maximum amount of thought to the message being received, leaving a minimum amount of time for mental excursions or sidetracks that lead away from the talker's thought. In their book *Listening to People* authors Ralph Nichols and Leonard Stevens outline four processes used by a good listener:

1. The listener thinks ahead of the talker, trying to anticipate what the oral discourse is leading to and what conclusions will be drawn from the words spoken at the moment.

2. The listener weighs the evidence used by the talker to support the points being made. *Is this evidence valid?* the listener asks herself. *Is it complete evidence?*

3. Periodically, the listener reviews and mentally summarizes the points of the talk completed thus far.

4. Throughout the talk, the listener listens between the lines, in search of meaning that is not necessarily put into spoken words.

Regarding listening between the lines, the listener pays attention to nonverbal communication (facial expression, gesture, tone of voice) to see if it adds meaning to the spoken words. The listener asks herself, *Is the talker purposely skirting some area of the subject? If so, why?*

Listening with an Open Mind

Although we often think that we listen carefully to what others say, in many cases we come to a conversation with certain expectations, goals, and preset outcomes in mind. We listen selectively to what is being said, so that we hear only what fits into our preconceived notion of how the conversation should go. If we are selling, we often spend a lot of time thinking how to get the conversation over with and get on to closing the sale. Instead of paying attention to what the other person says, we listen for remarks that confirm what we already think is or should be the case. Rather than listening for information from an impartial point of view, too often our emotions are involved; we hear what we wish to hear rather than what is actually said.

"Hear the person out" is a phrase that describes an essential part of true listening. It requires giving up or setting aside one's own prejudice, frame of reference, and desire so as to experience as much as possible the speaker's world from his point of view. Here are some proven techniques for increasing the quality of listening.

The "Visitor from Another Planet" Technique. Communications specialist Elaine Zuker uses the visitor-from-another-planet method to become a better listener. She says that if you approach new people as if you have just landed on their planet and are trying to gain information, you will have fewer preconceived ideas about how the conversation is going. If you were on another planet, you would have no expectations. You would ask questions because you genuinely wanted information. Does this person speak as you do? Does this person talk about things in the same way you think of them?

Simply gathering information without evaluating it makes for much better listening. If you avoid deciding in advance whether the information is good or bad, right or wrong, strange or familiar, you are much better equipped to understand what is being said. If you continue the planetary fantasy further, you can imagine that you must report on everything you learned when you return to your own planet. Thus you pay closer attention knowing that your information is important—and that it must be unbiased.

The "Looking for Negative Evidence" Technique. Learning to be unbiased in your listening is important. Most of us automatically have an emotional reaction to another person and what he or she says. Our inclination is to find evidence to support the emotional response, so we listen only for the words that confirm what we feel. Developing the technique to search for evidence to dispute our emotional first reaction helps us hear more clearly what is being said. Initially, this is not an easy task. It is much easier and more instinctive to find confirmation for our beliefs. It can be done, though, and it is helpful in understanding how another person perceives the situation differently. If we make up our minds to seek out the ideas that might prove us wrong, as well as those that might prove us right, we are less in danger of missing what people have to say.

Listen for Ideas, Not Facts. Sometimes it is easier to listen to the surface of a conversation, rather than delve deep to the essential ideas contained in the words. People want to communicate their ideas, not a conglomeration of facts, but we often latch onto the facts and ignore the ideas behind them. Facts are usually given as examples of the main idea or as supporting evidence for the idea. When we listen specifically to understand the ideas, the facts become of secondary importance. Grasping ideas is the skill on which the good listener concentrates. The facts are important, but only peripherally. Once you understand the idea, the facts will come easily to mind.

Once you've trained yourself to listen carefully, you'll see and hear things you would have overlooked before. You are likely to find that people are more intriguing or interesting to you. If you can suspend judgment, you're apt to discover a better sense of rapport with them.

WHEN IT'S YOUR TURN TO TALK

Quality listening is an exchange process that requires quality *talk*ing as well. Robert Watson, director of advertising services at AT&T, recalls a memorable meeting with a media sales rep for *Puck the Comic Weekly,* a syndicated newspaper section. The salesman was trying to convince Robert to give him business for Clearasil and other "teen" brands in his media group at Benton and Bowles.[13]

The salesman introduced himself, sat down, and immediately began an obviously prepared sales pitch. He spoke quickly and without pause about facts, figures, and the details of his magazine. Watson realized that he was hearing very little of the information, because he was almost hypnotized by the manner of delivery. Soon he became impatient at the nonstop babble and interrupted the salesman to ask what all that had to do with his specific clientele.

The salesman continued to talk—twenty minutes in all—without ever addressing Watson's concerns or questions. At that point, he had finished his presentation and took his leave. Watson had no inclination to place ads with this representative. Nor did he ever hear from the salesman again.

Effective salespeople listen and ask questions. Only then can they start to understand the prospect's needs, problems, and way of thinking. Ineffective salespeople do just the opposite: they spew a flood of words, covering every benefit, every aspect, of the product, believing that sooner or later, the prospect will hear something positive and buy. As in Watson's case, he observed and heard things that turned him off and lost his patience rather than winning his attention.

IDENTIFY YOUR CUSTOMER'S BUYING CYCLE

Although the canned sales pitch can be disastrous in developing a long-term customer, equally self-defeating is the salesperson who tries to close too soon.

Jan Ozer, an Atlanta-based marketing consultant, relates this experience[14]:

It was my first day with Barbara, our midwestern sales rep. The prospect was the Long Branch Inn, a resort recently purchased by a local businessman. Barbara had met with him twice before, once to interview and once to demo. She said the deal was ready to close.

We chatted briefly before Barbara summarized the benefits of the system and asked for the order.

Clearly surprised, the owner laughed and started in: "Place the order? What makes you think I'm ready to place the order? I haven't even started shopping yet!"

He pointed to the telephone on his desk. "You see that phone? It's part of a system I just paid $30,000 for. You know what I did before I bought it? First, I hired a consultant, because I don't know beans about telephones. He polled my staff to identify our needs. He arranged four product demonstrations. We visited sites and contacted references. We got proposals from all four companies. We selected two finalists and started negotiating. We got final offers from both and then we placed the order.

"I'm a businessman," he continued. "I don't make snap decisions. I'll be glad to speak with you next April, but I don't buy anything until I do my homework!"

Back in the car, I asked Barbara, "What made you think this deal would close today?"

"Well," she replied, "at training they said deals close after the demonstration. I demo'd last time, so I thought it would close today. How was I to know he wouldn't buy until April?" Barbara retorted defensively.

I responded, "You ask, Barbara, you ask!"

Barbara failed to distinguish between the seller's cycle and the buyer's cycle. In reality, a company buys at its own speed; the buyer has a selection process and timetable. It's important to uncover, understand, and confirm these needs before you begin to close.

LEARN TO THINK LIKE A SALES DOCTOR

Selling is a process of satisfying needs. A truly effective salesperson is able to describe a product or service to someone in a way that allows the person to see how the product or service satisfies a need. To do this, you must first ask the right questions to learn what the prospect needs.

In considering how to proceed effectively, think of yourself as a "sales doctor." That's the approach Sharp Electronics adopted to train its dealers several years ago. As Morton Cohen, a national programs manager, related, "A doctor's job is to find the pain and help the patient—the prospect—understand that it's urgent he get treatment."[15] The key to this approach lies in getting the prospect to discuss problems in the business, with specific emphasis on ones that your product or service can fix.

Writing in *Success,* Brian Azar illustrates Sharp's sales doctor approach with this dialogue:[16]

Never Begin with a Presentation—Ask Questions
Prospect: I should tell you, our present copier works just fine.
Sales doctor: Good. Can you tell me what you consider "fine"?
Prospect: I guess it jams sometimes, but overall, it gets the job done.
Sales doctor: So if it didn't jam, you'd be completely happy with it?
Prospect: Well, no. After we fix the jam, the next twenty or so copies are
     smudged, so we do them all over again.
Sales doctor: And that takes time?
Prospect: You bet it does.
Sales doctor: How do you feel then?
Prospect: Terrible! Our real work isn't getting done, and we lose money.

Probe Deeper
Already the prospect's mind is on a problem the salesman can correct—with a copier that doesn't jam. But the sales doctor needs to define the pain better.

Sales doctor: In your business, how important is a fast response to opportunity?

Prospect: Well, it's essential.

Sales doctor: How much money a year do copier malfunctions at your company cost you in time and opportunity?

Prospect: I never added it up.

Sales doctor: $10,000? $20,000?

Prospect: Close to $20,000, I guess.

Sales doctor: How does that lost $20,000 make you feel?

Prospect: Pretty awful.

Sales doctor: If you had a magic wand and money were no object, what would the solution be?

Qualify the Patient

The sales doctor still has to establish that the prospect has "health insurance." He asks, "What kind of budget do you have for your problem?"

If the prospect says, "We don't really have a budget now," ask him when he will. If that doesn't elicit a reasonable timetable, it may be time to "go for NO"—to end the sales call. Don't avoid rejection. Often, your worst answer isn't "no"—it's "I'll think it over." That leaves you both in limbo.

Now, Propose the Cure

If your prospect has the three key ingredients (pain, money to cure it, and authority to spend the money), you prescribe the cure—you make your presentation. Many salespeople want to present their whole routine anytime they see a prospect. The sales professional is willing to recognize that maybe the timing isn't right or that his product isn't a good fit and that there's no reason to go through the whole process:

Sales doctor: As I understand it, these are the problems we're hoping I can solve.

Then, summarize the problems. Pause every so often to "take the patient's temperature": Ask summary questions like, "Do you see how that would solve your problem?"

Just when you think it's time to close, ask a question like, "What should we do next?" When the patient answers that kind of query, he has, in fact, closed the sale himself.

Jeff Thull of the P.R.I.M.E. Resource Group sales consulting firm says this about the sales doctor "diagnostic" selling technique: "Diagnostic selling means understanding the customer's situations, fears and concern—his 'pain.' No two customers are alike, even two people in the same company or decision-making process. It might sound basic, but the starting point is to realize that all customers are different and unique; and you tailor your sales 'prescription' to fit each of their needs as closely as possible."[17]

Use your dialogue with a prospect to build confidence and trust by practicing two guidelines. First, avoid being a know-it-all. If you walk in the door with the attitude that you know everything, your credibility is already suspect. People want someone to help them find the answers to their problems, not someone who just tells them what to do. Second, help the prospect talk to you. If you are open and honest in your conversation with the prospect, it encourages that person to be honest with you. Trust is a two-way street. You disclose something to someone; and the prospect discloses something to you. Sharing your own ideas and concerns encourages your prospects to share theirs.

IT'S NOT JUST WHAT YOU SAY; IT'S HOW YOU SAY IT

Establishing rapport means more than providing information. It also involves verbal and body language resonance among people. Eye communication is highly important; communications experts suggest spending plenty of time looking at each person. Make contact for three to five seconds with a person to truly achieve eye communication. Body language is also critical in building rapport. Even while sitting down and presenting to a single buyer, make sure you use gestures to communicate your excitement about your product or service.

Humor can also be a valuable tool for building rapport. A good example of how a sense of humor can make a sale comes from Mustang Engineering. Today Mustang employs 280 people and earns annual revenues of $30 million, designing drilling platforms for clients all over the world. The company started out, however, at the beginning of the oil slump and saw conditions in the industry worsen steadily. To keep afloat, the company took whatever business it could find that was in any way related to what it did. When things were looking as though the company was going to have to lay off key employees, the founder of the company heard about a new bus maintenance facility that was being planned. Mustang bid on the contract to provide engineering and drafting services. The trick would be to get the job; why would a transit commission pay attention to a company whose expertise was oil field engineering? Paul Redmon, one of the three cofounders of the company, describes their presentation:

> We knew we would be the last to present, just before lunchtime. We gave each guy a big Snickers bar, saying, "We don't want you thinking about lunch during our presentation." The last member of the board was a woman, and we knew from my friend that she was two months pregnant. So I gave her a big Snickers and a little one, too, for her baby. That a got a laugh—they could tell we had inside information—and it broke down the wall. Then we sang a takeoff on the Snickers jingle, you know, "Snickers will satisfy you." We sang, "Mustang Engineering will satisfy you."[18]

Mustang got the job and managed to keep everyone working until the oil business began to generate enough to keep them busy and prospering.

Remember, feelings and emotions are usually far more persuasive than intellect. More energy is generated by feelings than facts. As someone once said, "Seeing's believing, but feeling's the truth."

PLAN YOUR RETURN CALL BEFORE YOUR FIRST CALL

A McGraw-Hill survey reported that six out of ten customers will say no four times before they say yes. This makes repeat calls a virtual certainty. "Reasons to return" can play an important role in turning a qualified prospect into a first-time customer. Involving the buyer's interest is crucial to making these return encounters effective. Here are ten constructive reasons for returning:

1. To gather more information
2. To add some important new data to your reply to a question the buyer asked last time
3. To take a tour of the prospect's facility
4. To explain a new or improved product or service
5. To talk about a promotion the customer might run to increase sales on his (and your) product
6. To follow up on literature sent
7. To congratulate the customer on a promotion or award
8. To accompany the prospect to a trade or professional meeting
9. To introduce other prospective team members
10. To entertain so as to show appreciation

Regardless of the reason to return by which the sales representative reconnects with the prospect, every sales contact should be planned with the objective of moving the prospect closer to a sale. Just because a salesperson isn't making a formal presentation doesn't mean that the call shouldn't be planned. In some cases, planning takes only a few seconds before a call. But in every instance, it's vital for the sales representative to answer one simple question: For this call to be successful, what should result?

Patience, persistence, sales planning, and lots of reasons to return were what won Guy Anderson, regional vice president of Stockholder Systems, a $1.5 million account with E. I. du Pont de Nemours, beating out a field of four keen competitors. Du Pont decided to replace its stockholder record-keeping system and estimated the project would take about twenty-one months from the evaluation stage to installation and in-house operation. Du Pont was determined to find out everything about securities systems vendors and make sure its own employees understood any new system that was considered. It was clear that making the sale would require patience, persistence, and serious involvement with the decision makers.

Anderson took advantage of the time involved in the analysis process to learn everything he could about Du Pont. He got to know the people who would be working on the project. He spent time watching, listening, and learning. He made repeated contact with the people who were evaluating systems. Instead of simply touting his product, Anderson called to see how everything was going and offered to provide additional information and resources. He assumed the role of partner in the process, rather than outsider trying to sell the company something.

By planning to stay in constant touch, Anderson gained an important edge over the competition. He learned about the people—their personalities, their likes and dislikes, their working styles—and he learned about the various objectives the new system would have to satisfy. With his newfound information, Anderson was able to satisfy both corporate and personal concerns about the new system.

To reassure Du Pont that his company would offer continued customer support, Anderson took its key people to visit some current satisfied customers and invited them to symposia where the product was demonstrated. Getting to know the system support people before buying the system reassured Du Pont that help was available if needed. Seeing big customers who were satisfied with the system also allayed fears.

As it turned out, Anderson's presence and persistence paid off. He won the competition by being there, by being concerned and helpful, and by subtly selling his product again and again. By the time the planning stage was completed, Anderson had the contract in the bag. His own planning had paid off handsomely, and his four competitors were left waiting to give their big sales pitch.[19]

RULES FOR ENDING EVERY CALL

A critical aspect of every sales call is how the call is concluded. As we have discussed, the purpose of every sales call is to move systematically toward a completed sale; there is no better place to ensure meeting that objective than to make sure you conclude your sales calls correctly. Consider these guidelines:

- Be sure you've uncovered the real points of interest about your product or service.
- Outline what you are going to do next.

- Tell the prospect what you need in order to provide the benefit they're interested in.
- Agree on the next contact; be specific.

Throughout your conversation with the prospect, and particularly as you are concluding your call, beware of overpromising and building unrealistic expectation. Build your communication in a way that influences the prospective customers to expect a little less service than they will get. For example, if your company can routinely get a package door to door in eighteen hours, guarantee twenty-four-hour service. If you do this, you are promising something you know you can deliver, and your prospects will be delighted to have their expectations exceeded. As customer service consultant Michael LeBoeuf says, "It's not the quality of service that you give but the quality of service that the customer perceives that causes him to buy and come back." Always keep in mind that as we convert prospects into first-time customers, we are not trying to merely make a sale. Instead, we are trying to develop a loyal customer.

WHERE THERE'S A WILL, THERE'S A WAY

Although many entrepreneurs and other professionals often feel that closing a sale is a life-or-death situation, in Sunny Graham's case this was no exaggeration. As a first-time salesperson, her commission-only salary was her sole hope of escaping likely imprisonment by her government. With no time for sales training or lackluster beginnings, the neophyte salesperson had a short three months in which to make her money. Sound like an impossible task? Here's how she did it.

In the summer of 1971, Graham, a native Filipino living in Meycauayan in the Philippines, had just graduated from the University of the Philippines. (As part of her degree, she had earned a scholarship and studied for a time in the United States.) Fearing martial law was near, she and her family were increasingly concerned that if she did not get out soon, she would be unable to leave the country at all. She had participated in the student movement on the University of the Philippines campus and was likely to be imprisoned for her activist work at the university.

In May 1971, upon receiving her college degree, Graham began looking for a job. She had three months to raise the necessary cash to leave Meycauayan for the United States. Time was tight. She had to get to the States by the end of the summer to qualify for a student visa to get into graduate school by the fall.

Through a friend, Graham found out that Compton's Encyclopedia (a division of Britannica) was just entering the Philippines and was hiring local sales representatives. She applied and got the job.

On the basis of a commission of 200 pesos, or roughly $25, Graham determined she would have to sell, on average, seven sets of Compton's a day, five days a week, for three months to save the money she needed. Having no experience selling this product or any other, it seemed an enormous quota, but to achieve her goal of leaving the Philippines, she had no choice. She went to work.

Graham selected her target market: the upper-crust families in her community and in the neighboring city of Manila. She began by contacting families she knew. Her sales message stressed the benefits of Compton's as an important educational extension. There was no public library system in the Philippines, so she emphasized the merits of the encyclopedia to families in search of more education for their children. The fact that she had successfully studied in the United States (no one in her community had ever gone to the United States on scholarship) made her recommendation even more credible.

Her first sale was to the vice mayor of her town. From that sale and others, she diligently asked for referrals. In addition, she also went door to door. On many calls, she went back two, three, and even four times before the sale was made.

Graham put in long hours and covered many miles. At first, sales were slow, but by the end of the summer she had met her goal, averaging a remarkable seven sets a day! In fact, her average daily commission of $175 exceeded her brother's monthly salary as a long-time government official.

She returned to the United States in September 1971, four months before martial law was declared. As she had feared, professors, student leaders, and protesters were taken to prison. Four of her closest friends ultimately died in prison. Several others, who did not die in prison, were brutalized and beaten during their incarceration.

Upon returning to California, Graham did additional graduate work. She married the son of her "foster" parents, and they have been married for more than thirty years. She and her husband now live in Dallas, where she heads an import-export business specializing in products from the Philippines.

What accounted for Sunny Graham's unlikely success? Was she a natural-born sales prodigy? Did she just experience beginner's luck? Was she at the right place at the right time? Perhaps the answer lies in a recent Harvard Business School study that identified the most common characteristics of top salespeople. According to the study's findings, most people who become top sellers do so by being willing to study, concentrate, and focus on their performance. Here are eight attributes identified by the study as being essential to successful salespeople[20]:

1. Did not take *no* personally
2. One hundred percent acceptance of responsibility for results
3. Above-average ambition
4. High level of empathy

5. Intensely goal-oriented

6. Above-average willpower

7. Impeccably honest with self and with the customer

8. Ability to approach strangers

No doubt, Sunny Graham's unfortunate circumstances gave her lots of incentive to sell. But the good news is that this same level of success, and more, is available to anyone armed with a well-conceived product or service and equal measures of focus, diligence, common sense, and integrity.

Today, in her import-export business, Graham enjoys a luxury of time with her customers that she did not have when she was selling encyclopedias. This enables her to focus less on making sales and more on developing customers. But her mastery of selling to first-time customers is a distinct advantage. It's an important first step to a long, profitable, lasting relationship with a customer.

LEARNING FROM A LOST SALE

Let's face it. Despite your best efforts, you will never convert every qualified prospect into a new customer. But take heart. Even a lost sale can give you valuable information about building future sales and loyalty. Here's how one company made it happen.

Several years ago, Tom Tjelmeland of T&K Roofing was faced with a problem of fallen margins and lost bids. In 1988, profit margins had dropped from 5 percent to 1 percent on sales of $2.5 million, and the chief executive of the Ely, Iowa, roofing company was ready to do almost anything to halt the downward slide of retained earnings.

Tom and his son, Kurt, T&K's vice president, decided to construct a form that would deliberately invite criticism from would-be customers who had awarded their roofing jobs to T&K's competitors. What emerged was the Lost Job Survey, containing twenty-two quick-answer questions. Among the most important information that came back from the one thousand surveys returned to T&K in a three-year period was that the respondents didn't want the indestructible, high-quality roofing that Tom thought they should buy. It was too expensive. "It forced us to ask prospects what they wanted, instead of offering them what we thought they needed," Tom said.[21]

The question on the survey form that prompted the most changes in how T&K would sell products asked customers if they had established a relationship with another roofing contractor. "If this was marked yes," Tom said, "it told me my people were out there slapping prices on jobs instead of developing relationships. Establishing a relationship takes time, but you learn more about what the customer wants besides a low price."[22]

T&K's Lost Job Survey did more than show the company how to make the difficult shift away from low-margin, low-bid contracts to the more lucrative, negotiated-bid contracts it had been losing before. The questionnaire prompted the company to assume a revitalized sales philosophy that changed the emphasis to a "best solution for customers" approach. In the process, employees who couldn't change their methods quit; other were let go. Since T&K began using the survey, its profit picture has steadily improved; sales have grown to $12 million. The company's unwavering focus on customers has reaped other rewards as well. In 2000, T&K became the first three-time winner of *RSI* (Roofing, Siding, Insulation) magazine's annual Roofing Contractor of the Year award.

The experience of T&K Roofing illustrates a key fact: even if a counted-on sale does not materialize, not all is lost. Valuable information can often be gleaned from the experience so as to identify problems and improve loyalty-building strategies.

SUMMARY

- It takes an average of seven contacts to turn a prospect into a first-time buyer. Research suggests that this "rule of seven" may be rising, because of deeper alliances between buyers and sellers and a tougher economy.
- A canned sales pitch no longer works; customers want people who listen to their needs, are honest and up-front, and diagnose problems and offer solutions.
- With permission or opt-in marketing (via the Web), prospects give their permission for you to send them communication. As such, the response rate can be substantially higher than for other nonpermission marketing approaches.
- It takes patience and time to build trust in a customer; once trust is gained, there are many long-term benefits.
- Plan your return sales call before your first call. Develop an array of constructive reasons for recontacting your prospects.
- Feedback from lost sales produces valuable information about how to make future sales and build customer loyalty.

GETTING STARTED

- Recontact some of your recent prospects that were not converted to first-time buyers to understand why the sale was lost. Apply this learning to improve your firm's prospecting, qualifying, and selling processes.
- Teach effective listening techniques to all employees, especially frontline staff. Make this a skill that gets ongoing practice and improvement.
- Seek out real-life stories within your company that demonstrate the patience and persistence often required to turn a prospect into a first-time customer.

Circulate these stories to reinforce the importance of effective qualifying, needs-based selling, and so on.

• Work with your sales staff to establish a list of reasons-to-return that are specific to your company and product or service line. Use the latest experience of the sales staff to regularly add to the list.

CHAPTER SIX

Turning First-Time Buyers into Repeat Customers

W hen an American husband and wife purchased a faulty Sony compact disc player at a Tokyo department store, they received a lesson in customer loyalty that completely overwhelmed them and turned their anger into amazement.

The couple, who were staying with the husband's parents in the outlying city of Sagamihara, had tried to operate the disc player the morning after the purchase and were disappointed when it wouldn't run. Further investigation proved there was no motor or drive mechanism in the case.

Annoyed and perplexed, the husband practiced the scathing denunciation he planned to register by telephone with the manager of the Odakyu Department Store on the dot at 10:00 A.M., when the store opened.

But at 9:59 A.M., the phone rang and was answered by the husband's mother, who had to hold the receiver away from her ear, so vehement was the barrage of Japanese honorifics that came from the other end of the line. The caller was none other than Odakyu's vice president, who clamored effusively that he was on his way over with a new disc player.

In less than a hour, the vice president of the company and a junior employee were standing on the doorstep. The younger man was laden down with packages and papers. As they met the customer at the door, both men began bowing enthusiastically.

Continuing to bow, the younger man began explaining to the customer the steps they had taken to rectify their mistakes. On the day the customers had left

99

the store, a salesclerk had discovered the problem and requested security guards to stop them at the door. Since they had already left, the clerk reported the error to his supervisor, who reported to his supervisor, and so on, until the vice president learned of the error. Since the only identification the store personnel had was an American Express card number and name, they began there.

The clerk called thirty-two hotels in and around Tokyo to ask if the couple were registered. That turned up nothing, so a staff member was asked to stay late at the store, until 9:00 P.M., when the American Express headquarters in New York would be open.

American Express gave him the couple's home phone number.

When the employee called that number, at almost midnight Tokyo time, he reached the wife's parents, who were housesitting. He learned the couple's address in Tokyo from the wife's parents.

The young employee, breathless from his recitation, then began offering gifts to the customers: a new $280 disc player, a set of towels, a box of cakes, and a Chopin disc. In less than five minutes, the astonished couple watched the vice president of the store and his employee climb back into a taxi—after profuse apologies for having made the customers wait while the salesclerk rewrote the sales slip. They sincerely hoped the couple would forgive the mistake.

Most stores replace defective merchandise. How many would go to such lengths to make an unhappy customer a lifelong buyer? Certainly, top management would rarely even know that such a mistake had happened. It's this type of spirit, intent on heroically preserving the good opinion and esteem of the customer, that builds the loyalty of the first-time buyer.

FOUR REASONS FIRST-TIME BUYERS DO NOT RETURN

Consultant Richard Shapiro, president of MJ Associates, specializes in keeping management on track in pursuing customer retention. He reports that for many firms, the rate of first-year account attrition is often more than double that of older accounts. After performing a series of extensive "exit interviews" with a cross-section of a software company's former customers, Shapiro discovered four essential reasons first-time buyer attrition is so widespread[1]:

1. *Early problems sour the relationship.* If a problem develops during the first three to six months of a customer's life cycle, the customer assumes the situation will occur frequently and may feel buyer's remorse. Suspicion that there will always be problems can quickly sour the relationship and block any opportunity for future sales.

2. *No formal servicing system.* The same company that spends months or even years pursuing a new customer often fails to set up tight account management functions to ensure that an order is processed and fulfilled satisfactorily.

3. *Communication breakdown with the decision makers.* Organizations rarely communicate regularly with decision makers in the customer's business. They usually end up continuing their dialogue with users or technical buyers. Although these individuals may have been involved in the purchasing cycle, they are not usually solely responsible for retaining an organization as a supplier. As communications with the decision maker weaken, the supplier is at risk. In addition, if an original decision maker leaves and a new one takes over, the organization leaves itself vulnerable to competition if there is not consistent communication.

4. *Easy return.* If the customer is still doing business with a former supplier, it is easy for the customer to return to that supplier if problems develop.

THE REAL SALE BEGINS AFTER THE "YES"

As the management at the Odakyu Department Store so aptly demonstrated, the real sale begins after the customer says yes. It's how you perform after the customer buys that determines whether you keep him or her as a loyal customer. Consider this short story.

A man died and went to Heaven, where he was told he had a choice between Heaven and Hell. He decided to take up this unusual offer and check out both options. Heaven was serene, bathed in a pleasing white light. A lot of people were walking around in white robes singing hymns. Nice, but a tad boring for eternity, the visitor reasoned. On his visit to Hell, he was surprised to find people having fun. They were playing golf, they were playing cards, and it wasn't at all hot. He had an easy decision: he told the angels at the Pearly Gates, and headed back to Hell.

But when he got there, everything was different from his first visit. It was hot and terrible, and people were miserable—a lot like his original expectations.

"What happened?" he worriedly asked the Devil. "This isn't at all what I saw when I visited."

"When you visited, you were a prospect," the Devil told him. "Now you're a customer."[2]

This humorous account is a sad-but-true commentary about how some businesses operate. The rapport and trust established during the selling process can quickly fade if a new customer's needs are not met. Just log on to any of the many complaint Websites (complaints.com, problems.com, defective.com, concerns.com, criticisms.com, among others) and you'll find countless scenarios where first-time buyers lament disappointment about the postsale experience. Consider this new buyer's Web posting:

Only two weeks after purchasing my new notebook computer, it began having problems booting on power-up. After three weeks, the hard drive crashed and because it was defective, the recovery disks wouldn't work either. After [I spent] about an hour on hold [on the manufacturer's help line], the [rep] agreed to replace my system, since it was less than a month old. When I called back the following week, they had no record of me or my return authorization information. Again, I spent about forty-five minutes on hold only to learn that [the manufacturer] was out of stock of my model. The rep said they did however have a similar model. Needing a computer desperately for law school, I agreed to take it. The rep said I would have the system in two days. Three days later, still no system. When I called, they were unable to tell me whether my system had been shipped or not and seemed, once again, to have no information on my matter. They assured me that "most likely" the system shipped and that if I didn't receive it by Monday, then to call back. On Monday I called back and the rep proceeded to tell me that not only hadn't my order been shipped, but that the reason it wasn't shipped was because they were out of stock! At that point I told them to cancel my order and I demanded a full refund. Point of the story? Avoid [this manufacturer] at all costs! And if you've already purchased their product, only hope that you never have to deal with customer service![3]

FOLLOW THE ORDER

In the movie *All the President's Men,* which chronicles the Watergate scandal, journalists Carl Bernstein and Bob Woodward receive inside information from an unidentified contact called Deep Throat. Deep Throat's most frequent advice is "Follow the money." To anyone interested in developing loyal customers, the advice could easily be "Follow the order." Why? Because every customer's experience is greatly determined by a company's order management cycle (OMC).

Writing in the *Harvard Business Review,* professors Benson Shapiro, Kasturi Rangan, and John Sviokla encourage managers to track each step of the OMC by working their way though the company from the customer's point of view rather than their own. Say the authors, "In the course of the order management cycle, every time the order is handled, the customer is handled, [and] every time the order sits unattended, the customer sits unattended. Paradoxically, the best way to be customer-oriented is to go beyond customers and products to the order; the moment of truth occurs at every step of the OMC, and every employee in the company who affects the OMC is the equivalent of a front line worker."[4] It is the order, say the authors, that connects the customer to the company in a systematic and companywide fashion.

Here's an outline of the ten steps, from planning to postsales service, that define a company's OMC. Opportunities for improving overall operations and creating new competitive advantage can be found in these ten steps[5]:

1. Order planning
2. Order generation
3. Cost estimation
4. Order receipt
5. Order selection
6. Scheduling
7. Fulfillment
8. Billing
9. Returns and claims
10. Postsale service

Follow the order is an apt description of what Gen. Robert F. McDermott did when he assumed the position of chief executive of USAA in 1968. (As an insurance and financial services company, San Antonio–based USAA has been serving members of the U.S. military and their families since 1922.) McDermott describes the situation he found:

> There was paper everywhere. We had 650,000 members at that time and three thousand employees. Every desk in the building was covered with stacks of paper—files, claim forms, applications, correspondence. You can't imagine how much paper. Stacks and piles and trays and baskets of it. And of course a lot of it got lost. On any given day, the chances were only fifty-fifty that we'd be able to put our hands on any particular file. When I first started, I would often stay late and go around putting little marks on papers and files, then I'd check the next night to see if they'd been moved. A lot of people moved no paper at all.[6]
>
> We constantly got letters and phone calls about poor service. Most of our members were sticking with us because our premiums were lower than anyone else's and because we were good on claims. It certainly wasn't because of our prompt and dependable service in any other area.
>
> There were fifty-five steps associated with every new insurance policy USAA processed. The first person would open the envelope, remove the paper clips, and pass it to the second person, who would check addresses on big Rolodexes and write in corrections with a pen, then pass it to the third person, and the fourth person, and so on—fifty-five steps. The average employee stayed with the company for eleven months. We were giving terrible service and boring our employees.

Contrast that with the company today, and the transformation is truly remarkable. With twenty-two thousand employees, the nation's sixth largest home insurer and seventh largest private vehicle insurer serves 4.7 million members and manages $62.5 billion in assets. Among its officer core members (the group longest served by USAA), the company's retention rate is a remarkable 98 percent.

Still today, USAA's phenomenal success can be attributed to the company's customer-centered philosophy of following the order.

This focus began in earnest in the early nineties, under Gen. McDermott's leadership, when the company created an AIE (an automated insurance environment) that includes policy writing, service, claims, billing, customer accounting—all aspects of the OMC. McDermott explains:

> Now when you want to buy a new car, get it insured, add a driver, and change your coverage and address, you can make one phone call—average time, five minutes—and nothing else is necessary. One stop, on-line, the policy goes out the door the next morning about 4:00 A.M. In one five-minute phone call, you and our service representative have done all the work that used to take fifty-five steps, umpteen people, two weeks and a lot of money.
>
> We get about 150,000 pieces of mail every morning, of which 60 percent to 65 percent are checks. Of the remainder, less than half ever leaves the mailroom. All of our policy-service correspondence is imaged, indexed, prioritized; it's then instantly available anywhere in the company.[7]

Gen. McDermott illustrates:

> Suppose Colonel Smith has sent us a letter asking for a change in his homeowner's insurance, and he calls and wants to know if we've received it. The service representative says, "Yes, sir, I've got it right here." "You do?" he says. "Yes," the rep says, "I have it right in front of me. What can I do for you?" The colonel's impressed. We received his letter only that morning, but it's already been imaged, so it's instantly available to every service representative in the building. Now let's say Colonel Smith calls back the next day with some additional information we've asked him for and talks to a different service rep, who also has his letter "right here in front of me." Now the colonel's impressed and amazed.
>
> Let's say the service rep, who has not only Colonel Smith's letter but his entire file available on the screen, goes on to explain how the change Smith wants to make in his homeowner's coverage may reduce his need for umbrella liability and thus lower the cost of that policy. Now the colonel's impressed and amazed and very pleased. And so are we, because the whole transaction's taken five minutes.[8]

Look closely at USAA's operations today and you'll continue to find a company aggressively working to serve the customer by following the order. Explains David Travers, senior vice president of policy service for USAA's Property and Casualty Insurance Group, "We have successfully integrated our account administration systems across all our products. That means a member only has to contact us once with a change of address, for example, and that new information will be incorporated across all the member's accounts—whether it's banking, life insurance, investments or property and casualty. One contact is all it takes. Likewise, the company's Internet site, usaa.com, is linked with the company's imaging system so that once a member completes a form online it can pass to the image system for permanent record keeping. Again, one contact is all that is required."

This one-contact dependability standard, says Travers, took on additional meaning in the wake of September 11, 2001, and the terrorist attack on the World Trade Center. Moments after escaping from one of the towers, a USAA member wanted to get word to her family that she had survived. Phone lines were down, but the woman discovered outbound calls could still be made on 1-800 lines. So she called USAA's toll-free number from memory and connected with a service representative who, in turn, notified the member's family that she was safe. Says Travers, "The fact that she thought to call us for help pleased us but didn't surprise us either. The basis of USAA's success is our ability to establish personal relationships with our members. We work hard to keep the transactional side of the business running well so we can focus on the all important relationship with our members."[9] What better reason to follow the order?

GIVING EMPLOYEES THE TOOLS TO PERFORM

USAA has identified and championed a key element of customer loyalty that other companies are now just beginning to understand: that the key to growing loyal customers rests first in creating effective employees. To succeed in today's hypercompetitive marketplace, a company must transform its internal operating systems into structures that empower rather than impede frontline success with the customer. No doubt, a firm's reputation for world-class customer care is built one customer and one contact at a time. Whether servicing customers face-to-face or through e-mail, phone, fax or self-service, frontline employees play a direct or indirect role in delivering the contact.

Successful management realizes it is essential that the employees who deal directly with customers have the necessary time, tools, and training and the complete support of the company. It is the performance of those frontline employees on which judgments of the entire company are made, and future sales made or lost. No sharp advertising campaign or glossy packaging can make up for a poor relationship between the customer and the company's representative who deals directly with him.

Making frontline employees effective means arming them with the information they need to serve their customers. No one understood this better than Mike Marino, vice president of customer development at Frito-Lay, an $8.5 billion division of PepsiCo in Plano, Texas. But Marino was grappling with a problem plaguing many sales teams in geographically dispersed locations. How do you pool information resources to serve a national customer on a local level? "There was knowledge trapped in files everywhere," says Marino, but with so many disparate databases, there was no way for his fifteen-member sales team to get at it. As a result, the sales team benefited very little from sharing best practices and other information collaboration. Field inefficiency spilled over into corporate double-work as well. For example, numerous salespeople would ask the corporate marketing staff for current private-label trends in their snack category. Support staff would supply the information again and again, performing the same task many times. Besides these inefficiencies, the sales team lacked a way to collaborate and brainstorm online. For example, if a sales team member in the Midwest received some research data and wanted feedback from account executives on the East and West coast, the opportunity for online collaboration was not available.

The answer? Build a knowledge management portal on Frito-Lay's corporate intranet. A KM portal is a single point of access to multiple information sources; firms such as Frito-Lay are awakening to the portal's ability to leverage intellectual capital and in turn make for a learner, smarter organization. Indeed, a recent Delphi Group survey found half of the eleven hundred organizations polled were interested in deploying a portal.

But Marino moved beyond interest to a pilot program. Starting from scratch in populating the test portal, Marino and his team began with an audit followed by expertise profiles to identify who's who at Plano headquarters. In doing so, people with know-how in such areas as promotion planning, cost estimation, or new product announcement could be readily called upon for assistance. Why is that critical? Because in large organizations a wealth of knowledge exists. Yet with little or no support someone new in the field can suffer many false starts trying to determine where and from whom to get the needed information.

Because the pilot team was working with confidential client information, security was a top concern. The portal was built so that different sections were password-protected. This allowed only pertinent users to access confidential information. As Marino explains, the particular customer "had custom information about sales performance that they shared with members of the Frito-Lay team, but we were contracted not to let that information get outside the team that worked with that customer."

A year after the test portal went live, the sales results were telling. While not disclosing exact figures, Marino says the test team doubled the growth rate of the customer's business in the salty snack category. Marino shares further that "the retailer is happy because they're doing more business in their market, and we're doing business at a faster growth rate with this customer than other customers." But the benefits don't stop there. Team members report more camaraderie and relationship building with each other. From a homepage list of team member birthdays to an automatic message feature that informs team members who is online, the portal is proving an invaluable tool for helping team members pull together on behalf of a customer. The employee retention rate has improved as well. In previous company surveys, sales people complained about geographic constraints and how they didn't feel connected and part of a team. Since the portal has been in place, not one person on the fifteen-member team has left.[10]

A CLOSER LOOK AT FIRST-TIME BUYERS

The purchase entails consequences for the buyer. They occur as a result of what consumer behaviorists call postdecision reevaluation. Every customer brings to a purchase a certain set of expectations. Following the purchase, the buyer compares what she received with what she expected. If the comparison is favorable, the buyer is said to be satisfied. If the comparison is unfavorable, the buyer is said to be dissatisfied.

The first-time buyer is in effect a "tryer." She is trying the new product or service, and her perception of quality influences her desire to buy again. If a first-time buyer is pleased with the first purchase, the likelihood the customers will buy again improves greatly. The second purchase is significant, because it represents a change from the first. This time, the buyer makes her purchase decision on the basis of a new set of criteria, what consumer behaviorists call nonrandom purchase behavior. This means that the buyer goes into the repeat purchase process with a substantiated preference about what, and from whom, to buy. This preference has been at least partly earned through the positive first-time purchase experience.

On the other hand, if a purchase expectation is not met, dissatisfaction results. Dissatisfaction is defined as "the degree of disparity between expectations and perceived product performance." When a disparity between performance and expectancy exists, the new buyer experiences a state of psychological inconsistency, or dissonance. The degree of postpurchase dissonance is a function of several factors[11]:

- The more important the decision, the greater the dissonance.
- The greater the number of alternatives considered before the purchase decision, the greater the dissonance.
- The more attractive a rejected alternative, the greater the dissonance.
- The more frequently the product or brand is purchased, the less the degree of dissonance.
- The more irrevocable the purchase, the greater the dissonance.

A state of dissonance is uncomfortable for the purchaser; if not appropriately handled, it can lead to increased dissatisfaction. This leads to lost sales, as seen in the case of US West Cellular.

How US West Cellular Fights Postpurchase Dissonance

US West Cellular had a problem. The company invests at least $700 to recruit a new customer, with a payback time on this investment of at least seven months. US West discovered that many accounts were canceling their service before the payback period was complete. In fact, 50 percent of all new accounts never made it to long-term status. Financial analysis indicated that if the monthly cancellation rate could be cut by just 0.1 percent, approximately $1 million could be added to US West Cellular's bottom line.

Unlike many firms that regard a past-due account as simply a collection problem, US West Cellular determined that 75 percent of all overdue payment disputes were actually customer service problems. A dissatisfied customer is not as prompt in paying a bill as a satisfied customer. Recognizing this fact, the company merged its financial service and customer service departments and made John Suhm, a company accountant, head of customer service.

Suhm and his staff soon discovered that a large percentage of the company's new customers were canceling service soon after receiving their first bill. Why? The first bill includes a charge for the first month's service, long-distance charges for all calls placed that first month, and charges for the next month's service. As a result, the total bill is usually two times more than the customer expects.

To help cycle customers through this first "buying" period, the service reps on Suhm's team place "welcome new customer" calls with the purpose of thanking them for their business, answering questions, and most important reassuring them that future bills will be considerably less. Through company research, US West Cellular found an interesting link between customer contact and customer satisfaction. It seemed that when customer representatives called customers periodically, those customers developed a perception that the cellular service itself was of a higher quality (less static, for one thing) than that perceived by customers who did not receive calls.

Another team of company employees, called the "retention group," focuses exclusively on handling customers who wish to disconnect their service. A rep earns the right to ring a brass ship's bell hanging prominently in the group's work area whenever he or she "saves" a customer from canceling. Moreover, US West Cellular created a companywide bonus plan that encourages every employee to take action to reduce customer loss. Referred to by Suhm as the "churn" bonus, even a file clerk receives a monthly bonus of $50 when company disconnect goals are achieved.

US West Cellular has seen dramatic results from these measures. The save rate has increased by 150 percent, monthly attrition has dropped by 30 percent, and according to Suhm the bottom line has improved by $8 million.[12]

The Right Information at the Right Time

Carefully selecting the means by which information is fed to the new buyer can help reduce postpurchase dissonance. One study that attempted to reduce dissonance among people who had just bought a refrigerator obtained mixed results: letters to the new customer appeared to get a favorable response, but a telephone call did not.

One-third of all customer complaints come from customers who do not know how to use the product, according to John Goodman, president of Technical Assistance Research Programs, a customer service consulting organization. Service visits, mailings, and other forms of active communication can educate customers about product use and help keep them satisfied. For example, Armstrong found that many purchasers of its no-wax floors cared for them improperly and complained when they deteriorated. In response, Armstrong prominently stamped an 800 number on the surface of each floor with the message "Call for instructions on how to remove this number." The number comes off with water, but callers also receive instructions on how to care for the floor. The result? A significant increase in repeat purchase from satisfied customers.[13]

Even doctor-patient relationships can improve with the right information, according to the findings from a test by two cancer specialists in Sydney, Australia, who were looking for a way to improve the patient's perception of care. The study showed that when doctors write letters to their patients repeating what they told the patients in the office, the patients feel a higher level of contentment with their medical care. The researchers reported that they tested the idea on forty-eight cancer patients who came in to see one of the specialists for follow-up consultation after treatment. Half of the patients were randomly chosen to receive a letter dictated by the doctor immediately after the patient's visit. The letter summarized what had been discussed during the visit.

In the ensuing three weeks, all forty-eight patients were interviewed and asked to rate the visit, on a scale of one to five. The patients who received the letters rated the doctor visit higher than those who didn't receive a letter. Of the twenty-four letter recipients, thirteen rated their visit a five (highest possible), while only four of those who didn't get a letter gave this top score.[14]

WHAT GOOD SERVICE REALLY MEANS

As we saw in Chapter One, customers increasingly want more than just a one-night stand with the business from which they buy. Consumers are becoming more concerned about service and how they are treated when they purchase something than they are about the price alone. Nurturing customer relationships is the cornerstone of a growing number of new customer marketing strategies, as reflected in the prevalence of offering of a long-term guarantee on products, service packages, investments, and other similar incentives. What kind of service turns a first-time buyer into a repeat customer? Perhaps part of the answer can be found in how customers perceive the concept of service after the sale.

The five dimensions of service quality were first identified through a model developed by researchers from Texas A&M University and then validated again in a study by the Forum Corporation. In comparing customers' expectations of service quality with their actual experience, both studies identified five dimensions of service as most important to a buyer[15]:

1. *Reliability:* the ability to provide what was promised, dependably and accurately

2. *Assurance:* the knowledge and courtesy of employees and their ability to convey trust and confidence

3. *Tangibles:* the physical facilities and equipment and the appearance of personnel

4. *Empathy:* the degree of caring and individual attention provided to customers

5. *Responsiveness:* the willingness to help customers and provide prompt service

The research further found that three of the factors—assurance, tangibles, and empathy—are closely tied to demonstration of responsiveness and reliability.

Let's take a closer look at these two critical dimensions and their implications for giving customers a positive service experience.

Reliability

Customers put reliability first in assessing service, yet salespeople and sales managers still perceive that customers regard responsiveness as more important. One possible reason for this disparity is that, unlike reliability, which is a wider organizational issue and takes an investment of time and money, responsiveness is most often provided by sales and service people and therefore is an easier dimension for them to control. Research reveals that salespeople and sales managers even make references about reliability less often than their customers.

Research has also shown that honesty plays an important role in reliability, according to Jennifer Potter-Brotman, a Forum senior vice president. Explains Brotman, "If a customer requests a product on a Monday, yet reality dictates a Wednesday delivery, being open with the customer significantly increases the chances of earning his or her trust and establishing a long-term relationship. Customers have considerable empathy for the seller's position, yet they have little patience for sellers who overpromise, don't establish the proper expectations, or bring the customer in on a problem when it's too late for them to contribute to its solution.[16]

Responsiveness

With the advent of the Internet, a customer's perception of responsiveness is changing. More and more, customers are coming to expect round-the-clock customer service. Although many companies are migrating their customer service function to the Internet to better serve customers, few are prepared for the challenge this increase in customer access creates. Most companies do not realize that when they take their business to the Web, customer inquiries typically double or even triple, leaving even the most competent customer support staff besieged. A recent Jupiter Communications survey found that almost 50 percent of the most well-known online sites are overwhelmed by customer inquiries and take five or more days to respond, if at all, to even the simplest customer requests.[17]

To earn repeat business, loyalty-driven companies are increasingly understanding that today's customers arrive on a Website time-starved and eager to locate answers quickly. Three online tools are helping with consistent delivery of responsive service.

Self-Service. Self-service, delivered through accurate and pertinent Website content, offers the quickest and most cost-effective means of answering most customer questions. Research shows as much as 70–90 percent can be effectively handled with self-service.

This immediacy better serves the customer and can help increase the probability of a customer continuing the relationship. Consider the case of the California Chamber of Commerce, which had three hundred to nine hundred callers lighting up the phone lines each day seeking answers to topics ranging from customer service to tourism. The staff adequately managed the call handling, but the process lacked efficiency for both callers and staff and there was no tracking mechanism or means to effectively route questions and issues through the chamber's various departments.

The Chamber established an answer center on its Website with question-and-answer pairs on a host of subjects (employment law, tourism, how-to for business, and customer support issues). E-mail queries were available to customers who needed assistance beyond the FAQs. Callers were directed to the online answer center by the Chamber's after-hours and on-hold phone system messages. The result was that messages on the after-hours phone system dropped by 50 percent. Moreover, an incident summary is now run once a week, reporting the FAQs that are requested the most. Says the Chamber's Internet manager, "We finally have a handle on what information is most important to our constituents. . . . We now have the information to back up and show what we need to do."[18]

E-Mail Management. As an alternative to self-service, e-mail management can serve as an effective escalation for customers who have a preference for this type of interaction or a unique query not yet addressed in the knowledge base (FAQs and the like). Sorted by workload, expertise, or even customer temperament, e-mail can be intelligently routed to the appropriate customer service agent. E-mail management makes it possible to send an auto-response or assist an agent in searching the knowledge base to locate an answer. Each closed inquiry is then posted to the knowledge base, reducing future need for similar customer queries.

When Air Canada installed an e-mail management system, its ten thousand monthly e-mails dropped to four thousand, a reduction of 60 percent. For the same period, traffic increased dramatically on the self-service section of the Website, suggesting that effective e-mail management can increase self-service efficacy as well.[19]

Live Chat and Web Callback. Live chat and Web callback options can yield personal, one-to-one interaction with a customer at a critical transaction time. Consider the case of IBM.com. Its call center agents handle an average of ninety-five sales calls and thirty-eight service calls every minute. IBM reports 70 percent of customers who make a purchase on the Website contact the call center to complete the order. Says Fred Fassman, vice president of IBM.com centers, "They still want to talk with someone who's a systems expert and who deals with their problems everyday." According to Fassman, orders placed by live chat and Web callback customers are twice as large on average as those from people calling the toll-free number. Fassman admits that "we don't know if that's a chicken-or-egg situation. We do know that when the chat or callback buttons are clicked, it's a high priority."[20]

CALL CENTERS: THE NEW FRONT LINE

As we have already discussed, the key to growing a loyal customer rests first in creating an effective frontline employee. Increasingly, for many enterprises the employee front line is a customer contact center where agents interact with customers. You may know it as a call center or customer interaction center or telecenter or help desk. The performance of its frontline employees determines how judgments of the entire company are made—and future sales made or lost. Indeed, many firms have traditionally considered call centers little more than a tactical, reactive point of contact for the customer. More visionary companies, however, are now looking at inbound calls as an all-important servicing function that retains existing customers, cross-sells new services, and helps increase the company's overall share of a customer's budget.

You'll recall from Chapter Two that giving the customer multichannel access points has been shown to have a positive effect on customer loyalty and profitability. These multichannel benefits are motivating more and more companies to develop converged call centers that integrate the various ways of interacting with customers into a single customer information system and contact center. Gartner Group estimates that 70 percent of North America's call centers will migrate to multichannel contact centers by 2005. That's the good news. The bad news is that with increasingly sophisticated communications channels for customers—including real-time Web collaboration, Web callback, e-mail, live voice chat, and cobrowsing—the skill level required of call center agents is rising sharply.

Although both the technology and demand for giving customers numerous communications channels is enticing, little attention has been paid to how to handle people resources—specifically, hiring and training agents to field more than just phone calls. Increasingly, call center agents need strong writing skills as well as verbal skills. Dianna Booher, author of *e-Writing: 21st Century Tools for Effective Communication*, shares these insights[21]:

- *Recognize the dangers of poor writing.* In addition to being a risk to a corporation's image, poor writing can also be a liability risk. Misstating company policies and the like in a customer e-mail, chat text, and so on can have severe legal consequences for a company.

- *Train all front liners to write effectively.* Even as late as five years ago, a firm's "official" letter writing was reserved for management. Now, frontline agents are expected to respond. In today's call center, every frontline person needs effective writing skills. Attempting to reserve e-mail writing only for agents who are already good writers does not work in the long run. Your system will be plagued with bottlenecks. Arming all your front liners with adequate writing skills is the wiser approach.

- *Revise corporate style guides.* Many corporations already have a style guide illustrating acceptable formats for internal memos, customer proposals, and so on. The style guide should now be updated to include professional guidelines for composing customer e-mail and the like.

- *Make a writing test part of the hiring process.* Test a prospective agent's writing skills. For example, devise a writing exercise in which the prospective agent writes an e-mail message in response to a simulated e-mail from a customer. Evaluate the prospective employee's e-mail sample for thought process, clarity, and grammar.

- *Build boilerplate text that is easy to customize.* Perhaps the only thing worse than an e-mail full of ambiguous sentences and grammatical errors is a canned response that fails to answer the customer's real question in the first place. Make sure suggested response templates and prescribed chat phrases allow appropriate customizing.

Keeping call center reps focused and productive in a multichannel environment requires more than effective writing skills. Attention to multichannel skills as well as morale and culture issues is also critical[22]:

- *Train agents to excel in multiple channels.* Agents working in a multichannel contact center have to switch gears from channel to channel effectively and possess a good grasp of the Web—in particular, the nuances of their own company site. This is why coaching call center agents on how to efficiently access resources from the Cisco Website is a key training focus for Cisco's frontline employees. For example, Cisco's Customer Response Center's escalation team uses the Cisco Collaboration product, which provides Web-sharing functionality, to enable an escalation agent to help a frontline agent remotely navigate to a specific contact on the Cisco site.

- *Keep an agent's workload balanced.* Agent burnout is a common problem in many call centers. To help combat agent overload, many companies are using departmental or workgroup e-mail addresses rather than individual ones. This allows a dedicated group of representatives to monitor inbound activity and balance its distribution.

- *Have agents contribute to online knowledge bases.* You'll recall from our earlier discussion about Frito-Lay that a knowledge base (referred to in that example as a knowledge portal) is a single point of access to multiple information sources. Because of their customer contact and direct experience, frontline agents should be key contributors to the knowledge base. Pharmaceutical giant GlaxoSmithKline answers ten thousand customer queries per month, primarily by phone and e-mail—with only thirteen agents. An efficient online search index and file folder system simplifies information retrieval for the company's agents. "This knowledge-base protocol was totally developed by our call-center agents," says Laurie Garvey, manager of consumer information at GlaxoSmithKline. "And they continually add new items based on customer questions."[23] Garvey knows that people support what they help to create. The online knowledge base is no exception.

- *Carefully measure an agent's performance.* Self-serve Websites and knowledge bases are designed to let customers resolve for themselves questions that have simple answers. That's why building a knowledge base with the sole intention of reducing agent talk time can backfire. In fact, knowledge management can actually cause talk time between customer and agent to *rise.* Yet many companies discourage the agent from spending adequate time with a customer by rewarding agents who have the shortest call cycle. A customer survey that measures the agent's performance (Was the issue fully resolved for the customer? Was the customer pleased with the outcome?) is a better gauge. Measuring the rate of agent referral of questions to others is another meaningful metric. You want the agent answering as many questions without referral as possible. "Ninety-five percent of questions that come to our agents stay with our agents," reports Garvey.[24]

FIFTEEN ACTIONS THAT ENCOURAGE FIRST-TIME CUSTOMERS TO RETURN

Here are a number of steps a business can take to encourage customers to return. Consider each one in light of your business's particular needs, and choose those most appropriate for your specific situation.

1. Say Thank You for the Purchase

Thanking the customer after a purchase is overlooked as a loyalty-building marketing technique by many companies. A customer can be a first-time buyer only once. Passing up the chance to thank the customer for his or her purchase—especially the first one—is a big opportunity lost on the road to building loyalty. Murray Raphel shares this personal experience[25]:

Within the past few months I bought a $5,000 air conditioner, a $600 TV set, a $17,000 car, and a $50 pair of shoes. Following these sales, I heard from none of the businesses—except my shoe salesman. He thanked me for coming in to buy and hoped I would "receive much comfort" and remember him the next time I wanted another pair of shoes.

There's something wrong here.

I called each of the retailers (except the shoe store) and asked if they ever thought of writing thank-you letters after the sale. These are the actual answers:

The air-conditioner dealer: "I don't think we ever did that. Well, once in a while our financing company writes a letter to all the people they carry on their books." (What for? He wasn't sure.) "Listen, we know it's a good idea and I know you're going to ask why we don't do it, and the answer is, I guess we just never got around to it. There's so much to do in this business."

The television dealer: "Sending a thank-you letter is the best thing we ever did. Absolutely. We stopped about eight or nine months ago. We're so backed up with all the paperwork in warranties and finance deals that we just don't have the time anymore. But I'll tell you something—from the customer's point of view, it was terrific. We used to get a big response. We have to get back to that sometime."

The automobile dealer: "Are you kidding? Why, that's the first thing we do. The day the car is delivered, the salesman sits downs and writes a thank-you letter right away. Positively."

Well, that was a month ago. No letter yet.

A simple thank-you letter is an easy and inexpensive way to help reassure the new buyer that he has made a good choice by shopping at your business. All it takes is a couple of sentences that say "Thank you for your recent purchase. Hope you enjoy using your [name of product]. If you have any questions or need more information on [name of product], please call me." Do not fall into the trap of sending a generic letter addressed "Dear Valued Customer." That approach, though often used today, can do more harm than good. If a customer is worth having, then all written communication should appear personalized.

A letter of thanks can go a long way toward sowing the seeds of loyalty in a new customer. Since so few marketers do it, it can set you apart and allow you to connect with the customer more personally. As Stan Rapp, CEO of the international marketing firm Rapp and Collins, so aptly describes marketing, "Winning share of mind is giving way to winning share of heart." Thank-you letters can be an effective first step for doing just that.

2. Seek Customer Feedback Early and Respond Quickly

An enterprising sales director for the AmeriSuites Hotel in Dallas found client follow-up to be an important way to anchor the loyalty of both the traveler and the secretary who made the travel arrangements.

The key was to call the secretary and inquire about the visit during the guest's stay. Most travelers communicated with their office daily, so the strategy worked nicely. In the event there was a problem, the sales director could help remedy the situation while the guest was still in the hotel. In one instance, the guest, informed by his secretary that the hotel had called, came out of his room, searched out the sales director, and said, "I want to shake your hand and thank you for following up with my secretary before I even leave to make sure that everything is OK. I'm impressed!" This follow-up technique helped the hotel sales director forge relationships with both customers, the secretary/travel arranger and the hotel guest.

Sometimes a more high-tech solution for capturing customer feedback is called for. Ask Justin Lacey, whose customers are among the wealthiest and most finicky in the world. Investing $50,000 to quickly evaluate customer service delivery using a customized survey application and Palm VII handheld seemed like a bargain. That's because Lacey's employer, Flexjet, a division of Bombardier Aerospace, sells fractional ownership of luxury corporate jets, complete with cushy swivel seats, gourmet food, and personal video screens that show DVD movies. Fractional ownership prices range from $418,000 to $5.6 million.

What has Lacey, director of business development and planning, learned about winning repeat customers among this base of billionaire clients? It's the small things that can cause the biggest service problems. Explains Lacey, "Catering is funny—it's a big deal. They want to make sure the caviar is cold, the champagne is from the right region, the wine is from the right years." Because clients are often entertaining important guests or business associates, a no-surprises flight is important. "They don't want to be embarrassed. When things go wrong, we have to find out about it so we can work through the problems."

Flexjet had relied on voice mail to track service quality of its 110 jets, each of which routinely made two to three trips a day. Flight crews would leave daily phone messages detailing how each trip went, and then the headquarter staff would decipher and transcribe the voice messages. This inefficient system made for delayed data analysis and slow-turnaround on solving service problems.

In a brainstorm meeting, Lacey's boss looked at the Palm VII lying on his desk and asked, "Can we use this thing to solve the problem?" Flexjet's new means for gathering customer feedback was born. Working with a Palm software developer, Flexjet created an easy-to-complete customer survey. Toward the end of every flight, an attendant hands the Palm to the client who, in about a minute or so, enters answers to the electronic survey on the screen. The cockpit crew and attendants complete separate parts of the survey. When the plane lands, a crew member raises the Palm antenna and sends survey results via e-mail to Flexjet headquarters. The formatted survey results are automatically grabbed by the e-mail server and fed into a customer feedback database from which quality assurance analysts run daily reports. Jon Maxfield, Flexjet's manager of owner services, says, "We can see how well our different vendors are providing services to customers at different airports. We can cut the data in a lot of ways."

Since its launch five years ago, Flexjet has been steadily building business and gaining ground against its formidable rival, NetJets, owned by Warren Buffett's Berkshire Hathaway. Up against NetJets' 40 percent market share, Flexjet is depending on flawless customer service to help turn first-time customers into repeat customers and loyal clients. Rapid analysis of customer needs is an important means for getting there.[26]

As AmeriSuites and Flexjet both demonstrate, creating customer loyalty begins with pleasing the first-time customer. Would you buy a second Acme widget if the first one did not work? Of course not. If your customers are to buy from you again, they must perceive your product as having solved their problem. Follow up the first sale with some form of customer contact soon after the sale. Ask your customers if they are pleased with the product or service. If they have a problem with the product, correct it. Make this follow-up strictly for evaluating performance and not for soliciting another sale. With this feedback in hand, you are better equipped to start the process for winning a repeat purchase.

3. Use Indoctrination Mailings

Another reason a first-time customer may not repurchase is that the customer fails to use the product or service. For example, how many home computers have you seen family and friends buy that now sit, dust-covered, in a back room?

If a customer does not use your product or service, he or she will probably lose interest in continuing a business relationship with you.

The indoctrination mailing, sent after a purchase and telling the new owner in painstaking detail how to use the product or service, helps motivate your customer to use the product. The mailing tells the customer why the decision to buy was a wise one and how to get the most out of what was bought. Design your mailing to draw the first-time customer's attention back to the product and to reinforce the person's original interest in it. Send the mailing out to your customer immediately after she receives the product or uses the service. Along with the letter to your first-time customer, provide an offer that encourages her to use the new purchase. For example, a computer retailer could offer free introductory word processing lessons to the new computer owner, or give her half off the next printer cartridge replacement if she brings it in within six months.

4. Constantly Reinforce Your Value in the Customer's Eyes

Good service is not enough. It counts only when your customer recognizes it. One company that understands the importance of reminding customers of its value-added service is Allcounty Plumbing and Heating in Brooklyn, New York. The competition among plumbers in the Brooklyn market is fierce, with twenty pages of phone book ads to prove it. A customer has plenty of opportunity to go elsewhere. To help keep customers loyal, Allcounty sends a thank-you letter to the customer after a service to help build and reinforce perception of quality. Here is a passage from one such letter. Notice how Allcounty presents a generic offering in an exceptional, customer-driven light: "Our effort to please you started with the carefully considered selection of each and every employee, from receptionist and dispatcher to servicemen and supervisory staff. It continued with the commitment to be there seven days a week, day or night, should you ever need us." The letter continues: "You probably have noticed our one-year guarantee, proof of our commitment to your satisfaction. Should you ever need help or have a question, we have a customer service number: (718). . . ."[27]

Office Depot is the world's largest seller of office products, with more than 982 warehouse stores in nine countries. From its three-store start-up in 1986 to its current size of almost one thousand stores, the company has won loyal customers among small- and medium-size businesses with its wide selection of brand-name office products at everyday low prices. The company does not use a central warehouse but maintains inventory on the sales floor of its no-frills stores. Office Depot is able to offer its customers a broad in-stock selection at prices generally 40–60 percent below manufacturers' suggested retail prices.

Recognizing that everyday low prices are what its customers value most, Office Depot provides a unique pricing comparison at two important points during the customer's shopping trip: at the shelf during selection and on every customer's receipt. I recently stopped in at Office Depot in Austin to buy a flipchart pad for an upcoming presentation. My sales receipt had a series of lines that read:

> Catalog list price would have cost you $15.75.
> Office Depot's low everyday price $8.29.
> You saved $7.46.
> Thank you for saving at Office Depot.

How about adding value each time you communicate with your customer? Consider this strategy: whenever you contact your client, have a bit of interesting news at hand to help him or her run the business better. It could be something you read in a trade magazine or newspaper or heard from a colleague. For example, when you call your client, you could say, "Pat, I'm calling today for a couple of reasons. First, I want to share some information I read in the *Harvard Business Review* that could have an impact on your business. Second, I'd like to tell you about a new product that might be of interest to you."

The value-added strategy can help businesses earn future contracts and orders. Says People's Bank Vice President Ken Weinsten, "We try to make sure that we are building a relationship instead of forcing a relationship. You want customers to use more of your services, but you have to earn it. Customers are looking for value."

5. Capture Customer Information and Use It

When CIO Ron Ward and CFO Scott Little signed on at the Hard Rock Café in 1998, their joint vision was to use the Internet to help capture customer information and drive repeat business to the 104 cafés in thirty-six countries. The duo, recruited from Disney, were promised significant leeway in putting much-needed IT systems in place to help boost repeat business. Revenues had stagnated after 1996, and in 1999 sales declined from the previous year's $396 to $388 million. "Our goal and our desire is that we can capture people coming out of the Café and they would go to our Website," Ward says. "And the goal with our Website is first and foremost to drive traffic back to the Café."

At the heart of this two-pronged strategy is a CRM system that tracks users both on the Web and in the restaurants. Ward explains that "if somebody had a phenomenal time in Paris, they go home to Cleveland, and there is a follow-up e-mail from the general manager to come in and experience the local café, again increasing the frequency of a customer's visits."

The Hard Rock has developed some sure-fire ways to drive diner traffic to the Website; in turn, this allows the company to capture important customer information including age, address, and musical preferences. At the bottom of every restaurant receipt is an identification number, unique for every meal, that can be entered into the Website. The Web visitor can then earn a five dollar gift certificate by entering some personal information, filling out a survey evaluating the Hard Rock experience, and naming their favorite bands. The Hard Rock, in turn, notifies the customer when the band is in town or when that band or a similar one will be performing via Webcast at the local café. As another means for driving customers to the Web, restaurant diners can have a digital picture shot among the posters and guitars and then find the picture online for download on Hardrock.com.

How is this repeat business strategy working? So far, so good, according to three early indicators. First, customers are completing the online survey via the reference on the receipts. Although the exact completion rate is not disclosed, Hard Rock reports that it is in the "substantial double digits." Compare this against the standard direct mail completion rate of 2–3 percent, and Hard Rock's numbers are impressive.

Secondly, an impressive 70 percent of people who get their picture taken at the café go online to claim it, which suggests the drive-diners-to-the-Web portion of the strategy is working. Finally, the firm's bottom line is improving. For the first half of 2000, sales were more than $200 million, promising to outpace 1999's $388 million and reverse the company's sales trend decline.[28]

Fischer Florist in Atlantic City, New Jersey, understands the importance of repeat customers. Founded in 1876 and one of the top hundred FTD florists in the United States, this veteran retailer sends to customers who have bought flowers on repetitive occasions (birthdays, anniversaries, holidays) a reminder in the mail. If our president, George W. Bush, were a Fischer Florist customer, his 2002 reminder letter sent in early June might read as follows: "On June 14, 2001, you remembered Laura on her birthday. Remember this important occasion again this year by giving us a call at Fischer Florist. We have enclosed a selection guide of gift ideas appropriate for the occasion." The florist encloses a brochure for easy gift selection along with the letter.

The program was originally administered by hand with a card file, but thanks to modern technology the process is now computerized. Owner and CEO Charles Fischer, Jr., reports that the reminder program is a mainstay of the company and is a cost-effective method of producing repeat purchases. Fischer adds that customers have grown to see the reminder as a service; once, when the florist missed a mailing, several customers called, annoyed because they'd failed to receive their reminder!

Fischer Florist and Hard Rock Café are only two of the thousands of retailers, service companies, manufacturers, and distributors that are discovering the benefits of customer relationship marketing. As discussed in Chapter Three, at the heart of CRM is a simple concept: collecting information about prospects or customers, then using the information to create specially targeted offerings.

In its first pilot program with database marketing, Saab Cars USA, the importer of luxury automobiles from Sweden, undertook an ambitious program to use database marketing to sell models such as the 900 CS and CSE sports sedans to American drivers.

Approximately two hundred thousand owners of new and used Saabs were mailed brochures, letters, and enticing offers such as a coupon good for $2,000 off the purchase price. The result was that spending $200,000 to mail letters expressing "appreciation of our customers' loyalty to the Saab marque" was one of the key factors that helped generate sales of an estimated $62 million worth of Saabs. "To build sales, you have to build a relationship with the customer," said Holly Pavlika, executive vice president and creative director of Fox Pavlika, the agency handling Saab's direct response programs. "You have to create a sense of value, a sense of trust, and reinforce the fact the customer has made an intelligent decision."[29]

Customer databases are helping aggressive pizza delivery companies win the "pizza wars" around university campuses. One of my marketing students at the University of Texas, Steve Lassiter, shared this repeat-buyer experience with me. Steve was in his apartment near campus one weekday evening around 9:00 P.M. (just about the time other fast-food "Aren't you hungry?" type ads begin to appear on TV). A Pizza Hut representative called and said, "Steve, we're calling to tell you that when you place your next order with Pizza Hut, you will receive a $2 savings." The Pizza Hut representative continued, "If you'd like to order now, we'll get a hot pizza right out to you."

Steve thought for a second, decided a pizza sounded good, and said yes. The next question for Steve was "Do you want your usual large with pepperoni and extra cheese?" Think about it. Pizza Hut already had all the information required to get the next purchase—even down to what the customer ordered last time. Now it simply put the information to use. Right customer, right time.

The database can serve as an easy tracker of who your customers are, of what they are (and equally important are not) buying from you. Brad Hale, who runs a lawn maintenance company with annual gross sales of about $150,000, uses his database to cross-sell lawn care services that his current customers aren't already getting.

George Watts, proprietor of the George Watts and Sons crystal and china store in Milwaukee, uses his database of more than forty-three thousand customers to target mail to groups of five hundred to six hundred people interested in sought-after sterling patterns, notifying them of any upcoming sale. He also lets customers know when their particular china pattern is being discontinued, tipping them off to potential clearance bargains. Timing is everything with customer communication, and e-mail is making it increasingly easy for firms like George Watts to stay in real-time communication with database customers.

As useful and effective as customer database programs can be, it takes time and effort to implement them. One of the most complex data problems facing many companies is the lack of one centralized, companywide database. For example, a company's service center, marketing department, and billing department typically have separate databases with no effective way to tie all that knowledge together into a 360 degree customer view. To effectively implement a sound customer relationship strategy, you need to implement all touch points into one centralized database. Yes, it can be a daunting task, but some firms are rising to the challenge. Saturn is creating a Web-based information system that links all four hundred of its U.S. retail facilities with each other and with customers and partners. This data system makes it easier for the car buyer to shop multiple dealerships for their choice of model as well as help owners schedule a service appointment regardless of where they are.

If maintaining a centralized database with information that is easily retrievable and kept up to date isn't enough to worry about, here's another potential trouble spot. Privacy issues surrounding your customer database require careful management (see the next section). If they are to work, all these areas require a commitment of company resources and people. A business that organizes a plan and carries through with it finds that a well-conceived database offers a big advantage over competitors using the shotgun approach to marketing and managing the customer relationship. The key is to start collecting the customer information with the buyer's very first purchase.

6. Carefully Guard Customer Privacy

Database marketing is on the rise, but so are issues surrounding customer privacy. Rest assured that in the years ahead many of your customers will become increasingly concerned about privacy and want to know how their personal information is used and what sort of safeguards have been put in place to protect the data. Lawsuits may plague unprepared companies.

Just ask Computer City in San Diego, which was sued by a customer. When paying for his original purchase, the buyer noticed the clerk typing his name and address into the computer. He asked the clerk if his name would be added to a mailing list and the clerk responded no. The buyer then wrote on the back of his check that he would sue Computer City for a particular amount if the company violated the agreement not to put his name on any mailing list. Sure enough, he began receiving mailings from the company; he sued and won. The judge ruled that the buyer's check served as a legally binding contract violated by Computer City.[30]

To stay in your customers' good graces, follow these privacy guidelines:

- Rule number one: always ask your customer for permission.
- Explain to customers why you need specific information.
- Give your customer the privilege of opting out at every information gathering juncture.

- Establish a clear privacy policy and make sure it is accessible across all media, with particular attention to direct mail and Internet.

- Communicate extensively with staff about your privacy policies and practices; make frontline training part of this communication process.

- Build a well-documented privacy compliance program; make audits a part of this program.

- Tread carefully on data mining, and pay attention to customer feedback; if customers feel you are abusing your information privileges, data mining could cost you far more in goodwill and lost loyalty than it's worth.

- Make it easy for customers to provide feedback concerning your company's privacy practices; take action on what you learn.

7. Communicate Your Full Range of Services Continuously

Business consultant Howard Upton tells of a recent experience. He was in the office of the president of a petroleum equipment company that stocked and sold pumps, valves, and other such equipment used in service stations. In recent years, the company had been heavily engaged in installing underground storage tanks. As Upton and the president were conversing, the company's service manager stopped by briefly and said, "You're not going to believe this, but I've just been talking with the executive vice president of K-Plus, and it turns out he didn't know we do tank installations."

(Upton explains: "K-Plus [not the real name] owns and operates four hundred service stations [and] is one of the principal customers of the equipment company whose president I was visiting. Yet here was the company's service manager reporting that the top operations executives at K-Plus had been unaware of one of the major services offered by this company.)

"Oh, you must be mistaken," the equipment company president responded. "Everyone knows we do tank installations."

This experience demonstrates an important fact: in an increasingly complex business environment, customers and prospective customers rarely comprehend the full range of services offered by any company until the services are spelled out for them. Even then, the customer will have a short memory and must be reminded. Company brochures, newsletters, direct mail letters, and sales calls are some of the ways a company can keep reinforcing to the customer its range of services. "The most serious marketing mistake management can make is to assume that everybody knows what we do," says Upton. "In subtle ways, each company differs from all similar companies in the industry. These unique differences must be repeatedly communicated to clients and prospective clients."[31]

8. Paint a Picture of Future Possession

A friend of mine has been quite successful as an independent interior designer. She works with clients in redecorating existing homes and furnishing new ones. Her ability to turn a first-time buyer into a long-lasting client is evident from the many client relationships originating from her first year in business. One of her keen abilities is to "paint a picture of possession" with a new customer. It's rare that anyone can completely refurnish a home or even a room all at one time. Recognizing that, my friend provides a master design plan, complete with specifics on major furniture pieces, accessories, color swatches, and even artwork. She then guides the customer through initial purchases on the basis of the available budget.

Using the master plan as her guide, she touches base with each customer periodically to encourage and support the person on the next acquisition. Comments like "I'll be going to the High Point market next month; why don't we talk before the trip and decide what kind of rug you would like me to look for?" sound less like a sales pitch and more like a service call. The master plan concept has also helped to inspire anniversary, birthday, and holiday gifts within her client families.

The concept of painting a picture of possession has application across a range of industries. From residential landscaping to computers, hair care, or antique cars, many a company can benefit from painting a picture of possession with the first-time buyer well beyond the first purchase, and then assisting the buyer in achieving that vision over time.

9. Turn Repeat Purchasing into a Service

The dispenser containing the black gooey makeup that women use on their eyelashes can be a haven for bacteria if not replaced regularly. If this bacteria-infested mascara gets in the eye, a serious eye disorder may result, even blindness. Jana Beatty is a cosmetic specialist in Waco, Texas. Recognizing the awareness that many women have about the hazards of mascara, Jana identified a way to help them practice a safe make-up routine and at the same time turn the first-time mascara buyer into a regular customer. Here's how she did it.

When Jana sells a tube of mascara to a new buyer, she explains the importance of replacing the tube every three months and how, as a member of her "mascara club," the buyer can receive fresh mascara delivered to her home four times a year. Jana provides a sticker on the tube with the date of the purchase. She then sends a fresh tube of mascara to the buyer in the mail before the three-month period is over. Jana tells me that before she mails the mascara, she calls her customer and ask whether there is any other makeup item she needs. Jana says that, more often than not, she also receives a request for other products.

How does Jana Beatty convert a first-time buyer into a repeat customer? By identifying a specific need and then filling it.

10. Treat Customer Service Costs as a Worthwhile Investment

Expenditures made to help strengthen customer loyalty can be cheap when compared with the cost of losing a customer. Recognizing the possible future income from repeat business and favorable referrals, Ford authorizes its dealers to spend up to $250 per customer of goodwill money to correct, without charge, problems the customer sees as the fault of either the dealer or the company. Ford considers the $250 well spent to protect profits from future sales.

One extraordinary act can earn a customer's loyalty forever. When a ride in Disney World broke down, the part manufacturer, Premier Industrial, found a replacement part in Chicago and had an employee fly and drive it to the Florida amusement park within five hours, for a charge of $14. Disney executives were embarrassed by the low fee and offered to pay more, but Premier refused. Premier CEO Mort Mandel sees it this way: exceptional service really is not costly, because it is needed only once every couple of years per customer. But the loyalty it generates among customers, says Mandel, drops right to the bottom line.[32]

11. Nurture and Protect Communication with Decision Makers

When a company is selling to a large organization, several individuals can be involved in the final decision to purchase. These purchasing professionals form what can be called a "buying center." The parties may include the user (the person using the service), the influencer (the individual who determines the specifications), the buyer (the person who has formal authority to select the vendor), the decision maker (the one who has final authority for vendor selection and terms), and the gatekeeper (the person who controls information flow into the buying center).

Once the initial purchase decision is made, a fatal mistake often follows: sales and service personnel and even senior management often end up dealing with the day-to-day users in the customer organization, not the decision maker. According to Richard Shapiro, "When relationships are built with users and not decision makers, employees feel less comfortable approaching senior management within the customer's organization. This may occur because they have lost touch with their customer's organizational structure and strategic direction. All the while, competition is continuing to reach decision makers within the customer's organization and informing them of newer technologies, better approaches or more cost-effective ways of providing services."[33]

This situation can be prevented, says Shapiro, by initiating a program of collecting direct feedback through a structured interview process. This process affords a sales or service representative a legitimate reason to schedule an appointment with the decision maker to review how the organization is meeting the customer's needs. As Shapiro explains, "This formalized process will also provide an opportunity [for the sales representative] to communicate improvements currently being planned and explain new policies or procedures that may have been recently implemented."[34]

Shapiro suggests a number of questions as an effective way to open dialogue with a decision maker as well as garner valuable input for an organization:

- What do you like best about dealing with our organization?
- If you could change anything about the relationship you have with our organization that would reduce frustration and make it more effective, what would it be?
- How does our organization stack up against our competitors?
- Which additional products and services should our organization provide as part of our overall offering?
- If you were president of our organization, how would you go about retaining customers?

To benefit from the customer feedback, determine when first-time customer data will be collected and who will be analyzing it. Additionally, you will want to decide how this information will be processed and disseminated within your organization.

12. Develop Customer Reward Programs

Beginning with the first purchase, many companies are developing programs to anchor the relationship. Over the past five years, Mitchell's auto dealerships in Simsbury, Connecticut, have offered a "Mitchell preferred customer" card to new customers purchasing a vehicle. Free car washes in the first year, a loaner car or shuttle service during repairs, and discounts on certain auto accessories are among the privileges of the holder. "We are trying to say that it is more than just the price. We want to offer you a relationship," said David Tefft, general sales manager of Mitchell's Pontiac, Dodge, Volvo, Volkswagen, and Subaru dealerships. "We have to spend money on our customers to maintain them."

One specific type of customer reward program is the "family promotion." This is a special event or happening that only customers and clients are notified about. Family promotion is an effective way to make customers feel they are getting an opportunity that is reserved only for those people who have earned it with their patronage. Direct mail postcards, letters, e-mail, and telephone calls are good ways to communicate a family special.

13. Develop "New Customer Welcome" Promotions

A "new customer welcome" kit can be an effective way to help motivate first-time customers to return. A hair salon in my neighborhood designed such a kit for its new customers. The kit contains a "salon sampler" card with special introductory savings on a variety of products and services throughout the salon. These savings are redeemable on the second, third, fourth, and fifth visits. (In the hair care industry, five consecutive visits is the average number required to turn a first-time buyer into a solid, repeat customer.)

The kit also has a brochure outlining the salon's unique services, such as the "emergency haircut" for busy customers who may need a spur-of-the-moment haircut to look their best for an important meeting. A comprehensive list of the salon's services and prices is also included as part of the brochure.

Finally, the kit contains a "recommend a friend" card, outlining how the new customer can enjoy special gifts and treats by referring friends to the salon.

These three pieces are delivered to new customers by the receptionist upon "checkout" in an oversize envelope, labeled the We Want You Back Pack. The receptionist acknowledges the customer as a first-timer, thanks her for the visit, presents her with the kit as a token of the salon's appreciation, and invites her to return.

14. Offer Product Guarantees

Bombay is one of the hottest retail chains in North America. The company sells replicas of eighteenth- and nineteenth-century English furniture in roughly four hundred mall stores throughout the United States and Canada. Using a worldwide network of supply channels, the company manufacturers its own lines. The company's prices are 30–60 percent below competitors', and no item in the stores costs more than $500. With sales of $232 million, Bombay's average sales per foot are $340, well above the industry average of $110.

An unconditional guarantee is a primary component of the company's customer support policy. Explaining that the best time to capture a customer for life is when he needs a refund, the president and CEO, Robert Nourse says, "We'll take the thing back with no hassle, no questions, no guff about 'Where's the receipt?' The cost of that is peanuts compared with what you gain in customer loyalty. Too many retailers have forgotten what service means. When you treat customers like a million dollars, they'll come back."[35]

For a guarantee to truly assist in winning customer loyalty, execution is critical. If a customer encounters difficulty in getting a guarantee honored, the trust and goodwill felt toward the organization can be greatly damaged.

15. Develop Value-Added Promotions

When Leo Spellman, director of advertising for Steinway and Sons in New York City, talks about customer relationships, he thinks thirty years into the future. "We are trying to engage our customers in not just a one-purchase deal, but in building a relationship," says Spellman. He continues: "We think of things that will add value, or perceived value, to the purchase." This philosophy is what led

Spellman and Steinway to begin giving dealers an option of offering zero-coupon bonds of ten-, twenty- or thirty-year maturity as a buyer incentive.

During the monthlong promotion period, anyone who purchased a Steinway piano received a zero-coupon bond equal to the piano's purchase price. A zero-coupon bond is bought at a discount to the face value. No interest is paid on the bond until it matures, at which time the bond is redeemed at face value. For example, the buyer of a Steinway with a $20,000 purchase price would receive a zero-coupon bond for the same amount. After thirty years, the $20,000 zero-coupon bond can be redeemed for $20,000.

Clinton's of Hartford, a piano retailer and one of Steinway's one hundred dealers, participated in the recent bond promotion. Clinton's manager, Harold E. Niver, was attracted to the promotion for one key reason: a typical customer who purchases a Steinway piano—they vary in price from $10,000 to $70,000—considers the purchase an investment and often hands the piano down as a family heirloom. Says Niver, "If [customers] held [the bond] to maturity, they would realize the price of the piano," and when the bond does reach maturity, customers "still have the product, which has actually appreciated in value."

Niver's instincts proved correct. The promotion helped boost the store's Steinway sales to about $100,000 for the month, representing a 50 percent increase over normal sales for that period. What's more, the promotion helped ensure that the name Steinway was kept alive in the mind of the purchaser's family for years to come, further increasing the likelihood that any future piano bought by a family member will also be a Steinway.

In his book *Winning Through Enlightenment,* Ron Smothermon offers his observation about relationships and loyalty: "There is something curious about loyalty. There is something that must be in order for loyalty to endure: it must be noticed. If you simply remember that no one owes you anything, loyalty will be easy for you to notice and acknowledge. If you begin to think 'they' owe you loyalty, you are in trouble."[36]

There is no more important place to start noticing patronage and nurturing its beginnings than with the first-time customer. Turning the first-time customer into a repeat customer is a major passage on the journey to earning the customer's long-term loyalty.

SUMMARY

- First-time buyer attrition is often double that of older accounts. Turning the first-time buyer into a repeat customer requires the constant attention of the seller.

- In every company, the order is a surrogate for the customer. When the order sits unattended, so does the customer. The best way to be customer-oriented is to go beyond customers and products to the order.

- People judge an entire company by the performance of a frontline employee. The employee must have the time, tools, and training to perform. For many companies, the employee front line is a customer contact center (tele-center) where agents interact with customers. It is becoming increasingly important that these agents have proficient writing skills as well as verbal skills.
- Customer database technology can be extremely helpful in building a strong relationship with the customer and turning a new buyer into a repeat customer. With database marketing on the rise, guarding customer privacy will be of increasing importance to the customer.
- Most companies lack a centralized database and instead have multiple databases with no effective way to tie all the knowledge together. A centralized database that has a 360 degree view of the customer is important in growing repeat customers and clients.
- Three online tools are helping companies consistently deliver responsive service: self-service, e-mail management, and live chat and Web callback.
- Steps should be taken to help reduce the amount of dissonance experienced by the first-time customer.
- To help keep an account loyal, nurture the relationship with the user of your product or service as well as with the account's decision makers.
- Indoctrination mailings, "new customer welcome" promotions, and customer reward programs are a few of the marketing tools proved to be effective at turning the new buyer into a repeat customer.
- Never take a customer's loyalty for granted. For loyalty to endure, it must be noticed and acknowledged.

GETTING STARTED

- Carefully and continuously track the percentage of first-time buyers who become repeat buyers. Research the reasons first-time customers do not rebuy. Apply what you learn to increase the rate of repeat purchase.
- Stay in close touch with frontline employees to identify new and better ways to effectively serve the customer. Consider holding regular brainstorming sessions with front liners to identify recent customer problems and possible ways to address them. Use this information to improve internal processes companywide.
- Monitor call quality and e-mail quality of call center agents. Conduct training where needed.
- Regularly check complaint Websites for customer comments about your company and its products and services. Contact unhappy customers and attempt, at minimum, to neutralize their displeasure. Apply what you learn to improving internal systems and processes.
- Establish a clear privacy policy concerning customer data and make it

accessible to customers across all communication channels. Make a well-documented privacy compliance program, including audits, part of this policy. Communicate extensively with staff about your privacy policies and practices.

CHAPTER SEVEN

Turning Repeat Customers into Loyal Clients

Ireland's supermarket mastermind, Feargal Quinn, knows a lot about turning a repeat customer into a loyal client. In fact, some of his most profound lessons were learned in childhood. "If you've got the chance to be born again," he says with a twinkle in his eye, "do your best to be born into a family that runs a holiday camp. It's a smashing way to grow up—and a smashing business education."

Today, Quinn is executive chairman of Superquinn, a nineteen-store chain with annual sales of $700 million and fifty-six hundred employees. Considering its tiny size (Tesco, its fiercest competitor, has annual revenue of $30 billion), the chain's brand name and market impact are nothing short of remarkable. But then again, Quinn's early business lessons were also profound.

Growing up in Ireland, Quinn spent school breaks working at his father's Red Island holiday camp on the coast of northern Dublin County, doing whatever was needed, from page boy to waiter to bingo caller. One big lesson for young Quinn was his father's rule of always charging guests at the beginning of their stay for their entire holiday. Explains Quinn, "It was set up so that no matter how hard we worked to give our guests a great experience, we wouldn't increase our profit from their stay. The only way we could judge our success was if the guests came up to my father and said, 'Mr. Quinn, I had a great holiday, I'm rebooking for next year.' Every single thing we did was centered on one overriding aim: to get people to come back. I learned that if you look after getting repeat business, profit will largely take care of itself. When faced with any business decision, any call on your time or resources, you need to ask, What will this do to help bring the customer back?"[1]

This same philosophy on earning repeat business drives the Superquinn chain today. From working with exclusive suppliers to develop "destination products" (made-to-order sausage, a custom-designed potato) to embracing some of the world's most leading-edge retail technology (including self-scan checkout and digital shelf labels), Superquinn is constantly searching for a way to add more value for existing customers. This dedication to earning repeat business gets results for the chain. The privately owned company enjoys market leader status in the greater Dublin area and a hefty 9 percent of Ireland's $11 billion grocery business.

So, what's Quinn's best advice for winning customer loyalty? Focus on one key trait: humility. In fact, he counsels business leaders to concentrate on five lessons in humility: "My customers know more than I do. My employees know more than I do. Neither my employees nor I can be creative all of the time. What I knew yesterday is not enough for today. I'm not responding fast enough for my customers."[2]

Quinn's humility philosophy reflects a basic loyalty truth: a business that fails to show strong appreciation for its customers and instead takes them for granted is a business with a short future. The fact of the matter is that a loyal customer is an increasingly precious commodity. No longer can customers be regarded as an endless stream of convenient cash machines that buy the products offered to them without complaining about poor service, failed promises, arrogant or inattentive salespeople, or company policies that place more emphasis on profit than on service and performance. Economists are predicting tough competition ahead, reflected in the slower growth rate of the population, of income, and of retail sales.

As we have seen from earlier chapters, analysts who study business profiles to determine who will remain successful in tough competitive times have discovered a number of realities:

- Most businesses get their profit from long-term customers. Says Frederick F. Reichheld, "New customers are actually money losers. Much money is spent to attract them, but many do not make it past the first-time customer stage."

- The average business invests six times more money in acquiring a new customer than it does in retaining a customer. Yet it is estimated that customer loyalty is worth ten times the value of a single purchase.

- Customer retention produces profits, since a long-term customer costs less to deal with. This customer knows a company's personnel and procedures, and the company knows the buyer's tastes.

How can a business, as a matter of policy, upgrade repeat customers into loyal clients and keep them loyal? The answer is quite simple: the company must deliver value—as defined by the customer—by continually enhancing, improving, or even changing the basic product or service to increase its payoff to the customer.

The importance of value, and the role it plays at this later stage in loyalty development, is partly illustrated by Stephen Covey's concept of a person's emotional bank account. Covey describes it as operating on deposits and withdrawals, just as an actual bank account does. We get "overdrawn" with others when, in their eyes, we've "withdrawn" from them more than we have "deposited." The same concept applies to our customers. To upgrade a customer to loyal client and to keep him loyal, we must deliver value so that he continues to feel we have deposited more in his account than we have withdrawn. In other words, in his eyes, we have given more value to him than he has given to us.

The concept of delivering value is not new, but how customers define it is. Historically, customers have viewed value as being a combination of price and quality. Today's customers have enlarged their definition of value to include such factors as reliability, purchase convenience, and after-sale service.

THREE TYPES OF VALUE

The companies that have attained a leadership position over the past two decades achieved their success by narrowing the business focus and delivering value in one of three categories: operational excellence, customer intimacy, or product leadership.[3]

Operational excellence means giving customers reliable products at a competitive price and with minimum difficulty in purchasing.

When college student Michael Dell began selling computers out of his dorm room at the University of Texas, he based his business on operational excellence. His approach was a radical departure from market leaders Compaq and IBM, both of which embraced dealer distribution and king-of-the-hill technology. Dell pioneered a telemarketing system that bypassed dealers and sold to customers directly. In doing so, he created a low-cost corporate culture that enabled PC buyers to buy state-of-the-art technology easily and affordably. From such sparse beginnings in 1984, operational excellence has helped drive Dell Computer to a remarkable $31.8 billion in annual revenues and made it the world's number one computer systems company.

The second value category, customer intimacy, means segmenting and targeting a market with exact precision and then customizing the offering to meet the demands of that niche. Two factors are critical if a company is to excel in customer intimacy: detailed customer knowledge and flexible operations. Combined, they make it possible to respond quickly to customer needs and special requests. Unlike operational excellence, which depends on a lean and efficient operation, customer intimacy requires that a company look beyond the value of a single transaction to the customer's lifetime value and do whatever it takes to ensure that the customer gets exactly what he or she truly wants.

Home Depot, the $45.7 billion Atlanta-based retailer, has established the customer-intimacy gold standard within the home improvement and hardware industry. Throughout the company's thirteen hundred stores across the United States and in Canada, Mexico, and Puerto Rico, knowledgeable salespeople, frequently recruited from the ranks of electricians and carpenters, are urged to spend lots of time with the customer to determine what product is required to solve a particular home repair problem. Home Depot also routinely offers free demos on everything from putting in a complete bathroom to simple installation of a home lighting fixture. Made-to-order service is the way Home Depot delivers value. The customer whose overriding concern is price is outside the corporation's target market. Home Depot's approach has struck a cord with homeowners, as evidenced by healthy earnings and a 25 percent annual growth rate.

In the third category, product leadership, a company makes its value contribution by giving the customer leading-edge products and services that make competitors' goods obsolete. For example, in the sport shoe category, Nike has product leadership; in eye care products, it's Johnson and Johnson; in computer software, Microsoft excels. With product leadership, a company must constantly challenge itself to pursue new solutions and make its own technology obsolete. Otherwise, a competitor will do it.

In determining how to best deliver value, a company must take into account its capabilities and strengths as well as those of its competitors. Both Dell Computer and Home Depot chose their particular type of value by carefully analyzing market conditions as well as their own resources and capabilities. Through analysis, planning, and in-market experience, these companies have determined how to best deliver value so that the repeat customer becomes a loyal client. The same can be true for you. But to lock in loyalty, you must determine what your repeat customer values most and how to best provide it.

As discussed in Chapter One, the loyal-client stage is most critical in regard to potential profit payoff. At the repeat-customer stage, the customer's momentum is in your favor. He has bought from you at least twice. Now is the opportunity to lock him into a consistent pattern of buying from you. The key here is to firmly anchor his loyalty rather than let it wane.

Whether it's operational excellence, customer intimacy, or product leadership, value delivery can take a number of forms, depending on the nature of the firm's products and services, its competitors, and its customers. Nonetheless, there are a number of factors that should be considered in formulating any strategy for transforming a repeat customer into a loyal client. We examine these issues in the remainder of this chapter, beginning with the all-important role of customer research.

RESEARCHING YOUR CUSTOMER

True loyalty is not measured by what a customer says; it is measured in terms of buying habits as they relate to your products or services. The objective of customer research is to discover who the largest customers are, what they are buying, and why they are loyal. This information is critical to any plan for upgrading loyalty. Most companies don't know the answers to these pertinent questions, yet they can be gotten without a great deal of digging. You can review a customer's buying habits by going back to purchase records and evaluating such patterns as visits per year, spending per visit, year-on-year comparison of units shipped, and products and services purchased.

Who Are Your Best Customers, and What Do They Buy?

Rank your customers by sales dollars and unit volume. Look carefully at who is at the top of the list. As a rule, the people in the top one-third of your list do indeed represent the source of your profits. These are the people who contribute cash to your bottom line reliably and repeatedly. Your return is usually highest with the customers who buy the most and have been associated with you for the longest time. They are one of the few appreciating assets in your company. Next, evaluate which products and services your best customers are buying. Identifying the products or services your customers are buying most can give you a valuable clue as to how to increase future sales.

Joan V. Silver, president of Reeves Audio Visual Systems, found her secret weapon for identifying a way to build sales and loyalty in a surprising place: her sales receipts. Silver directs an industrial audiovisual equipment company in New York City, offering both sales and service. Silver's marketing breakthrough came when she wanted to increase sales of a new $16,000 Sony video projection system she had recently added to her offerings. Silver began going through her receipts to determine which of her clients could not afford the system. Most could, she reasoned, since she believed that 90 percent were Fortune 500 companies. But Silver got a big surprise. Receipts revealed that just 58 percent of revenue came from these large corporations. The remainder came from smaller companies, many with less than $1 million in sales.[4]

Silver analyzed the receipts (including invoices and purchase orders) in more detail and established a ranking of her top twenty customers by sales. Next she identified what they were buying most. More surprises were in store. Many of her larger accounts had disappeared owing to mergers and cutbacks. Advertising agencies and insurance companies had taken their place. Ad agencies were buying custom-designed turnkey editing systems. Rather than subcontracting out the work, they were setting up their own editing suites. Insurance companies were buying TV production equipment to make in-house training tapes.

Armed with this information, Silver adopted a new strategy: she searched through her receipts for ad agencies and insurance companies that had not yet bought such equipment. She sent out personalized letters with a simple sales message: "Your competitors are bringing their production work in-house. Shouldn't you?" She concluded her letters by outlining Reeves's full-service audiovisual capabilities.

As for the smaller accounts, her analysis showed that because they usually need service on the spur of the moment, they rarely have the luxury to bid out the work. Since they do not have in-house support, they often need both support and service. This makes profit on such an account higher. To accommodate that business, Silver enlarged her product lines and offered three-hour delivery. She has now replaced her larger, unfocused quarterly mailing of the past with a simpler monthly mailing targeted to these smaller identified markets. Since launching this new strategy, the company's response rate has jumped 10 percent.

Another technique for identifying your best customers is to apply the concept of customer lifetime value (CLTV). With CLTV, a firm views the customer as an asset and estimates CLTV as the net present value of the profit to be realized on the customer across a given number of years in the future. Although Silver used historical data to rank customers, firms using CLTV rank customers according to their future-oriented estimate of value. This CLTV ranking in turn helps a company make effective choices concerning acquisition, retention, and win-back expenditures and which customers and CLTV segments are most worthy of investment.

Moreover, a firm using this approach looks for a way to increase the CLTV of its customers using one or more of three avenues: (1) increase the *lifetime* by raising either the retention rate or the number of years a customer can remain a customer, (2) increase *sales* by raising the firm's share of customer purchases or the customer's referral rate, or (3) decrease the *cost* of serving the customer.[5]

When manufacturer Kimberly-Clark, maker of Huggies disposable diapers, considered CLTV, one thing was certain: even among its best buyers, profitability was stalled because of the eighteen-month life of a Huggies customer (that is, the period of being a baby). Moreover, market research found parents felt guilty if their child was still in nappies after eighteen months but also felt guilty for rushing a small child who was not ready for pants. Kimberly Clark introduced trainer pants that fit like real pants but still have the absorbency of the conventional diaper. This new product extended the customer life by about six months (or 33 percent) and in turn dramatically improved the CLTV (and resulting profitability) of Kimberly Clark's customer base.

Why Do Your Customers Buy?

Another vital part of customer research is for a company to carefully evaluate what makes its customers loyal. In other words, which particular aspects of the company's products and services create the loyalty? Is it the attitude of the employees? Are customers impressed by the company's policy regarding guarantee, return, or exchange? What exactly does the company do that engenders loyalty? Many companies make a mistake by assuming they know the answer.

When Mac McConnell, owner of the Artful Framer Gallery in Plantation, Florida, conducted a poll of three hundred of his customers, six years ago, he got the surprise of his life. Price, which he believed was the factor that ensured customer patronage, was last on the list of his customers' priorities. Until the survey, McConnell had always competed on price and believed he had no choice. Now he discovered that the customers' first requirement was quality, followed by uniqueness.

The same survey indicated that word of mouth brought in a third of his customers. So McConnell set about reinventing his business to give people more reason to tell their friends about his shop. Because repeat customers wanted quality, he abandoned his low-end framing options: "We made museum framing the standard." He answered the need for more creative framing options by stocking eighteen hundred frame samples. He began offering a lifetime guarantee on all work and started calling customers a month after purchase to see if they were satisfied. When he knows an order might be delayed, he calls the customer and gives plenty of notice.

He taught his salespeople to take a more consultative selling approach, by talking first about where the customer plans to hang the art, followed by discussion of price.

With these changes, the store's average invoice increased from $67 to $167. Over four years, sales tripled, with net profits up 26 percent. McConnell reports that "when we changed our focus to making great frames, the money came."[6]

After nine successive new product failures, Techsonic Industries, a manufacturer of sonar devices for fishermen, decided to listen to customers. But the next decision was the toughest. With profits on a steep decline, would the company commit the $20,000 necessary to do the necessary focus group interviews among prospects and customers? Despite an industry with revenues of roughly $55 million, market research was simply not done in this business, and Techsonic Chairman Jim Balkcom wasn't sure he wanted to be any different: "If you're going to invest money, you think about what you'll have when you're through. Spending money on this [research], all you have is a folder with some stuff in it. It's not an asset, like a [design] mold."[7]

Balkcom was even more uncomfortable when he saw the results: $20,000 for a single sheet of paper with a bunch of phrases ranked one through forty-five.

"Sunlight" was the number one problem consumers had with their depth finders, according to the sheet and its ninety-four pages of support data.

From the focus group findings, a more quantitative telephone survey was conducted. More than eighteen hundred fishermen were surveyed to determine a ranking of problems consumers had with their depth finders. The findings were surprising, to say the least. "Sunlight" indeed reigned as the number one complaint, reflecting fishermen's problem with reading a fish finder in bright sunlight.

"We really had no idea how important that was," said Balkcom. Complaint number two? Fishermen generally found their fish finder too complicated. Once again, Balkcom was shocked: "Our conventional wisdom was that fishermen liked to press buttons."[8]

Long story made short: focus group feedback, combined with quantitative research, enabled the company to identify a gap in the industry and fill it with a new fish-identifying technology called LCR (liquid crystal recorder). The company sold more than 100,000 units of the product in its debut year, an impressive number given that 96,280 units had been the record for the company's biggest seller in its best year.

This experience with market research made a believer out of Techsonic, which was out in the marketplace with its LCR soon after introduction, seeking feedback for future upgrades.

Getting actionable results is the key to any customer loyalty research plan. My company conducts quantitative loyalty research for clients whereby attributes are divided into four actionable categories (see Figure 7.1 for more details):

1. *Loyalty drivers.* This area is most important to your customers; this is where your performance is highest. Stay the course. Your efforts are already producing loyalty.

2. *Improvement candidates.* This area is important to the client, but your performance is lacking. To improve loyalty, invest more resources to improve here.

3. *Hidden opportunities.* Your customers may have emerging needs in this area that they themselves are yet to identify. Additional communication and investigation may be warranted.

4. *Overinvestment candidates.* Since customer importance is low in this area, avoid overspending. Trimming costs may be wise.[9]

As we've seen, Artful Framer Gallery and Techsonic are practicing the art of, and profiting from, a key customer loyalty principle: probe customers to find out what is creating loyalty and what your company can do to increase and extend it. The most successful companies know that this is a never-ending process.

Figure 7.1. Customer Motivation Window.

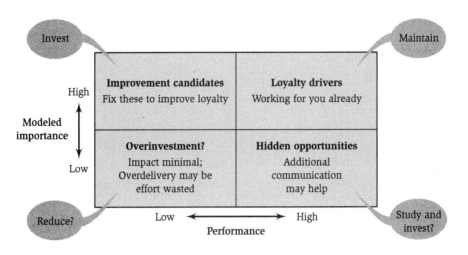

Customer needs are constantly changing. The business must continue to ask "How are we doing?" and "What can we do better?"

FROM REPEAT CUSTOMER TO LOYAL CLIENT: EIGHT GUIDELINES

Staying close to customer needs through regular research is an important step in moving a repeat customer into a deeper loyalty zone. But there's more to do. Here are eight additional considerations for moving your repeat customer to a higher level of loyalty.

1. Insulate Your Best Customers from Competitive Attack

As you know, your best customers are your competitor's best prospects. This means you must carefully guard your customer relationships at all stages in the Profit Generator, but particularly those that you've raised to repeat-customer status. Remember, the more advanced your customer is in the Profit Generator, the more profits she typically represents to you. It would be a shame to lose her now.

This is why, upon learning that two new competitive supermarkets were moving into the neighborhood on the same day, Green Hills Farms went to work to insulate its best customers from attack. Located in Syracuse, New York, this family-owned store of twenty-two thousand square feet has a heritage of more than seventy-five years of outperforming the competition and, in doing so, earning weekly sales of $16 per square foot, while the industry average is roughly $8 to $10. So it's not in the nature of CEO Gary Hawkins or his staff to just sit back passively and watch competition take away valuable customers. Instead, they quickly mobilized to defend against the new competitors.

First, Lisa Piron, director of information services, generated a list of best customers by department (produce, meats, bakery, and so forth). Next, she composed a letter thanking them for their strong patronage and enclosed a Green Hills certificate for a gift basket tied to each one's favorite department. When the customer came in for the basket, the department manager handed the basket to each customer with a personal thank-you for the business. CEO Hawkins reports the store not only "held its own against the new competition but even gained sales."[10] Taking steps to insulate your best customers during intense competitive activity (new product, store launch, promotional blitz) can be critical to retaining repeat customers and turning them into loyal clients.

2. Make Top Spenders Your Biggest Priority

Green Hills Farms categorizes its customers into four buyer groups: diamond, at the top of the spending scale; followed by ruby, pearl, and opal. Roughly three hundred customers qualify as diamonds, regularly spending $100 or more weekly, while about a thousand customers are rubies, spending $50 to $99 on average each week. (The firm's frequent-buyer program, was launched in 1993; the store collects data through an orange-and-green card held on the customer's key chain.) When the store first started categorizing customers, Hawkins was convinced he could graduate lots of customers to a higher level.

Experience taught him otherwise. Although some customers consistently shop the store every two months or so, some top spenders visit three to five times a week. Hawkins found the gap is too wide, and trying to convert price shoppers is ultimately self-defeating. Lisa Piron agrees: "There aren't a lot of things you can do to get lower-spending households to spend more."[11] So the company works hard to make sure big spenders get lavish attention. For example, the company hosted a black-tie party in the store to get better acquainted with more diamonds and rubies. More than two hundred customers attended.

As the store's database guru, Piron carries out ongoing tracking of whether best customers are truly getting their fair share of discounts. If they are not, she simply devises a new promotion to make sure they do. Unlike most stores, which simply measure the effectiveness of a promotion by the overall redemption rate, Green Hills pays close attention to *who* redeems the offer. Too many opals and pearls redeeming, and not enough diamonds and rubies? The promotion gets redesigned.

3. Harness Your Supply Chain to Deliver Better Customer Value

Some world-class companies are winning customer loyalty by combining supply chain management and customer relationship management into a digital loyalty network. Consider U.S. furniture manufacturer Herman Miller. Competing in the traditionally slow-moving furniture industry, the company knows that product differentiation is not enough to earn customer loyalty. So the manufacturer is creating a digital loyalty network that is increasingly capable of differentiating, in real time, the entire supply chain response to individual customers according to their lifetime value, requirements, and total cost to serve. This means best customers can design and order custom-configured furniture and have it delivered directly to them from the assembly plant. Also for best customers, Herman Miller has streamlined its Web page, called EZ-Connect, to enable these customers to place an order at special pricing.

On the supplier side, the company has developed Internet capability so that critical manufacturing and inventory data can be coordinated with the five hundred or so members of the worldwide supplier network. This enables suppliers to reduce their inventory cost and make supplies, parts, and materials available to Herman Miller on a just-in-time basis for final assembly. The bottom line is that more than a week has been shaved off the time required to build and deliver most orders; on-time shipments have risen from 75 percent five years ago to almost 98 percent today. In an industry known for sluggish fulfillment and delivery, such differentiation helps Herman Miller earn continued loyalty from the repeat customer.[12]

4. Build a Frequent Buyer Program That Really Works

The right frequent-buyer program can be a strong force for turning a repeat customer into a loyal client. Look no further than casino operator Harrah's, whose frequent-buyer program goals are straightforward: build loyalty and increase business by rewarding the customer for cumulative purchases through targeted communications, incentives, and performance tracking. Simple to state. Much harder to do, reports Harrah's. Here's their story.

Go to the Strip in Las Vegas, and every quarter of an hour you'll see tourists rush the erupting volcano outside of MGM's $750 million Mirage hotel and casino. If the Mirage is lucky, a handful of these visitors will stroll into the casino and spend a few thousand dollars in a few hours of gambling.

In stark contrast, on the other side of the street stands Harrah's hotel and casino, looking downright dowdy and deprived. But like many things in Las Vegas, looks can be deceiving. The reality is that the financial performance of the company, with casinos throughout the United States, is two to three times better than any of its competitors. In 1999, Harrah's doubled revenue from two years earlier and saw same-store sales grow 14 percent from the year before.

The secret is that although most other casinos invested money in creating glitz, Harrah's took the road less traveled and built a companywide information network as the backbone of the firm's frequent-buyer program, Total Rewards. Harrah's coast-to-coast customer database is an industry first and enabled the company to have the first integrated, nationwide system that allows real-time communication between all of its properties. This means that Harrah's in Las Vegas can know the gambling, eating, and spending preferences of a visitor from New Jersey. This customer insight enables the company to tailor services to the visitor through customized comps such as free dinners, hotel rooms, show tickets, and the like. Thus when the New Jersey customer comes to Harrah's in Las Vegas, customized service can follow.

What's more, Harrah's can better target its marketing promotions so that the customer is more likely to bite. For example, a customer receiving a mail promotion phones Harrah's call center for more information. The call prompts an array of customer information to pop up on the computer screen of the Harrah's customer service representative. From knowing the customer's tier (platinum, gold, or diamond) to seeing how much he's won or lost, and even possibly to having an estimate of his financial worth, the rep is armed with key information to help turn the caller into a confirmed reservation.

Harrah's Total Rewards program enables the company to leverage an important marketing principle: profits are driven not simply by increasing share of market (which Harrah's has also accomplished) but by increasing share of customer. Says William Schnitt, executive director at the Canadian Imperial Bank of Commerce, Harrah's "has been able to retain those lower-end players by calling them up to ask about their trips. Retaining a customer is one-tenth the cost of getting a new customer."

But Harrah's customer relationship vision wasn't always so clear. Before developing the Total Rewards program, the operational philosophy assumed that a customer was loyal to one particular location; therefore each Harrah's casino operated independently. In effect, they competed with one another. This meant each property had its own player card program, the card was only useable at the casino issuing it, and therefore the information generated at each casino was not shared. But the company's customer research—as far back as 1988—indicated that customers did indeed patronize a variety of Harrah's sites; there was real customer value in extending its card player program so that customers could use their cards at any Harrah's casino.

Despite growing evidence that an integrated customer database and coast-to-coast network were needed, the company's IT improvements had to wait. Legalization of gambling on riverboats and Indian reservations spurred Harrah's into a rapid expansion period in the early 1990s, prompting the chain to triple the number of casinos to twelve locations by 1997.

But by the midnineties, with expansion slowing, Harrah's management finally turned its attention to creating a marketing program that would allow the firm to compete and grow revenues without pouring bricks-and-mortar capital into properties. Harrah's went to work to consolidate its far-flung IT systems and information silos across all the casinos. Major IT problems soon appeared, including how to make the company's mainframes compatible with its Unix systems. Says John Boushy, Harrah's senior vice president of brand operations and information technology, "There were times during this project when the single greatest challenge we faced was convincing the IT people we could do this."

To implement the information strategy, Harrah's senior management faced other challenges as well. Regional and site property managers were conditioned to think of each Harrah's property as a separate fiefdom; they worried that promoting other Harrah's destinations would pull business away from their own property. But senior management, convinced they were on the right track, aggressively preached the merits of cross-market visits and eventually sold their managers on the new strategy.

The company hasn't looked back. Since Total Rewards was rolled out in 1997, the number of customers playing at multiple Harrah's properties has increased 72 percent, while cross-market revenues have soared from $113 million to $250 million. Of the company's 1999 profits of $594 million, $50 million can be directly attributable to revenue from cross-marketing visits. By a factor of two to one, more players today carry Harrah's player cards than any other in the industry.[13]

Harrah's experience conveys a trio of valuable lessons surrounding frequent-buyer programs. Lesson number one is that successfully developing and managing a frequent-buyer program requires a big commitment across the firm. Lesson number two is that it's not simply the Total Rewards program itself that fuels Harrah's success; instead, it is how the company leverages the customer preference information generated by the frequent-buyer card that drives creation of loyalty. This means a robust companywide information system is required to support such an effort. Without it, the real benefits from your program can never be fully realized. Lesson number three is that a companywide anything brings to the surface company culture issues. A frequent-buyer program is no exception. This is why strong program support must start at the top and trickle down.

Think carefully before committing to a frequent-buyer program. Include these questions when exploring whether this program is the right choice for your company:

- *Does your product or service have a frequent and regular repeat purchase cycle?* The most successful programs are those that occur when the customer has an ongoing need for your product or service.
- *Do your customers perceive little differentiation between your product or service and your competitors'?* If your customers perceive your product as replaceable and if they can be persuaded to buy from a competitor, then a frequency marketing program may be useful.
- *Will your customer perceive the reward as valuable?* The customer must consider your frequent buyer benefits to be valuable and definitely worth working for.

- *Are you and your staff willing to commit to the program for the long run?* A frequent-buyer program is not short-term. It requires long-term commitment if it is to work.
- *Will you have frequent and ongoing communication with these customers to build a long-term relationship?* Many companies send periodic statements to accomplish this.
- *Does your product or service lend itself to easy collection of proof of purchase?* Either the company or the customer must track purchases. The easier you make it for the customer, the better.
- *Can you afford the program?* The rewards, tracking, regular communication, and customer inquiries associated with the program require significant time and monetary resources.
- *Do your competitors offer a frequency marketing program?* If they do but you do not, you may want to give serious consideration to a program.

5. Establish Barriers to Exit

Creating value "barriers" that make it increasingly difficult for the customer to leave you is another effective way to upgrade a repeat customer into a loyal client. Here's one example.

I operate a small consulting company with an office located on the perimeter of the University of Texas. (UT is arguably our nation's largest university, with a student body of fifty-five thousand.) For years, the closest quick printer to my office was a national chain, open twenty-four hours, that primarily served UT students. My staff and I always got adequate service from this chain store, but the print staff didn't know us from visit to visit and there was always a line. About five years ago, I was excited to see that a small, independent firm called Print Depot was moving to my neighborhood. I watched eagerly as they set up shop. Once they looked ready for business, I stopped in with a quick copy job.

I was greeted by Suzi, the manager, who regretfully informed me that the shop was one day away from opening and although their copiers were ready to go, their business license did not allow them to officially transact business until the next day. "But seeing that your job can be a quick one," Suzi offered, "let me do it now while you wait and I'll hold the receipt and you can come back in and pay us on your next visit."

Wow, I thought. When's the last time I got an offer like this? "Sure," I said. "That works fine."

About a week later, I returned with another job (and paid the bill for the first job as well). This time, Suzi asked a key question: "Do you do printing on a regular basis?" I explained that someone in my firm typically had a print need on average once a week. Suzi asked me whether I would be interested in setting up a corporate charge account so that my company could be billed monthly rather than for each visit. I said yes and returned to my office with a credit application, which I filled out immediately and faxed back the same day. The very next day, Suzi called with good news: our references checked out and my corporate account was in place.

On one of my visits a month or so later, I carried in a magazine in which my *Customer Loyalty* book had been featured. I wanted to make copies of the article for some clients. Suzi studied the piece and then asked whether I was likely to recopy this article again in the future. "Sure," I said; "I plan ultimately to make it part of my firm's press kit."

That said, Suzi recommended that Print Depot start a chronological file for my company, where originals such as this article would be placed. Then, when I need copies, I would simply call the store and place my order, and they would be ready when I arrived. "Sure," I said for the third time. "Great idea."

What was Suzi's strategy? She was masterfully establishing exit barriers around my business. By setting up the charge account and the chronological file, Suzi made it increasingly difficult for me as a repeat customer to leave. How? By paying close attention to my specific needs and finding more and more ways to serve me—on my terms.

Each month, I receive a bill from Print Depot. Do I know exactly how much on a per-copy basis the firm charges me? I don't. And honestly, I don't care. I do know Print Depot's prices are competitive, though maybe not the absolute lowest. But that's fine with me because Print Depot has found a way to serve me that goes well beyond price. Quite simply, the convenience of doing business there is my barrier to exit. For this reason, I don't even look twice at any of her competitors.

Ask yourself this: What are your repeat customers' top priorities? What's on their worry list? How can you help address these needs? Your answers can help you establish barriers to exit and, in doing so, turn repeat customers into loyal clients.

6. Find Ways to Demonstrate "I Know What You Need"

As we've already established, loyalty increases in direct proportion to the value the customer perceives. You want to take actions that create a positive response from the repeat customer, one that might go like this, if the customer were to put his thoughts into words: "I'm glad to buy from you because you let me know you know who I am and what I need. You recognize in dozens of small ways the fact that I have been doing business with you for a long time. That makes me feel appreciated, and I keep coming back because the experience is productive and pleasant and personalized."

The online economy is allowing firms to personalize the customer experience as never before. There is no simple way to reconfigure a physical store or reproduce a customized catalogue for the individual shopper, but it is easy to tailor information when dealing with a customer through e-mail, the Web, or even a call center.

Walter Janowski, research director of the CRM team at Gartner Group, offers two important directives about personalization. First, don't view personalization as simply a Web strategy for your firm, but instead consider it a cross-channel strategy. He explains: "If a customer logs on a company's Website and is recognized as a customer but then picks up the phone and talks to a call center rep who is unable to match that same level of recognition, the goodwill falls apart. The customer expects consistency regardless of the channel."

Second, personalization is useless unless it delivers real value to the customer. Most of the personalization that is out there today is what Janowski calls "gratuitous personalization," in that it does little or nothing to add real customer value. For example, consider the "Welcome back, Bob" that greets you upon your return to a site. Yes, it's nice that they remember your name, but what do you as a customer get out of it? Not much. That's why companies like Fidelity Investments are working hard to marry personalization with real customer value.

Janowski offers this personal example. Upon joining Gartner roughly a year ago, he was informed that Fidelity managed the company's 401(k) program, in which he was included. Soon after, he logged on to his Fidelity account (he was already a Fidelity customer); a pop-up message appeared and asked him if he would like his Gartner 401(k) account added to his account summary. "Through no interaction from me—I didn't tell them I had joined Gartner or that I had this new account—Fidelity was able to identify me as an existing customer and through its actions demonstrate its ability to make my life simpler through account consolidation."[14] Finding a way to constantly demonstrate to a customer "I know what you need" turns a repeat customer into a client.

7. Hire and Train for Loyalty

To make any loyalty plan work well, the employer first has to realize that the employees, the people on the front line, are the ones in direct contact with customers. The employee represents the company's products or services for better or worse and can win loyalty for a company or turn a customer away.

Management must deal with the fact that it is not in charge of performing for the customer. Rather, it is the employee who talks to the customer. Many companies lack an effective program for hiring and training employees. A few companies have pioneered especially strong training programs that have reinforced their customer loyalty culture.

Employee teamwork and empowerment are a concern for any company building a loyalty-focused culture. Disneyland interviews prospective employees ("cast members") in groups of three so it can watch how they interact. Do they show respect, for example, by paying attention when the other employees speak? At the Four Seasons, it takes four or five rigorous interviews to sort out applicants with a friendly nature and a sense of teamwork. When the chain opened its Los Angeles hotel, it interviewed fourteen thousand candidates for 350 slots.

More and more, companies are realizing that it takes an employee empowered with know-how and initiative to build a loyal customer. As a result, they are giving the employee the authority to resolve a customer complaint on the spot, in a way that's bound to satisfy. Companies with programs of this kind are making empowerment potential a factor in the selection process; if you aren't willing to empower this employee, then do not hire him.

"We have thousands [of guests] who stay with us more than seventy-five nights per year," said Roger Dow, vice president of sales and marketing services for Marriott.[15] By estimating that this customer spends about $125,000 during ten years, Dow suggested that for every eight of those guests who turn to a competitor, Marriott loses $1 million in sales. To retain customers, Marriott began testing an empowerment program in 1988; since then, it has introduced formal training that stresses how much money can be lost if a steady customer decides to check in at a competitor's property.

Empowerment training is producing loyalty-building behavior in Marriott staff. Each employee feels a sense of responsibility for the customer's satisfaction. In one case, a bellman accidentally damaged a customer's word processor. Faced with the possibility of an angry guest taking his business somewhere else, the bellman and other employees found a solution and replaced the word processor with a new, undamaged machine. On another occasion, a guest who was leaving the hotel mentioned to the staff member carrying his luggage that his breakfast had been improperly prepared. The staffer immediately escorted the guest back to the desk, where his breakfast charges were completely refunded.[16]

Companies that develop strong customer loyalty have at least three things in common:

1. Management clearly understands what builds loyalty for a company and trains its staff members to encourage customer loyalty.

2. The required behaviors are written in clear, straightforward, easy-to-understand guidelines. The behavior is measurable.

3. The company has a written credo that is reinforced constantly to staff members at staff meetings, in memos, and in attention-getting displays.

Frederick Reichheld put the importance of employee training in sharp perspective when he said, "In a service business, knowledge and information are the raw materials and the assets are loyal customers and employees. Accounting systems don't measure these."[17]

Nissan has gained a reputation for having some of the most customer-oriented dealers in the business; it's largely the result of innovative training and customer service systems. The company operates a six-day boot camp for dealers of its

Infiniti luxury automobile. All dealership employees must attend, including clerks and receptionists. "The receptionist probably talks to more customers than any other person in the showroom," says Ken Petty, an instructor. "Our receptionists can tell you how the cars handle on the track, and they have driven the Lexus, Infiniti's key competitor, too."[18]

That's part of the plan to equip every employee at a dealership to answer any question about the Infiniti lineup. These same people are taught buyer demographics, or how to pitch an Infiniti to various age groups and people of different lifestyles, and they can even compare the merits of their car and the competitors.

Once employees are well trained, a company must retain them. Before you can have a loyal customer, you must first have a loyal employee. Says Republic National Bank treasurer Thomas F. Robards, "The most explicit quality technique is to get good staff and retain them."

One of the most common reasons for losing good employees is that a company sets high customer loyalty standards without giving the employee the capability and tools to perform to that expectation. In today's competitive marketplace, customer loyalty systems may require hefty spending on technology to ensure that the frontline employee has the tools needed to be loyalty-driven. A leading financial brokerage firm understands that not all customers require the same level of service or generate the same revenue. The company recently installed a telephone-computer system that recognizes individual clients by their telephone numbers when they call. Large accounts and callers who make frequent transactions are automatically routed to their own senior account representative. Those customers who place only an occasional order may be routed to a more junior representative. In either situation, the customer's record appears on the representative's screen before the call is taken.

Such a system entails a host of service benefits for the company and its customers. For example, similar accounts can be grouped under one rep who specializes in that instrument, removing the need to train every rep on every financial tool. In addition, the company can direct certain value-added services or products to only those clients it knows would be interested.

Another example of technology playing a major role in a customer loyalty system is United Parcel Service, which has outfitted each driver with an electronic clipboard that includes a stylus and a pressure-sensitive receipt pad. Consignee signatures are downloaded overnight, and by the next day, volume senders who subscribe to a special service can log on to UPS's database from their PC to check on the status of key packages.

8. Motivate Your Staff for Loyalty

American business is suffering today from a "hyped out" employee. The techniques for inspiring the workforce with things such as compensation, a benefit plan, and motivational seminars aren't as effective as they used to be. It's hard to get anyone excited about simply generating profits for someone else. The key is to encourage employees to be part of the building process. They will be more cooperative if they can see some of their own ideas put into action. If you really want to build customer loyalty, put your staff in charge of building it; give them the autonomy, training, information, support, and rewards they need to do what is already natural to them. Your employees are just like your customers. Treat them with respect and allow them to make their own decisions, and they will treat your customers in the same manner. But equally important, don't tolerate in employees a casual regard for loyalty.

This sharing of corporate goals by employees at every level is similar in spirit to the labor methods operative in plants owned by Applied Energy Services (AES). The energy-producing company has a clear corporate philosophy that places responsibility for job effectiveness on the individual, not in a policy manual. There is no personnel department at AES ("It's too important to be left to experts"); there is no legal, finance, public relations, or engineering department. Instead, the 413 staff members of AES group themselves in cross-functional teams designed for specific tasks. According to Dennis Bakke, the company president: "Economists have done us a major disservice by seeing people as labor, as machines. And engineers have stressed the notion of efficient organizations, which I reject. It may be effective in some areas, but not in a company like ours. But don't get me wrong; people have to be accountable."

Accountability at AES causes job leveling in the interest of the company's combined production and altruistic objectives, and it facilitates communication from the top down. All senior executives are expected to spend at least one week each year working alongside technicians at the plant level. "I spent my first night in the plant on my hands and knees, trying to clear clinkers from the bottom of the furnace," Vice President Roger Naill remembered. It was during a graveyard shift one night that Naill, with the help of those in the mechanic shop, worked out the company's generous performance incentive scheme, which his group at the head office had been wrestling with for months.

Creating and giving customer value—as your buyers define it—is the secret to customer loyalty. Nowhere is value more important than in transforming the repeat customer into a loyal client. A smart company builds programs that support this process. A host of tools (customer research, digital networking, frequent-buyer programs, staff training and motivation, and so on) all can be designed to support the organization's overall objective of providing value and building a loyal customer base.

Transforming the customer from a person who does repeat business with your company to a loyal one who has an emotional attachment to it is critical to the whole system of managing customer loyalty. A company failing to realize the importance of the loyalty-bonding process is going to fall by the wayside in the future.

SUMMARY

- In terms of potential profit payoff, the loyal-client stage is the most critical.
- Successful companies deliver value in one of three categories: operational excellence, customer intimacy, or product leadership.
- Knowing who your most valuable customers are and what and why they buy is crucial to building and sustaining customer loyalty.
- In developing any plan for upgrading a repeat customer into a loyal client, a number of actions should be considered: (1) insulating your best customers from competition, (2) making top spenders your first priority, (3) harnessing your supply chain to deliver better customer value, and (4) finding a way to demonstrate to customers "I know what you need."
- The most successful frequent-buyer programs build loyalty by rewarding customers for their cumulative purchases through targeted communications, incentives, and performance tracking.
- Customers have valuable information and are willing to share it if you are willing to commit financially and organizationally to capture feedback.
- Offering key services builds barriers to exit and increases your customer's reluctance to switch to a competitor.
- Before you can gain loyal customers, you must have loyal, empowered employees.

GETTING STARTED

- Devise a formula by which you estimate your customer's lifetime value (CLTV). Rank your customers by CLTV. Next, rank them according to historical sales. Compare the two lists. Ensure that the customers with highest historical sales *and* highest CLTV receive top-priority focus and attention.
- Regularly survey your best customers to monitor their evolving definition of value and how your firm can maximize customer value delivery.
- Educate staff about barriers to exit; teach them to pay attention to how other firms practice the barrier-to-exit strategy. Regularly brainstorm with staff to generate new ideas on unique service offerings that could create new barriers against customer defection.
- Regularly meet with your supply chain partners to identify untapped ways to work together in delivering improved customer value.
- Aggressively seek out ideas from staff about how to better empower employees to serve customers. Test the most promising ideas and roll out the most workable methods companywide.

CHAPTER EIGHT

Turning Loyal Clients into Advocates

Once, *The Road Less Traveled,* by psychiatrist M. Scott Peck, was just another book on psychology and relationships languishing on bookstore shelves. Then a few people read it, told their friends, and started a chain reaction that's still going on. Today there are millions of copies in print, and the book is a record-setter for being on the *New York Times* best-seller list for more than nine years.

Initial sales of the book were largely generated by two people who became convinced that it offered an outstanding message. One was the publisher's sales representative, who was so impressed that he insisted book buyers at stores read the book. The other was a teacher in Buffalo, New York, who gave copies to colleagues and ministers she knew. Word of mouth created demand for the book. Two churches invited the author to speak, and the local Buffalo bookstore began selling hundreds of copies. Impressed by what was happening, the publisher, Simon and Schuster, took another look at the book. A promotional tour boosted sales, which continued to rise. The author has now published a teaching guide to the original book and a new book expanding on the original ideas, *Further Along the Road Less Traveled.*

When a customer becomes an advocate for your products or services, you have achieved a relationship of great closeness and trust. This is the most valued and sought-after level of bonding, where word-of-mouth advertising can flourish. This chapter examines why it is not enough for a loyal customer or client to buy exclusively from your organization. To fully leverage your opportunity with a customer or client, your company needs to recruit new prospects and customers through that client.

We discuss word of mouth or third-party endorsement and why it is so powerful. We then consider proven strategies for getting the word out and keeping the word out through client advocates.

BLITZED AND DECEIVED?

As discussed in Chapter Four, it is estimated that each American is exposed to well over three thousand marketing messages per day. This unending assault of advertising and marketing messages has had a pronounced effect on American buyers; they remember advertising less and less. For example, the market researcher Video Storyboard Tests says viewer retention of television commercials has dropped significantly since the mid-1980s. Moreover, even when consumers remember advertising, their retention is scarred by cynicism, or at best indifference.

Silicon Valley marketing consultant and author Regis McKenna reports that "increasingly, people are skeptical of what they read or see in advertisements. I often tell clients that advertising has a built-in 'discount factor.' People are deluged with promotional information, and they are beginning to distrust it. People are more likely to make decisions based on what they hear directly from other people—friends, experts, or even salespeople. Advertising, therefore, should be one of the last parts of a marketing strategy, not the first."[1]

If there's any doubt about the awesome power of word of mouth, consider the movie industry, one that rises and falls on word-of-mouth marketing. "Seen any good movies lately?" is that oft-asked question among friends that every movie executive knows can make or break a newly released film. Positive word of mouth can take a low-budget movie that has little or no advertising support and turn it into a multimillion-dollar hit. "Word of mouth is like wildfire," says Marvin Antonowsky, head of marketing for Universal Pictures.[2]

For example, *Home Alone* seemed to sneak into theaters one Thanksgiving as just another children's movie. But word of mouth made it a wild success and helped foster several sequels. Likewise, *The Blair Witch Project* was a low-budget, 1999 summer movie that earned a high talk factor and stunned everybody by becoming a hit. And how about *The Sixth Sense?* As a result of a much-talked-about surprise ending, the film catapulted to top-grossing status and raked in almost $300 million in U.S. box office revenue.

In the same way that good word of mouth can help a movie gross millions, bad word of mouth can move the needle in the opposite direction. *Harper's* interviewed some of the movie industry's marketing whizzes, and their comments were quite revealing. For example, the talk factor is so powerful that movie marketers concede that soon after a movie is released, the influence of studio marketing quickly evaporates. Says Joe Nimziki, executive vice president of a Hollywood advertising agency, "After about two weeks [from the date of release], it's mostly word-of-mouth. Our job is pretty much over."[3]

Commenting about the gratification of getting enough people to see a bad film on the opening weekend before reviews and word of mouth dissuade other people from spending their money on it, Mark Gill, senior vice president of publicity and promotion for Columbia Pictures, says, "If [a movie] opens big and then crashes, that's when you know that the marketing campaign was absolute perfection."[4]

As in many industries, the Internet has created a whole new realm of promotional opportunity for creating and sustaining movie buzz. But some studios are learning the hard way how to leverage this new frontier. Fearing loss of control, Warner Brothers and Lucasfilm, for example, threatened legal action against unauthorized fan sites. (As producer of *Harry Potter and the Sorcerer's Stone,* Warner Brothers sent letters to Potter Webmasters, among them fifteen-year-old Claire Field. After Field protested by organizing a boycott of Potter merchandise, the studio backed away.)

But partnering rather than panning fan Websites is proving to be Gordon Paddison's secret to success. As interactive marketing vice president for New Line Cinema, Gordon and his team are responsible for creating Web buzz for *The Lord of the Rings: The Fellowship of the Rings,* the first of three film adaptations of J.R.R. Tolkien's twelve-hundred-page literary trilogy. As such, New Line is responsible for all aspects of the film's official Website, LordoftheRings.net.

Unlike some of the other movie studios' online strategists, Paddison saw the potential for working with the existing online fan community and leveraging it to help spread word of mouth: "It would have been arrogant to say, 'We are Lord of the Rings, come to us.' The thought was, let's leave the sites alone and just become another silo of information on the Web." So where did Paddison and his team begin? They developed an early version of the *Lord of the Rings* site nearly *two years* before the film's official release and then reached out to the Webmasters of more than four hundred existing fan sites to drive traffic to the site.

Recognizing Tolkien's books had a strong and leverageable fan base, Paddison explains, "I wanted to establish a relationship early on with the influencers, people that I felt would be a conduit of information. We had to take advantage of the vastness of this community."

Take Michael Regina, the twenty-three-year-old cofounder of TheOneRing.net, a popular, unofficial Lord of the Rings fan site. Regina gets regular e-mails and calls from Paddison about the latest additions to the studio's official Website. Regina, in turn, is happy to post this information on his site and further spread the word. Says Regina, who runs his site from of the basement of his parents' Montreal home, "Gordon always lets me know when something cool is coming." Regina's support has its own rewards, he says: "I've actually been invited to the [movie] set twice. The director, Peter Jackson, is a big fan of our site."[5]

This reach-out-and-touch strategy has worked to drive phenomenal traffic to the movie's official site well before the first film's mid-December 2001 release. In April 2000, a record-breaking 1.7 million people downloaded a clip of the movie the first day it was offered by New Line. An e-mail newsletter launched in August 2000 has maintained a weekly circulation of five hundred thousand.

From downloadable screen savers to bulletin boards to interviews with the cast and crew, Paddison and his development team provide an array of take-aways and tips that make the casual fan feel like an insider. How has all of this affected movie ticket sales? Dramatically. As a *USA Today* headline reported, "'Rings' Lords over Box Office," with the movie grossing $94 million in its first week in theaters.[6] But the first movie release signals just the start of New Line and Paddison's efforts to generate and sustain online buzz. With two more films to follow, New Line has a weekly content change schedule for the site through 2004 when the third *Rings* film, *The Return of the King,* is scheduled for home video release.[7]

Though negative word of mouth can destroy a business, positive talk can make one thrive. Let's examine the factors that make word of mouth such a powerful force in the marketplace.

WHY WORD OF MOUTH CAN BE SO POWERFUL

Referral is the most powerful pathway for any business to recruit new customers successfully. Referrals are so effective because they come from an objective second party. The words come from someone who knows you and your products and services, is confident of your ability and reputation to follow through, and has no financial motive for touting your product. Many times, your product is sold before you even meet the new customer or client. When a new prospect comes to you through a second-party endorsement, you have three distinct selling advantages.

First, less selling time is required. Sales statistics indicate that you spend half the time selling the referred prospect that you do selling a nonreferred prospect. Why? Because much of the selling has already been accomplished by your referral source. Think about Chapter Five and its discussion of how to turn a qualified prospect into a first-time buyer. There I established that trust and believability are key factors in making the first sale. Winning trust and believability takes time. These important factors become almost a nonissue when people get a referral from someone they know and respect.

Second, these prospects have greater loyalty potential. People who buy because of a personal referral tend to be more loyal than those who buy because of an advertisement. Consider the experience of Laura Peck (no relation to M. Scott Peck). She used to advertise her workshops, but due to financial problems she discontinued the ads and instead began cultivating her own network of friends and acquaintances for clients. Now, two years later, her business is thriving. She says, "When I advertised, I seemed to attract people who came because of the discount I offered. These clients often did not return, would cancel sessions and generally were not repeaters. The people who were most enthusiastic, most loyal, and continued with their sessions were almost always clients who had been personally referred. Had it not been for the economics involved, I would probably not have learned this important lesson; personal recommendation is the best advertising there is."[8]

Third, people come ready to buy. One industry that evokes mistrust and fear is auto repair. Who hasn't heard a horror story of an auto repair that was unjustified or was never done right? So why does a customer who comes back to Direct Tire in Watertown, Massachusetts, spend $173 during an average visit while a new customer who has been referred by someone else spends $224?

According to President Barry Steinberg, the answer is quite simple. These big spenders have usually been putting off a major repair or purchase until they can find a repair shop they trust. Once they hear about Direct Tire's service, they come in and spend.[9]

A reputation of trust, reliability, and terrific service has made Direct Tire a profitable, flourishing business. The nearby Goodyear outlet sells tires for a Ford Taurus for $50 to $100 apiece, while Direct Tire sells the same tire for $60 to $120. Steinberg, who has spent his entire adult life in the tire business, says, "On average, we are consistently 10–12 percent higher than just about everybody else." Direct Tire does not sell on price; it sells on service. This formula works, as evidenced by its profit margin (twice the industry average) and client base; about 75 percent of the company's monthly sales are recorded from repeat customers.

EARN WORD OF MOUTH: FOUR PROVEN STRATEGIES

No doubt, getting happy customers to spread the word is your best source of advertising. Here's how to do it.

Give 'Em Something to Talk About

Bonnie Raitt, the popular blues and country cross-over artist, had a *Billboard* chart hit entitled "Let's Give Them Something to Talk About," which told how a good story travels fast. The same philosophy is the key in creating a high talk factor between customers and their friends. Two companies that have given their customers something to talk about are Windham Hill Records and, again, Direct Tire. Here's how they did it.

William Ackerman literally learned the record business from the ground up. In the mid-1970s, as a contractor and carpenter, Ackerman operated a Palo Alto contracting business called Windham Hill. Ackerman was hired to build warehouses for two small, folk-oriented record companies in the San Francisco area. In between his sawing and hammering, he got a bird's-eye view of the companies' daily operations and got to ask a lot of questions. During work breaks, Ackerman and his friends played guitar on the back of their pickup trucks.

In his spare time, Ackerman played guitar on campus at Stanford University. Although lacking only a few credits to graduate (including a course in Chaucer taught by his father), Ackerman had dropped out of the university, but he still got requests to perform. People were constantly asking to record his music on their own cassettes. With $5 each from some sixty people and a small loan from his friend and eventual partner, Anne Robinson, Ackerman recorded *In Search of the Turtle's Navel,* an album of guitar solos.

"The sum total of my ambitions consisted of selling three hundred records, which was the minimum order the record pressing plant demanded," said Ackerman. "I fully envisioned a closet in my house laden with at least one hundred extra records for the rest of my life."[10]

After selling approximately sixty copies to friends, Ackerman gave some extra records to ten FM radio stations and listeners began calling the stations to inquire about his music. Soon a few record stores contacted him, and orders began slowly flowing in.

Today, Windham Hill is part of RCA Records Group. Windham Hill, along with BMG, its classic label, generate more than $90 million in annual revenue for RCA. Robinson and Ackerman attribute word of mouth in the early years as fundamental to the label's early success. Robinson says: "We found there were a lot of people who became evangelistic about our music. We got letters from people who said that they went to their friend's house for dinner and heard our music. Then they had to have it because it spoke to them, so they went out and bought it and then played it for their friends."[11]

By accident, Windham Hill moved into an audiophile line in 1976. It happened through a chance meeting at an engineers' convention. Ackerman's engineer ended up sitting next to Stan Ricker, the premier half-speed-mastering engineer in America. At that time, few people had heard of half-speed mastering or its deeply enhanced sonics. As a result of the meeting, Ackerman's company adopted Ricker's recommendations of using quality pressings on high-quality imported vinyl, double-laminated covers, plastic inner sleeves, and superb graphics.

"'Quality begets quality' is the summary," Ackerman insists. "You need to be economically viable to be able to do any work in this society, but there are so many people whose principal desire is to see quality fostered in the marketplace that if you stand for that, people will come to you."[12]

Rod Watts, an early Windham Hill convert, observes, "In a record store, Windham Hill is the first place I head for. I'd much rather buy one of these albums, even if I haven't heard it, than buy some other musician or label cold."[13]

Explaining his company's strong commitment to customer satisfaction, Ackerman says, "You haven't made the sale just in selling the record. You've made the sale when somebody gets home and feels utterly happy with the record. I did that when I was building houses, too. The last handshake when you walked out of the house was when you sold the house, not when you signed the contract to build it; it's leaving them happy with what they've bought. In the long run, it brings about an audience loyalty that can't be overemphasized as an element of our success."[14]

Direct Tire President Steinberg sees the whole purpose of customer service very simply: to keep customers coming back and to get satisfied customers to tell others. Virtually everything that takes place at Direct Tire is directed to these objectives. Need to buy some tires and be in and out in an hour? Direct Tire will schedule an appointment whenever it's convenient for you. Need transportation immediately? Direct Tire offers one of the company's seven loaners to use. You can pick up your car on the way home. What if a new tire blows out after thirty thousand miles, or if for some reason you are simply not satisfied? Direct Tire guarantees the tires as well as any service work the shop does—forever.

How does Steinberg know these services are important and worth the necessary expense? Consider his large loaner fleet. Says Steinberg, "Three years ago, before I had the loaners, I was doing $50,000–55,000 a month in service work. Today I'm averaging $120,000 a month and the gross margins on service work are 30 percent higher than on tires. People will call up and say, 'I understand you have a free car I can use while you work on mine.' We'll say, 'Yes, that's right,' and they'll schedule an appointment right then. A lot of them don't even bother to ask what the work will cost. I'm going to add more cars."[15]

Typical of the length to which Direct Tire will go to keep a customer happy and loyal was the case of the customer whose car was sitting on a lift for front-end alignment. The customer had called in ahead of time to make certain there would be no delay for him to get to work. But Bobby Binnall, an employee who transports customers to and from work, was delayed elsewhere in a car that had stalled. The customer was getting edgy, and Steinberg had an inspiration: "I called the local taxi company, and in five minutes they were here and took the guy over to his office. The cab fare was $17, but can you imagine how many people he's going to tell this story to? It was the best $17 I ever spent."[16]

It is this kind of reasoning that has allowed Steinberg to maintain his high net margin, even as he increased his investment in customer service. But he measures his return on that investment with a satisfying fiscal picture that shows how effective he has been in turning one-time buyers into regular customers. Direct

Tire's revenues continue to increase steadily, as they have every year since its founding in 1974, despite generally flat sales for the industry as a whole—all because he wins over customers who tell other people about their positive experience at Direct Tire.

Find New Ways to Earn the Talk Factor

When this book was first published, a computer check-writing program called Quicken had become the most successful personal finance program ever released, holding an impressive 60 percent market share. Said Jeffrey Tarter, editor of the industry publication *Softletter,* "It has become the brand-name product in what would otherwise be a commodity business. It's the Kleenex or Xerox of its market."[17]

Back in the early nineties, Quicken was (and still is) carried by Target, Wal-Mart, and other retailers and computer chains nationwide. How large was the company's sales force at that time? It comprised exactly two people. But Scott Cook, then CEO of Intuit, the maker of Quicken, didn't think simply in terms of company salespeople: "Really, we have hundreds of thousands of salespeople. They're our customers." Scott speaks of his customers as "apostles" and states that Intuit's mission is to "make the customer feel so good about the product they'll go and tell five friends to buy it."[18] That early focus on customer advocacy continues today and has fueled the company's tremendous growth. Today, with more than fifty-two hundred employees, Intuit has greatly expanded beyond the original Quicken check-writing product to provide such offerings as Quicken.com, the leading e-finance Website; QuickBooks for the Web; Quicken Turbo Tax; Quicken Loans; Pocket Quicken (for the Palm Pilot); and others. The company's financial track record is equally impressive. Its 2001 net revenues were $1.2 billion, with $185 million in net income. What's more, the Quicken product line dominates its market, with more than 75 percent of retail dollar market share.[19]

But things weren't always so rosy. According to Cook, May 1, 1985, was the worst day of his life. His company, Intuit, was less than two years old and he had to tell his seven employees that, because he could no longer pay their salaries, he had to let them go.

Cook's flagship product, an easy-to-use check-writing program for personal computers, had plenty of potential. What he lacked was money. Cook had started the company with $350,000, a sum raised from a combination of family loans, his life savings, credit cards, and home-equity credit. Attempts to interest venture capitalists got him nowhere, and now his start-up capital was nearly gone.

By the summer of 1986, the little company had just $125,000, generated primarily from Intuit sales in bank lobbies. If he wanted to catch the all-important Christmas selling season, Scott had to roll the dice on a make-or-break ad campaign. He wrote the ad himself and spent all of the $125,000 on the campaign.

It worked. Scott's all-or-nothing ad campaign, coupled with his uncompromising efforts to create a product that truly satisfied its buyers, paid off.

To create this phenomenal word of mouth with such potential mass-market appeal, the Quicken program had to be fast, cheap, hassle-free, and above all easy to use—so easy that anyone as a first-time user could sit down at the computer and start writing checks. Intuit is on a constant crusade to meet these objectives. One such example is Intuit's Follow-Me-Home program, in which Quicken buyers from local stores are asked to let an Intuit representative observe them when they first use Quicken. This way, Intuit gets ongoing feedback on how the product might be made just a tiny bit easier for first-time users. "If people don't use the product," says Tom LeFevre, chief programmer, "they won't tell their friends to use it, either."[20]

Get Your Product in the Hands of Influencers

Conventional wisdom says that to get a group of opinion leaders to earnestly spread the word about a new product, its maker must first give the product away.

Not so with Approach Software, a start-up in Redwood City, California, which found a way to earn initial sales from opinion leaders and then triple the number of people who purchased its product on the advice of friends or associates in the six months following the product's launch. How did the company do it? By offering a low introductory price and a ninety-day, money-back guarantee. The target of the offer: carefully selected, influential users, who were asked to try the company's first product, a database software program designed for nontechies.

Approach's limited-time offer of $149 for Approach 1.0 for Windows, plus free technical support, quickly got the innovative software into the hands of thousands of small-company CEOs and other targeted customers. The price was hard to beat, given the software's appealing characteristics (less than a half-hour to learn the program and seamless integration with other database software). Competing products were costing as much as $799.

Research finds that online word of mouth can be particularly powerful. A study by Burson-Marsteller and Roper Starch Worldwide found that one influential person's offline word of mouth tends to affect the buying attitude of two other people, on average. Online, the circle of influence jumps to eight. "You don't need to reach two million people to let them know about a new product," says Marc Schiller, CEO of ElectricArtists, an interactive marketing agency. "You need to reach the right two thousand people in the right way, and they'll reach two million."[21]

Turn a Center of Influence into a Full-Time Advocate

One unique application of word-of-mouth advertising in the Deep South proved how effective this form of prestige recommendation can be. Fifteen years ago, Jay Stein decided to expand the department store in Greenville, Mississippi, that his grandfather had founded in 1908. As a stroke of luck, several well-to-do women from Greenville volunteered to help out during the store's liquidation sale of some designer clothing. Commenting for the *Wall Street Journal,* Stein said, "They had firsthand knowledge of this better merchandise, because they had worn it for years." The experience convinced Stein that the concept was worth replicating. When Stein Mart opened its second store, this time in Memphis, he created a designer boutique department in the store, and he and his wife recruited socialite friends to operate it.

Today, to be hired as a Stein Mart "boutique lady" is a bit of a status symbol, as indicated by the waiting lists for the job at all fifty-one Stein Mart stores. "As soon as I heard they had an opening, I called to put my name in," reports Gay Kemp, who is married to an international marketing executive. "Everybody I knew was doing it and they kept talking about how fun it was. When you look at the women who are doing it—doctors' wives, women who have mansions on the river—well, it's a neat association."[22]

"The boutique ladies are our secret weapon," says Jay Stein. These women work one day a week, earn seven dollars an hour, and are excused from cash register responsibility and evening shifts. Instead, their activities are focused on spreading the word about designer merchandise. For example, when a shipment of $39 designer silk separates arrived at the Jacksonville Stein Mart, boutique lady Joy Abney, the wife of a former managing partner of Coopers and Lybrand, hit the phones. She called fellow board members at Wolfson Children's Hospital and "told them to get over here." Joy's friends obliged by spending $2,000 in her department that same day.

For many boutique ladies, it's gratifying to learn that women of a certain age and without a resume are still welcomed in the workforce. Many compare the job to volunteer work, since, as Kemp sees it, "you are busy helping people." The pay is a bonus. "It's fun to get a paycheck that's mine," says Kemp, who also adds that the employee discount of 25 percent is more important to her than her $40 paycheck. "I don't care who you are or how much you have, everybody likes a discount," she says.[23]

In return, Stein Mart enjoys a polished, loyal sales force of advocates. Joyce de la Houssaye of New Orleans wedges her boutique duties into a full schedule of Junior League, golf, and four grandchildren. She brings flowers from her award-winning garden to decorate her boutique department. After organizing a special store reception, she took off in her golf cart to deliver flyers to neighbors about the upcoming event.

Nurture an Online Customer Community

A powerful way for creating goodwill about your business is to give your customers and clients an online community through which to share. (Our earlier discussion about New Line Cinema's Lord of the Rings site is one example.) After all, this very purpose is how the Internet came into being in the first place.

More than twenty years ago, the Internet community was made up largely of software engineers who shared development tips and tactics through newsgroups and message boards. The same ability to connect a network of clients, dealers, and suppliers is available today for any company wanting to leverage the opportunity. Consider the case of Ace Hardware, the hardware cooperative based in Oak Brook, Illinois.

In 1998 the firm began building its AceNet 2000 intranet, largely to push out information to its dealers about product availability and pricing. What started as a composite of directories and message boards has become a meeting place for dealers to share practical and useful knowledge.

With the help of Participate.com, a specialist in creating and monitoring online communities for businesses, Ace created ACIS (Ace Commercial and Industrial Supply), a password-protected area of AceNet 2000 to help its three hundred dealers better sell to commercial customers. Says Participate.com spokesperson, Bill Perry, "[The dealers] exchange marketing tactics, copy for a pitch letter, information on where to find a certain part or piece of equipment, leads, or even the quality of the products that already exist."[24]

The ACIS bulletin boards have been the source of many sales successes. For example, when Bonnie Merkling, sales manager at Sunshine Ace Hardware in Dundin, Florida, had a potential buyer who needed a special adhesive that attaches mirrors to wall surfaces, she posted a note on the community message board. Thanks to a responsive fellow dealer, in one short hour Bonnie had the information she needed and landed the sale. That first sale has been a 'gift that keeps on giving.' Bonnie reports she has earned an incremental $3000 in business from that same customer for that one product alone and that he "comes in to buy it on a regular basis and buys other stuff at the same time."[25]

Similarly, when Mike Dooley, who handles commercial accounts at the Ace Hardware dealership in Bullhead City, Arizona, was having trouble getting a foothold into the nearby casino market, the dealer message boards became a fruitful source of advice. Competition was edging Dooley out by selling paint that boasted to buyers a paint-to-metal adherence rating. Mike asked his fellow dealers for advice via the message boards. One of the many responding dealers urged Mike to get the Ace paint tested for the same rating. Mike did just that. Happily, the Ace paint scored better than all the rival brands, and Mike used the test results to win an exclusive contract worth $500,000. What's more, other dealers followed in Mike's footsteps and, selling the advantages of the rating, closed over a million dollars in additional paint sales.[26]

But getting buy-in for the online community across the dealer network wasn't immediate. From the beginning, Ace corporate worked diligently to communicate and demonstrate the advantages and explain the resources to dealers, who were not accustomed to using computers, let alone the Internet. One way Ace encouraged dealers to participate was to post leads online from customers who filled out information-request cards from magazines or at conventions, or who inquired about products through the company web site. Ace traditionally mailed magazine and convention leads to dealers, trying to distribute them fairly and without favoritism. Now, similar leads are promptly posted online for dealers to pursue on a first-come/first-serve basis.[27] This feature provides the dealer network with one more motivation to consistently log on to the online community.

The online dealer community is paying big dividends for Ace. Reports Tina Lopotko, manager of Ace's commercial and industrial division that was responsible for the community site's initial launch, "This gives us the opportunity to do a variety of things we would normally send paper out doing and makes information very timely."[28] By eliminating substantial paper costs and lag time, the online community provides major savings for Ace.

Perform an Internet search and you will find a host of how-to resources to help you with the details for building and managing a successful online community. But for starters, consider these key guidelines:

- *Remember: community is not an end in itself.* Begin your online community development with a clear vision on how an e-community will help your audience. It is imperative that the community site supports your firm's existing business model and provides people with clear reasons to participate. For example, diet company SlimFast's community site includes a personalized virtual buddy system. The company anticipates that socially connected customers will more likely stay committed to their diets and, in turn, their SlimFast product purchases.[29]

- *Set high usability standards.* The site's reason for being is to present information the community finds relevant, useful, and profitable. Identify clear performance measures and on a regular basis, report on the progress. Such measures might include percentage of best customers using the site's message board, average lapse time between user's information request and answer provided, and so forth.

- *Keep a watchful eye on content.* Giving customers a forum to communicate comes with watchdog responsibilities. Unprofessional online behavior by users, message board questions that linger unanswered, and online coaching sessions that veer off topic ultimately reflect poorly upon your company. Assign a staff member to watch over all content to ensure the resource remains professional, reliable, and user-friendly.

- *Evaluate the ROI.* Yes, your online community is designed to help users and in doing so, it creates and sustains deeper loyalty for your company. But it takes resources to effectively manage your site, which means the site should produce a measurable return on investment. Noting a substantive return from the company's online community for the year 2001, Ace Hardware CEO Shankar Hemmady, reported an estimated $10 million in new revenues and costs savings as a direct result of online feedback, ideas, and relationships. Says Hemmady, "The community features are part of our inbound and outbound marketing strategy. This strategy has worked out remarkably well."[30]

GETTING THE WORD OUT ABOUT YOU

Once you have developed a loyal client, you then have the opportunity to multiply that one client by a factor of two, three, five, or more. Each person you sell to can be multiplied by the number of his or her associates who are prospects for your offerings. It all depends on getting the word out through your client advocates. Let's examine the tools you need to maximize your talk factor.

What's in It for Your Endorser?

An advocate, or endorser, is someone who goes out and advocates your cause. Is this a totally selfless move on the part of your endorser? Not entirely. To an advocate, you are the best in the business, and his selfish motivation is to keep you in business. The advocate wants to keep you going so you'll always be able to continue doing business with him. Moreover, when you perform well for the new customer and he is satisfied, you make the endorser look good. In some ways, the new customer now "owes one" to the endorser. So the next time you are shy about asking for an endorsement, take into consideration the fact that giving an endorsement is not a totally selfless act on the part of your advocate. There is something in it for the advocate as well.

The Customer "Success Story" File

One invaluable sales aid is to keep a customer "success story" file. Make a point of adding a success story every week. Write it up, including the name, address, and phone number of the customer. Ask each one, in advance, for permission to use her name as a reference. When you're trying to win over a tough prospect, scan your file, identify a success story that nearly matches the prospect's situation, and invite the prospect to contact the customer directly for a reference. Among sales professionals, this technique is known as reference selling.

Reference selling is so effective that it can overcome hurdles that seem insurmountable, as Lynn Green, a sales engineer at Data I/O in New Hampshire, discovered. She was able to overcome legitimate price objections from a prospect by referring him to loyal customers. Though her company is the market leader, she says, "our pricing is usually the main stumbling block with a new customer who has used competitive products."

In one situation, she was selling a product for $15,000 against a competitor who was offering something similar for only $2,000. Lynn remembers that the prospect "called and asked why he should pay $15,000 when he could buy seven of the competitor's products for less money."

That was when she asked him to seek the advice of her own customers who had used the competitor's products in the past but had switched back to hers. "At the time," she says, "I didn't think I would get the sale because of the wide difference in price. But, once again, my existing customers made the sale for me."

Green stresses the importance of developing good rapport with your existing customer base. She found out that her customers enjoy assisting her. "If you and your company have a customer's loyalty, it can pay off in more ways than one," she relates.

The Testimonial Letter

Another approach to reference selling is a testimonial letter. It can be used in a number of ways—among marketing materials given to a prospective customer, for example. Or an excerpt from the letter can be used in a brochure.

Ask a satisfied customer or client to write you a letter on company letterhead outlining how your product or service helped that organization. Encourage your clients to identify concrete benefits they derived from you; make the benefits specific. Ideally, you should ask for letters from as many customers and clients as possible. Prospective customers like to see a testimonial from a company in their industry, and from their region of the country.

Often a client is happy to write a letter but asks for assistance in what to say. Show the person examples of other testimonial letters. Ask him questions about what he found most beneficial from your product or service. From the resultant description, you can suggest the thrust of what he can say:

- How long did he use your product?
- How does yours compare with others he has used?
- What was the scope of the project or sale?
- What were the tangible results?

Remember the customer advantage section discussed earlier and the benefits of comparing the after with the before? A statement of specific results can be powerful in building credibility. Here is an excerpt from a testimonial letter in my file referring to specific results for a hotel client: "Jill created a marketing and sales system for each of our five hotel properties. The result has been a 19 percent increase in corporate business this past year." From a distributor of a syndicated radio series came this one: "Jill's direct mail and telemarketing programs increased our response rate among prospective radio affiliates from 16 to 40 percent."

Perhaps you provide a product or service whose use is not so easily quantified. Ask for outcomes that are as specific as possible. From a state agency whose annual planning retreat I facilitated came this testimonial: "Not only were a large number of 'big ideas' conceived for next year's marketing plan but, as a result of the deliberations, our two groups have become even more effective in working together as a team. Your ability to keep a large group focused and motivated, and insistence that the discussions be interesting and fun, all contributed to the success of our retreat."

Make the testimonial letter development process easy for the client. I've had several clients suggest that I write the letter for them. I love it when this happens. They review it and may make some changes; from the draft, they finalize the letter.

The Preheat Letter

Juanell Teague, who operates a successful consulting business for established and aspiring speakers, suggests an approach called the "preheat letter" to turn a satisfied client into an advocate. Ask a satisfied client, she says, to write a preheat letter to between five and forty of his personal contacts. You get your client to give you names, addresses, and phone numbers, along with their letterhead and envelopes. You prepare the mailing, including postage, and return the letters to them for signatures and mailing. About a week later, you make followup calls. Obviously, the preheat letter is a warmup before you make a call on your customer's referral.

Juanell advises that a successful preheat letter accomplishes four objectives:

1. It explains the client's requirements that you filled.
2. It describes how he found you.
3. It outlines the work you accomplished.
4. It recommends you.

Here is an example of a preheat letter from one of my clients. This one was instrumental in helping me get several new assignments.

Dear Mr. Randall:
The first of a three-part seminar series on marketing and profitability in the salon was presented recently by Peel's Beauty Supply. The "Sharpen the Edge" seminar was created to address some of today's most pertinent salon issues.

To meet this need, we compiled some dynamic educators. Michael Cole and Jill Griffin were two of the participants. Jill Griffin was brought to my attention by Michael Cole after he heard her speak at Sebastian's Turning Point Conference in Las Vegas last November. Michael described Jill as a high-content, high-energy speaker with an in-depth understanding of salon marketing. The "Sharpen the Edge" audiences were extremely excited and enthusiastic about Jill's presentations also.

Jill presented a one-day course in "Power Promotions: Twenty-One Ways to Increase Salon Sales," and "Cash Comebacks: How to Turn Customer Service into Customer Sales." Using customized PowerPoint slides, audience participation, and attention-getting props, Jill effectively illustrated each presentation. Responses to Jill's presentation: "I got some fresh new solutions" and "Quickest two hours I've experienced in a long time." Our sales consultants were equally energized.

I would recommend Jill Griffin for any future educational programs your company may be considering. Jill's presentation was a straightforward, yet entertaining, attention-keeping approach to salon marketing.

For more information on Jill's marketing education programs, please direct correspondence to. . . .
Sincerely,
William C. Peel
President

Perhaps the simplest way to use the endorsement for selling is by asking your client for referrals and then promptly following up. Asking for referrals should be a natural part of your interaction with your client. As we discussed earlier, satisfied clients benefit by giving your referrals. Don't be shy. Just ask.

There is a right way and a wrong way to ask for referrals:

Wrong: You don't know anyone else who might be interested in my product, do you?
Reason it's wrong: based on a negative supposition; leads the client to say no

Wrong: Do you know someone who might need my product?
Reason it's wrong: gives the client the opportunity to just say no

Right: Who do you know that might appreciate knowing about my services?
Reason it's right: takes a positive, proactive approach that implies "I'm a problem solver"

Once you have been given the first person's name ask, "Who else do you know?" and repeat the process until your client runs out of referrals.

Ask permission to use the referrer's name with the question, "May I use your name as a reference when I contact them?" and then abide by her wishes.

Recommend-a-Friend Rewards

A profitable yet overlooked method for stimulating word of mouth and referrals is a recommend-a-friend promotion. The basic technique is to offer an incentive to a customer in exchange for the favor of referral. At Indy Lube, customers who send friends to the $3.6 million quick-lube chain get a $10 certificate toward their next oil change. It's a way to thank customers who take the time to fill out an Indy Lube referral card and give it to a friend. The new customer uses the card to get $5 off the first oil change. The Indianapolis company won thirty-five new customers that way in one month alone. When Indy runs a contest among its fifteen locations for most customer referrals in a month, CEO Jim Sapp says, he redeems as many as fifty referral cards per store.

Another twist on the recommend-a-friend promotion is the recommend-a-friend card, whereby a customer receives a special reward for making a referral. Experience has shown that you can expect a larger number of friends' names if your customer is guaranteed that his name will not be used in soliciting his friends. The rate of response from friends is higher, however, if you are allowed to refer to the friend who provided the name. Therefore, you may want to give the customer a choice of whether his will be used in solicitation by using this question: "May we use your name as our referral source?"

Response decreases in proportion to the number of names provided by the customer. Thus, if she gives you three names the response is likely to be greater than the total response from six names provided by another customer. Additionally, experience has shown that people list names according to likelihood of interest. Therefore, contact the names provided in the order of listing, giving priority to those listed first.

Companies that acquire names through customers find that the people listed are, with few exceptions, more responsive and ripe for conversion than those on most any list the business can rent or buy.

Learn to Say Thank You Every Time

Any action on anyone's part in referring a prospect to you deserves a thank-you. The rule is simple: thank the person in writing. Thank the person right away. Whether or not you convert the referral into a customer or client, the source for the referral deserves recognition. A thank-you message from a real estate agent might read, "Thank you for suggesting that Paul and Brenda Logan call me regarding their real estate needs. I met with the Logans on Tuesday and enjoyed talking with them. They mentioned how enthusiastic and complimentary you were in giving them my name. I truly appreciate your confidence in my abilities."

Notice what the note does not say: it does not say "I got the Logans' listing. Thank you." If the agent did receive the listing, then that piece of information could be incorporated into the thank-you note. But the most important thing about the communication is that the client is properly thanked for the referral. Period.

Keeping the Word Out About You

Have you had the experience of being out of touch with a colleague or client and then running into her unexpectedly and learning something to the effect that "I was just in need of someone with your know-how" or "My neighbor was just asking about . . . I completely forgot that you provide that service"?

The key is to keep yourself visible and top-of-mind with people by creating a simple yet effective system for staying in touch.

Blueprint for Staying in Touch Long-Term

Maintaining a network of clients and market influencers who are likely to give you contacts and leads for future business is essential to business success. The secret to a strong network is constant contact. Consider this system for staying in touch.[25]

Written Notes: Five a Day. Have some type of stationery with you at all times. This is important, because it's during those moments while you are unexpectedly waiting that you use the time to keep in touch. Note cards are great for this purpose. If you write five notes a day and are in business 250 days a year, that's more than twelve hundred extra contacts.

With five notes a day, you can create friendships from business contacts by simply taking the two minutes necessary to jot down a thought. Two to three sentences is all it takes to say to someone "I was thinking of you." A birthday, anniversary, or promotion is a reason to write, but why wait for a special event? A note that simply says "Hello" and "How are you?" can do the trick. Mailing a copy of an article you think may be of interest to a customer can be an added bonus.

The key to this tool is to maintain a current client address list; doing so is crucial to your ability to stay in touch.

E-mail, of course, makes staying in touch with clients easier than ever. You can take this same five-contacts-a-day principle and apply it to e-mail with excellent results. What's more, you'll know very quickly when an e-mail goes undelivered. Use an undeliverable e-mail as the perfect opportunity to pick up the phone, call the client, and say "What's up?" But as convenient as e-mail is, don't stop sending the occasional written note. The written connection stands out now more than ever since your competitors are unlikely to take the extra step.

Phone Calls: Five a Week. Make a minimum of five calls a week. Keep the calls brief. Two brief calls are better than one long call. You become the source. You are generating the communication, and you are building the network. Take the opportunity to ask the person you call his opinion on something you are undertaking. William James once said, "The greatest need of every human being is the need for appreciation." Let the person know you respect his opinion.

In-Person Contacts: Five a Month. Make five personal contacts a month. What's more, practice the "out to lunch" method by calling and inviting three clients to join you collectively for lunch. Pick a popular lunch spot. Mix new clients with long-term clients. Make it a social affair that can pay you business dividends. The numbers speak for themselves:

250 days x 5 notes/day = 1,250 contacts
50 weeks x 5 calls/week = 250 contacts
12 months x 5 contacts/month = 60 contacts
Total contacts = 1,560 contacts per year

What this means to you is:
- You can reach 260 people six times a year
- You can reach 390 people four times a year
- You can reach 780 people twice a year

Consider the impact of 1,560 additional contacts to your business!

PUTTING NEWSLETTERS TO WORK

An effective way to stay in touch with customers and clients and in doing so create camaraderie is to publish a newsletter. A newsletter can help establish a "club" feeling, giving customers a sense of belonging, of being special.

Any restaurateur will tell you that the secret to longevity in the restaurant business does not lie in getting customers in the door. The real task is getting them to return. The newsletter has become the weapon of choice for many a restaurant in meeting this important objective.

In the early 1980s, Jim Lark was searching for a means to let his customers know about the special monthly theme dinners he and his wife, Mary, were serving at their exclusive restaurant, the Lark, in West Bloomfield, Mississippi. A newsletter seemed like a logical choice. So Jim created a newsletter with a masthead that proudly proclaimed itself "America's first monthly restaurant newsletter." It contained prose that read like a letter to family and friends. The communication did the trick, and the special theme dinners, with the help of the customer newsletter, continue to be a sell-out two decades later.

With the exception of an occasional tombstone ad in a charity program, the newsletter is Jim Lark's primary way of letting customers know what's going on. The newsletter helps the Lark enjoy a healthy loyal clientele; Lark says "about 85 percent of our business is repeat business."[26] Consider this newsletter sampling: "Mary and I have just returned from safari. The African setting, the wildlife, and the camaraderie of the friends who accompanied us were all that we hoped for. What we did not expect was the exceptional cuisine, which took full advantage not only of the best wild game in the world, but the bounty of extensive orchards and vineyards of the surrounding area."[27]

Jim Lark's experience has taught him what companies in a wide cross-section of industries have discovered: a well-conceived newsletter that has a payoff for the reader in terms of education and information can help a company to

- Maintain contact with customers
- Foster long-term relationships
- Pass on product information
- Establish the company as an expert in the field
- Cultivate future sales

With the Web's growing popularity, online newsletters are becoming increasingly popular with both old economy and new economy businesses. Distribution is easy and inexpensive, but to be a success an e-letter must overcome one huge computer obstacle: the reader's Delete key. Fact is, it takes a reader less effort to hit the Delete key than to open the file, so you must make your e-letter worth the read. Consider these four tips for making your customer newsletter, online or off, an eagerly anticipated must-read:

- *Start out by drafting a statement of purpose.* Knowing what you want your newsletter to accomplish before you start development is critical to getting a world-class result. Explains Marketing Manager Steve McElroy, who is responsible for the client newsletter, *Inklings,* produced by the Canadian firm Hemlock Printers, "One of the chief objectives of *Inklings* was to nurture present clients and nudge them toward greater volume, while impressing prospects and ultimately making them customers. Our first step in developing this publication was to formulate a statement of purpose and objectives, as follows: '*Inklings will* focus firmly on the reader, his or her interests, problems, goals and aspirations, and thus will achieve its selling purpose through value rendered rather than overt persuasion and self-serving "advertorials." The reader will recognize *Inklings* for its excellence. As the avalanche of information competing for attention continues to rise, he/she will favor *Inklings* for its topical and incisive editorial content, its lively writing and dynamic graphics and its innovative ideas and superior reproduction quality.'"[28]
- *Create a subscription-quality newsletter.* Don't think of your newsletter as a client freebie. If you do, you'll likely not give it the critical attention it deserves. Says McElroy, "I advise [other] firms to think of their newsletter program as a service they could very well charge for. . . . Fashion your newsletter as if it were going to subscribers who pay. . . . Then, it seems, the whole creative attitude toward the venture changes for the better."[29]
- *Put your readers' needs first.* Says Jeff Rubin, owner of Put It in Writing in Pinole, California, which produces nineteen business newsletters, "I get far too

many e-mail newsletters that are much more me-oriented than about topics of interest to readers."[30] Avoid that trap by focusing content on your clients' needs and wants. Consider featuring clients in your newsletter. It's a great way to further build goodwill.

• *Offer choice.* Give your readers flexibility to receive your newsletter online or off. For example, my Austin accountant, Robnett and Company, gives me the choice of receiving their newsletter, *Client Line,* via e-mail or through a printed copy available by regular mail.

• *Reward your reader.* Consider "paying" clients to read your newsletter by peppering perks and bargains in the content. For example, a recent newsletter e-mailed to an Atlanta customer by Delta Airlines offered several Atlanta-based flights at special fares.

• *Remember: you are your newsletter.* In the eyes of your clients, you are what you publish. Clients and prospects alike are unforgiving of shabby work. From typos to boring articles, a second-rate newsletter can only hurt your business, not help it. Accept the seriousness of the decision to offer a client newsletter. Don't forget what your mom told you: do it well or don't do it at all.

BE READY FOR MORE CUSTOMERS

Think twice before you launch a plan to encourage personal recommendation referrals. Properly executed, it can produce dynamic results. But when a business is not ready for expansion, having a lot of new customers can threaten quality by reducing standards in order to meet demand. The result can be disastrous: disillusioned prospects, dissatisfied customers, low employee morale, and general frustration at not being able to provide good service. If this happens, unhappy prospects and customers will tell their friends, and a downward business spiral begins.

SUMMARY

• Word of mouth is the most powerful advertising your business can have.

• Referred customers require less selling time and are more loyal than other customers. They come ready to buy because in effect they have already been sold.

• Always remember to thank your customers, and realize that where they buy is a choice they make.

• Creating for the customers and clients an online community through which to share can be an effective tool for building customer value, and in turn customer advocacy.

• Use testimonials, customer files, and reward programs to increase the loyalty of customers and to build a strong reputation.

- Strive constantly to increase and improve your long-term contacts; they directly and indirectly increase your sales. As few as five notes a day, five calls a week, and five meetings a month with your network can give a substantial boost to your business.

- A client newsletter, offline or online, must present subscription-level value if it is to earn reader interest and build long-term loyalty.

- Be ready for more customers. Launch an aggressive plan for encouraging referrals once you have the systems in place to effectively handle them.

GETTING STARTED

- Experiment with the preheat letter method with a few clients. Tweak the approach based on what you learn. Roll it out to other clients.

- Establish a system for staying in touch with existing clients using multiple tools: written communication, including e-mail; calls; in-person visits; and so forth. Consider using a customer contact software program with built-in reminders to assist in implementing this process.

- Explore the possibility of a issuing a periodic newsletter. Carefully analyze the dollar costs and time requirements versus anticipated return on investment. Think about how to bring subscription-level quality to this communication piece. Query customers regarding their newsletter needs and wants.

CHAPTER NINE

Customer Loss

How to Prevent It and What to Do When It Strikes

I got a phone call today from one of our oldest customers. He fired us.
After twenty years. He fired us. Said he didn't know us anymore. I think I know
why. We used to do business with a handshake, face to face. Now it's "I'll get back
to you later." Well, folks, some things gotta change. That's the reason we're gonna
set out today with a face-to-face chat with every customer we have.
—United Airlines commercial

When a long-term client stops doing business with you, when in effect she or he goes "inactive," it's an expensive loss. As we saw in Chapter One, in terms of profit contribution, it is the long-term client who contributes most to a company's bottom line. When such a client goes inactive—stops buying from you—you lose a higher proportion of profit than when a first-time customer stops purchasing.

The loss is not a simple short-term loss. You forfeit future profit as well. For example, a grocery shopper who spends approximately $100 weekly on groceries for the family represents roughly $50,000 over a decade of purchases. The average lifetime value of a car buyer, excluding repairs, is around $150,000. The customer and her future buying potential represent a powerful appreciating asset for any business. So when a customer stops buying, the loss is far greater than simply one missed purchase.

In *Thriving on Chaos,* author Tom Peters states, "When the Federal Express courier enters my office, she should see $180,000 stamped on the forehead of our receptionist. My little twenty-five-person firm runs about a $1,500 a month Fed Ex bill. Over ten years, that will add up to $180,000. I suggest that this simple device, calculating the ten-year value of a customer, can be very powerful."[1]

But the losses are greater still. When a customer leaves, you lose more than just the person's buying power. You also lose referrals and word-of-mouth advertising. If an auto dealer's customer sells just one friend on doing business with the dealership, that customer's value appreciates from $150,000 to $300,000. With two referrals, the customer's value increases to $600,000.

Having a customer leave you is a double-edged sword. Not only do you lose that person's business specifically, but also you jeopardize gaining future business with new customers because of the negative word of mouth. A typical dissatisfied customer will tell eight to ten people about the experience. One in five tell twenty. If you're Robert Leone, you tell even more.

What if you hired a national moving company to transport your household possessions to your new home halfway across the country and the truck, the driver, and your possessions were lost for three months? That's precisely the predicament Leone found himself in the early 1980s, when he moved from Minneapolis to Austin to join the marketing faculty at the University of Texas.

Leone hired an attorney, took his case to court, and won. In the end, the moving company met all of his requirements for settlement but one: it refused to give him a letter of apology.

What was next for Leone? He began exhibiting the classic symptom of an unhappy customer. He told people—lots of people—about his experience. In fact, Bob Leone made a point of telling his story to all his introductory marketing classes at the university. Each year at Christmas, he would send a card to the president of the moving company and include a "running total" of how many people he had told thus far. Leone continued this tradition for ten years. In the early 1990s, he sent his last Christmas greeting to the moving company president. The number on the card: 3,503.

Just imagine if the Internet had been available. How many people could this tenacious, unhappy customer have shared his experience with? A lot. The lesson here is simple: never before has it been more important to keep customers happy and solve the problems of those who aren't.

THE LOST CUSTOMER DILEMMA: A CLOSER LOOK

This very minute, your best customers and clients are your competitors' most sought-after prospects. No one understands this reality better than Browning Ferris Industries (now a part of Allied Waste), which, like others in this industry, loses about 14 percent of its customer base annually to competitors. Competitors can easily spot the company's clients by simply touring streets and alleys looking for the blue Browning Ferris dumpsters.

Consider these facts: in 1992, Browning Ferris managed a net gain of 33,000 U.S. commercial and industrial hauling customers, increasing its total to 570,000. But that meant actually having to find 103,000 new customers, because 70,000 old ones were lost. The company's chairman and CEO, William D. Ruckelshaus, called the phenomenon a "tremendous customer churn"; in an effort to stop the attrition, he has embarked on a multimillion-dollar research effort to understand why people become unhappy.

Simply undercutting price is often enough to take business away, unless good service has created loyal customers. Browning Ferris's research is yielding understanding of what customers really want from their garbage collector. Customers frequently mention price when threatening to switch haulers, but they're usually angry about something else, too. Says Ruckelshaus, "If you solve that problem for them, the price issue goes away."[2]

Executives in other industries concur. At a recent roundtable session on customer service at *Inc.* magazine's conference for the fastest-growing small companies, American Teleconferencing Services COO Michael Twomey explained the effect the loss of a major client had on the Overland Park, Kansas, company: "We'll make up the sales loss, but it's devastating for the sales and support staff, who went all out." Says Twomey, "The client gave us high scores on customer service, but we lost out to a competitor that gave the equipment away."[3]

The advice from some of the twenty-two participating executives: "You probably lost the customer six months before. The relationship has usually soured by the time price becomes the issue."[4]

The Slow Leak

A longtime customer or client is yours to keep or yours to lose. By the time an account has gotten to the repeat-customer or client stage, there is a history, and both parties have invested a lot. After selling to this person over a period of time, you know his staff and his needs, just as he knows you, your staff, and your company. A considerable investment has been made by both parties.

Why, then, does a client leave? What prompts the decision to defect? In most cases, it's a feeling of discontent that develops progressively over time. The client leaves you when he finally feels that the cost of sustaining such a low level of satisfaction has gotten too high.

Like a car tire, businesses don't usually dissolve because of a blowout. Instead, it's the slow leak that kills them over time. Most businesses that fail don't do so because of a huge mistake or gigantic blunder. They fail because they slowly lose touch with their customers. In return, the customers become indifferent and open to the possibility of giving their business to a new supplier. As we saw with Browning Ferris, competitors are everywhere, waiting to capitalize on such indifference.

A Rockefeller Foundation study on lost customers found these reasons for customers leaving:

- Complaints were not handled (14 percent)
- The competition (9 percent)

- Relocation (9 percent)
- No special reason (68 percent)

If you look past "no special reason," you'll usually find customers leaving because of benign neglect. As the United Airlines commercial points out, many customers leave because they feel no particular connection with your company. You failed to tell them you cared. You failed to keep in touch. You took them for granted. The bottom line: you made it easy for them to walk away.

Reading Between the Lines

"Clients are funny," observed Ira Gottfried, vice president at Coopers and Lybrand in Los Angeles. "You'll suddenly find that the work stops and you don't get any new work. You seldom know why. It's a very rare client who will let you know they are having a problem. . . . The Christian ethic says you don't nail somebody; you just walk away."[5]

Indeed, statistics support what Gottfried has learned from experience. Only a small percentage of customers will complain. A typical business hears from only 4 percent of its unhappy customers. The remaining 96 percent go away, and on average 91 percent never come back.

Actions speak louder than words. This is an apt description of most customers; they do not voluntarily tell you they are unhappy, but their actions can. An unhappy customer often exhibits one or more of these purchase behaviors, each increasingly creating distance between you and your customer:

- Customer approval of your proposals comes more slowly.
- Access to upper-level management decreases.
- The flow of customer data slows down.
- Plans for future work become progressively more short-term.
- One or more of your products or services are discontinued.
- The volume of business they are doing with you is reduced.

These signs are often symptoms of developing dissatisfaction. When this is the case, it is useless to attack the symptoms directly. Instead, you must discover and address the customer's underlying dissatisfaction.

The Origins of Dissatisfaction

In many cases, dissatisfaction is a result of misunderstanding what is important to your customers. Although you meet the customer's general needs, you don't understand or deliver what is of primary importance to the person. For example, let's say your customer, Joe, wants blue widgets and you respond with yellow ones. Assuming that what he really needs is simply widgets, Joe may feel general dissatisfaction, because blue is his favorite color and distinguishes his machine from everyone else's. In other words, you have been concentrating on the wrong things, satisfying Joe in general but overlooking what counts most for him. The other possibility is that you accurately perceive what is important to him but do not deliver quickly enough. You have blue widgets custom made for him, but it takes six months for them to be delivered, and he counts on two. Time is money to Joe, whose dissatisfaction grows with every day that finds him behind in reaching objectives. Finally, the waiting becomes unaffordable and he severs the relationship with you.

Understanding Where You Stand

Identifying and continually assessing a client's "must list" and then delivering those things in a timely way is the key to Granite Rock's success. This construction materials company has established itself as the high-end producer in an industry that all but defines the term *commodity business.*

Based in Watsonville, California, the hundred-year-old family owned company, which has a dozen locations between San Francisco and Monterey, quarries granite and produces concrete, asphalt, sand, and gravel. In addition, the company buys and resells cinder block, drywall, and brick and masonry tools. Competing in an industry where customers are conditioned to take the low bid under the mistaken assumption that "all loads of stone are created equal," Granite Rock has taken the high road and chosen to emphasize high-quality rock supported by high-quality service. In return, Granite Rock customers pay, on average, up to 6 percent more than they would be charged by the competition.

Charging a premium and positioning itself as providing the best value in the industry put a real burden on Granite Rock to deliver. The company must constantly prove to customers that its products and services are worth the premium they pay. This means that Granite Rock employees must offer the kind of value customers are willing to pay for. How does the company accomplish this? With a three-pronged strategy: first, by understanding how its customers define quality and service (the customer's must list); second, by regularly gauging customers' opinions about Granite Rock's performance in comparison to the competitors; and third, by communicating all this information to its employees.

The company accomplishes the first step of the strategy by conducting, every three to four years, a lengthy customer survey in which its customer needs and wants relative to product lines are extensively probed. In this survey, customers are also asked to rank the most important factors in choosing a construction materials supplier. This survey is important because it helps the company determine whether it is concentrating on the right things: whatever the customer values most.

The second and third steps of the strategy are where Granite Rock really shines, by creating a report card of its performance versus that of the competition. Every year, the company conducts an opinion survey that compares its performance with that of competitors. All of Granite Rock's customers receive a survey in which they are asked to grade their top three suppliers on areas related to product quality and customer service.

Combining the long-survey data and the short-survey information, Granite Rock produces report-card graphs that are posted on bulletin boards throughout the company. Through these graphs, employees can see how they measure up when compared with their competition. Says Dave Franceschi, of Granite Rock's quality planning department, "We have a strong belief that if something is worth doing, it's probably worth measuring." Wes Clark, general manager of the company's three northern concrete plants, adds: "We believe that you don't stress a negative—you chart it. Our people are competitive. They will look at that negative and want to do something about it."[6]

In an increasingly competitive world market, a company keeps its customers by offering value every day. As business veterans Mark Hanan and Peter Karp explain, "Whether you are doing the wrong thing or doing the right things cost-ineffectively, the customer who is losing opportunities for enhancing his value will do you in. He cannot help it. He has no choice but to maximize his opportunities."[7]

No one understands that reality more than General Electric's Claudi Santiago. When he started in the GE Information Services (GEIS) office in Barcelona back in 1980, the company had local help desks to troubleshoot problems around the world. Customers would call the company via telephone, talk with someone in their own language, and get help on the software or network problem they were encountering. The electronic age and dramatically shortened response time have changed all that. As recently as the late 1980s, such GE clients as Chrysler, Caterpillar, and Chemical Bank would accept two-hour maintenance delays when a system crashed. No longer. Today, a ten-minute delay time can be all it takes to lose a client to a competitor.

"Customers are getting more and more demanding, and they are putting a lot of pressure on us," says Santiago. "They use our system to order raw materials or parts or to trade stocks and bonds. If an order gets lost or delayed, we can literally stop a manufacturing facility. Our clients' tolerance level for problems is close to zero. That's the reality."[8]

A decade ago, GE created Santiago's position. Today, he leads a staff of two hundred people worldwide who anticipate user problems; fix them rapidly, if and when they do occur; and prevent them from recurring in the future. To help meet these objectives, GEIS has created an innovative system for soliciting user feedback. The users respond to an electronic report card, grading the company daily on such areas as response time and service, with zero for "outstanding" all the way up to five for "disastrous." Results are tallied, and an overall grade is determined at the end of each week and each month. These monthly averages are compared against a target set by a client advisory council; if they meet the target, a predetermined percentage bonus is rewarded to every GEIS employee.

One of GEIS's most successful products is e-mail, so Client Talk, a special e-mail system on which customers can send and receive messages about the company's services, was a natural spin-off service. The newest Client Talk innovation enables the customer to flag a message for readership by GEIS management. The message is then published in the president's and vice presidents' daily reports. Another important Client Talk improvement is the ability to inform clients about user complaints elsewhere in their company. Explains Santiago, "Sometimes a client can have a distributor in Singapore who had a problem with an order and the client didn't know about it because we fixed it so quickly. Now they can see on a daily, weekly or monthly basis all the Client Talk problems that come up for them on a worldwide basis and how long it takes GEIS to fix them."[9]

It is clear that keeping clients loyal, and keeping them happy, depends on a company's ability to identify a problem quickly and respond immediately. If you don't know a client is having a problem with your company, chances are slim that the problem can be corrected before the client defects to a competitor. Constant monitoring and solicitation of customer feedback are essential to maintaining a loyal customer.

COMPLAINTS AS LOYALTY BUILDERS

Life in the real world means things don't always go according to plan. Problems are inevitable in any continuing business relationship. A hotel reservation gets lost, a car breaks down, a customer experiences difficulty in operating a new office machine. What's important is how the company responds to the problem. Some research suggests that people whose complaints are properly dealt with may become more loyal customers than those who have never experienced problems.

The company's eagerness to solve a problem and improve performance is what builds the customer's trust and translates into future business. Consider these statistics from McKinsey and Company:

- Customers who have major problems but don't complain about them have a repurchase intention rate of about 9 percent.
- Those who do complain, regardless of the outcome, have a repurchase intention rate of approximately 19 percent.
- Customers who have their complaint resolved have a repurchase intention rate of 54 percent.

- Customers who have complaints quickly resolved have a repurchase intention rate of 82 percent.

Notice that, in this study, the customer's intention to repurchase doubled (from 9 to 19 percent) by simply having a forum in which to complain. This is an exceedingly valuable observation. The large gains in intention to repurchase (54 and 82 percent) can take place only if the company is first aware of the problem.

No News Is Bad News

"One of the sure signs of a bad or declining relationship is the absence of complaints from the customer," says Harvard Professor Theodore Levitt, writing in the *Harvard Business Review.* "Nobody is ever that satisfied, especially not over an extended period of time. The customer either is not being candid or is not being contacted."

If you are not receiving complaints from customers, something is wrong. Don't be fooled into thinking there are no unhappy customers. Instead, it means that rather than complaining, your customer is probably leaving or, at best, reducing the amount of business he is doing with you. Moreover, the "iceberg effect" is alive and well when it comes to complaints. According to the Consumer Affairs Department, if one customer complains to a business, there are usually twenty-five additional customers with the same complaint that haven't been heard from.

Four Ways to Keep Your Customers from Leaving

An ounce of prevention is worth a pound of cure. Consider these ways of preventing defection.

Make It Easy for Customers to Give You Feedback. One of the most profitable activities a business can engage in is to seek out customer complaints, making it easy for the customer to give feedback. Ask customers regularly about their most recent purchase. Did it meet their needs? Was it what they expected? How could it be improved? Here's how one start-up company facilitated feedback from customers.

The marketing director at Restek, Neil Mosesman, knew customer calls were getting out of hand when he was taking them even while he was away at trade shows. Like any company that suddenly experiences an acceleration in growth, Restek, a manufacturer of lab equipment parts in Bellefonte, Pennsylvania, found itself bombarded with customer questions, comments, and complaints. To effectively deal with these calls, Restek adopted an unconventional solution. Rather than delegating call handling to a customer service department, Restek spreads the responsibility throughout the company by giving employees service training and incentives.

All employees are regularly updated on Restek's product applications, big customers, and primary competition. Job candidates are screened for their ability to converse with customers. Even a candidate for an R&D job must be comfortable in this role. Handling irate customers is a key part of the training received by Restek's technical staff.

To encourage employees to be concerned about customer loyalty, Restek offers a bonus program that includes a customer service component. Employees call two hundred to three hundred customers each month just to check in and make sure everything is going well. Many of these customers are first-time buyers. Employees ask if the product arrived on time, if the customer is having any problems, and if there are new ways the company can meet the customer's needs—through new or different products, for example. Restek's employees also contact customers who are showing signs of discontent, say, those who have returned a product or have not ordered within a year.

The callback program gives Restek the direct word on why customers don't come back and hard feedback on new products. "When customers complain about a product, the follow-up call might be made by the person who manufactured it or tested it," explains Mosesman, "so they really want to know why something didn't work. And they feel like they have to bend over backward to fix the problem. They can't say, 'Oh, that customer doesn't know what he's talking about.'"[10]

The callback program helped fuel Restek's continued growth. In the first two years the program was in place, the company grew more than 50 percent, from $6.4 million in first-year sales to nearly $11 million in year three.

At IBM Rochester, the Customer Partnership Call process thanks customers for purchasing IBM systems. A call is made ninety days after a system is shipped, and the customer is asked what she likes about the system, what she dislikes about it, and what suggestions she might have for improvement. These comments are then compiled into a database, analyzed, and distributed regularly to engineering, programming, marketing, manufacturing, and service teams to guide them in their work.

Federal Express has a toll-free number for the hearing impaired and an automated call distribution system for smoothing out demand peaks, relaying calls to the first available agent at any of its eighteen call centers.

Here are some other ways a company can encourage customer feedback:

• *Surveys.* Whether in writing, face-to-face, or by phone, a survey can be an excellent way to get customer feedback. Each year, Whirlpool mails its Standardized Appliance Measurement Survey (SAMS) to 180,000 households, requesting that people rate all their appliances on a variety of attributes. If consumers rank a competitor's products higher, Whirlpool engineers go to work (literally ripping the competitor's product apart) to understand why. The Web offers exciting new tools for surveying customers. For example, real-time surveys that pop up online following a specific customer transaction can quickly produce valuable customer feedback.

- *Order forms.* American Supply International gets customer feedback from a comment section incorporated directly into its order form. The mail-order company, located in Bryans Road, Maryland, helps overseas Americans find hard-to-get U.S. products. Among its biggest sellers are 9 Lives Cat Food and canned chili. The comment form, according to cofounder Steve Reed, has given the company new service ideas and contributed to an impressive 85 percent customer retention rate.

- *Newsletters.* Printing letters from readers motivates customer feedback through a newsletter. That's the word from Paul de Benedictis, communications director for Opcode Systems. Using newsletters has enabled the company to create a more personal, one-to-one rapport with its more than thirty thousand users.

- *Focus groups.* When Tyler Phillips founded Partnership Groups, a child care and elder care referral service in Lansing, Pennsylvania, he created an information kit to explain the range of his company's services. Phillips sold the kits to corporations and counted on his corporate clients to promote them to their employees. But when clients' employees were interviewed in focus groups, they said they wanted their questions answered by a person, not just a kit. That was all Phillips needed to hear to shift his company away from the kits and into more of a consulting service. Customers were given unlimited access to Partnership staff in getting answers to child care and elder care referral questions. Thanks to this increased interaction with employees, new options, such as "First-Nest" for infant care, were soon created. Ten years after focus groups helped redirect the company's service offerings, Partnership Group reports that the majority of its 109 corporate contracts are for three years and that the company is profitable, with sales of $9 million.

- *User groups and advisory boards.* SunWave Manufacturing of Leander, Texas, a maker of portable spas, uses a customer advisory board to stay in touch with customer needs. The advisory council is composed of SunWave spa dealers, who serve as a voice for other dealers in their region. SunWave coordinates these meetings to coincide with industry events and trade shows, thereby reducing cost.

- *Voice mail.* The Beef Box is an electronic mailbox that Homes and Land Publishing of Tallahassee uses to get feedback from its franchisees, which publish magazines containing real estate listings for a specific region. "Anything they want senior management to hear" is the way Ron Sauls, executive vice president, describes the comments or complaints franchisees call in with on the Beef Box. Sauls's assistant transcribes the voice mail messages and then passes them along to company staffers for quick follow-up.

- *Chat rooms and message boards.* As we discussed in Chapter Eight, an online community offers a company a real opportunity to gather customer feedback. Monitoring chat rooms, message boards, and the like on your own community site as well as other industry sites your customers frequently visit yields invaluable insight on customer opinions, problems, needs, and wants.

Collecting the information is only half the challenge. The information must be put into accessible form by the company so that it can be acted upon. Survivor Software, developer of a personal finance program, maintains a suggestion database. Reports Mike Farmer, president of the Englewood, California, company, "We have three categories: features that we'll implement immediately; features that are desirable, but we don't know how to do them; and features we intend to do on future revisions."

When Customers Need Help, Provide It Quickly. Once you get feedback from a customer, you must act quickly. If she calls with a complaint, you must respond immediately, preferably by fixing the problem, but at least by affirming your intention to fix the problem as quickly as possible. If she has to contact you more than once with a problem, she is much more likely to be dissatisfied, even if the second call results in a fix.

A TARP (Technical Assistance Research Programs) study conducted among the 800-number customers of 460 companies found that the number of customers

Figure 9.1. Customer Satisfaction Comparison, One Call Versus Two.

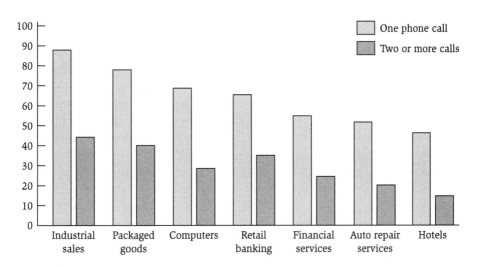

Source: "SOCAP 800 Number Study: A 1992 Profile of 800 Numbers for Customer Service." (Survey of 460 companies, about 25 percent of them small or midsize businesses.) Washington, D.C.: Technical Assistance Research Programs, for Society of Consumer Affairs Professionals in Business, in Alexandria, Va.

reporting complete satisfaction after one call was dramatically higher than when two or more phone calls were made[11] (see Figure 9.1). The TARP study reinforces another 800-number study, which revealed that customer dissatisfaction does not increase linearly; after the first period of delay, a customer's dissatisfaction appears to increases sharply.

Reduce the Hassle of Repairs, Refunds, and Warranties. Repairs, refunds, and warranties are often a source of frustration for customers. Consider how one business works to prevent dissatisfaction from brewing during this sort of encounter.

Barry Fribush learned firsthand how frustrating a repair can be when he became a spa owner in the late 1970s. Still running a printing business and advertising agency in Washington, D.C., he bought a spa when the product was still a West Coast phenomenon: "When I finally found one, it was terrible. It kept breaking down and there was no easy way to get it repaired. I figured I could do a better job selling and servicing them."[12]

Soon after, Fribush founded the Bubbling Bath Spa and Tub Works, in Rockville, Maryland. His early success stemmed from his ability to systematically provide good customer service. Well aware, because of his work in the ad industry, of the high price of advertising, he realized he could not afford costly ads as a start-up. The easiest and least expensive way to find customers was through word of mouth from satisfied customers. So he set about creating a service system that would spawn satisfaction and evoke enthusiastic word-of-mouth advertising. Here are a few of Fribush's principles, designed to make sure that problems are corrected early on:

- *Offer only quality products.* You cannot earn customer loyalty if the product you sell keeps breaking down. As a result, Fribush carries only those spas with a proven track record for reliability.
- *Trust repairs to the person who owns one.* All of Bubbling Bath's repair people are required to own a spa. Fribush makes them available at cost. It's the only way, he says, that his repair people will truly understand the product they work on. By experiencing the problems they are asked to fix, his repair people are better service providers. Their technical skills go up, and so does their sympathy for the customer.
- *Set the service hours according to customer calls.* Analyze when people call in for help and then staff as needed. For Bubbling Bath, a 9:00 to 5:00 service staff made no sense. Most of the service calls come in between 4:00 and 7:00 P.M., when people, home from work, turn on the spa and experience a problem. He runs a skeleton crew during the day and a larger staff during the evening rush.
- *Do it right or you won't get paid.* Every customer wants the repair job done right the first time, and if it's not, discontent escalates. In the beginning, callbacks were averaging 30 percent, or three out of every ten repair jobs. Fribush

instigated a new policy: if Bubbling Bath has to fix the same job twice within a four-week period, the person who did the initial repair work does not get paid for that repair. The policy has made a marked improvement in the company's service record. Callbacks now average only six a year!

Learn How to Comfort an Angry Customer. With an enhanced customer feedback and complaint system comes more customer interaction. The principles outlined to this point in the chapter are designed to help nip dissatisfaction at an early stage and prevent escalation of customer anger. But even in the best of companies, an angry customer occasionally surfaces. Still, an angry customer can be saved. Here's how.

When you come into contact with a customer who is angry, handle the person with care. It may help to visualize the irate customer as having a "psychological sunburn." If you touch him when the sunburn is at its worst, you may get a violent reaction. Help him recover from the sunburn by reducing the "heat." Give him relief by following these six steps:

- *Let the customer blow off steam.* Encourage the customer to share by saying something like "I'm sorry you've had trouble. Please tell me the circumstances so that I can help you." Remain quiet and listen attentively to all he has to say, and acknowledge his frustration. Do not act defensively; do not interrupt. You're already on the road to resolving the complaint by first letting him unload the discontent. When you do speak, ask open-ended questions, using such words as *why, when, where, which,* and *what.* By keeping the irate customer talking, you get more facts.

It's often helpful to remember that a customer's anger at times masks a far different emotion: fear. He may fear he is being taken advantage of, or perhaps he fears that this problem, left unresolved, will make him look foolish in front of his coworkers or friends. Next time you are fighting the urge to react to an angry customer's irate behavior, just picture a scared kid trying to find his way out of a dark room. Stay calm and see yourself as the customer's beacon of light out of the dilemma.

- *Let the customer know you understand his problem.* Paraphrase back to the customer his description of the problem. Your perception of the problem must match his if he is ultimately to be satisfied. In addition, if possible, let him know you are recording the information in writing. Such feedback as "Let me confirm this. We repaired your printer on Tuesday and by Thursday the problem had returned. Is that what happened? I want to write this down. . . ." helps the customer know you have heard him.

- *Find out what the customer wants.* A complaining customer does not want the problem handled; he wants the problem resolved. Does your customer want a replacement, a refund, a store credit? Always ask him how he would like the situation to be resolved, by using such questions as "What would you like us to do?" This question is also important because the customer can often be satisfied with far less than the company is willing to offer.

• *Suggest a solution on the basis of the customer's wishes.* If the customer's request is acceptable, then agree to the action and do it cheerfully and swiftly. In his book *Minding the Store*, Stanley Marcus says that giving customers what they ask for is better than bargaining. If you bargain, you are more than likely to lose their goodwill. Marcus tells of an experience early in his career when a woman bought a gown of handmade lace from his store. After wearing it once and clearly abusing it, she returned it and asked for her money back. Marcus gave it to her cheerfully, reasoning that it would cost more to replace her as a customer than the $175 cost of the dress. His instincts were right. "Over the years," writes Marcus, "this woman spent $500,000 with us."

• *If the customer is not happy with your solution, ask what she or he would consider fair.* Most customers will be fair. They are probably not asking for a refund or replacement simply to get your merchandise for free. If you have the authority, handle the request quickly. If you do not, find someone who can. If the customer leaves you unhappy with the outcome, the chances of winning future sales from the person are slim.

Several years ago, I treated myself to a series of facials and new skin care products. I purchased these products and services (which totaled almost $200) from the hair salon where I am a regular customer. Soon afterward, I had a reaction to one of the facial products. I had used about half of the cream before recognizing that the rash on my face was a result of one of the creams and not simply a result of changing my skin care routine.

I asked for my money back. The facialist refused, saying she could not return the product, given that so much had been used. She said she could do nothing about the problem. I took it to the salon owner, who refunded my money. But I never used the facialist's services or products again. Soon afterward, the facialist left the salon. She had not developed a large enough clientele to support her services. The point is this: most people will be fair. Don't sacrifice a customer over the one-time cost of a product or service.

Mike Ruettgers knows firsthand the brutal reality associated with unhappy customers and the extraordinary lengths sometimes necessary to save a customer from defection. Back in 1988, as data storage vendor EMC's vice president of operations and customer service, Mike was faced with company products (primarily disk drives) that were failing left and right at customer sites. As the company edged closer and closer to bankruptcy, Mike crisscrossed the country, meeting with angry customers in a desperate attempt to salvage EMC's reputation.

A low point was a meeting with a manufacturing executive, about Mike's age, who broke down in tears saying he was going to lose his job because of EMC's disk failures. His firm's business was essentially on hold because no one could retrieve vital information kept on EMC's data-storage systems. Shortly after that meeting, Mike made a bold decision: he insisted customers be given the choice of receiving a new EMC storage system or one made by key competitor IBM— but paid for by EMC. Many EMC customers chose IBM, so much so that during one quarter in 1988 EMC shipped more IBM units than their own. But customers took note and recognized EMC's ironclad commitment to stick by them in rough times. Once EMC put in place rigorous quality checks, many of these same customers began buying from EMC again.

Mike, who is now CEO of EMC, says: "What that proved to me, to all of us, was that when a customer believes in you, and you go to great lengths to preserve that relationship, they'll stick with you almost no matter what. It opened our eyes to the power of customer service." This profound commitment to customers has propelled EMC from sheer survival status in the late 1980s to world-class leadership today. With roughly twenty-three thousand employees, the company generates annual revenue of $8.9 billion and enjoys an unprecedented 99 percent customer retention rate.

But there's no resting on its laurels at EMC. The company continues to be vigilant in serving customers through fanatical devotion to service. For each hour EMC spends repairing fractured hardware and software, the company invests nine hours proactively safeguarding and preventing such situations. Using built-in sensors, EMC systems routinely check their own health status every two hours. If a problem or something questionable is detected, the system automatically "phones home" on a dedicated line to EMC's customer service center. Such unwavering customer service standards are earning high marks with customers. After recently surveying fifty large corporations about their technology suppliers, Carl Howe, director of Forrester Research, remarked, "EMC came out looking like God. It had the best customer-service reviews we have ever seen, in any industry."[13]

• *Make a follow-up call.* This is your opportunity to firmly anchor the resolution and leave the customer more loyal to you than ever before. A follow-up call reinforces your commitment to service. A well-resolved complaint is a rarity in today's world. When you go the extra step to call back and confirm, you really stand out!

HOW TO WIN BACK A LOST CUSTOMER

Murray Raphel tells about Frank Buck, the famous lion tamer in the 1940s who put on his circus act throughout the United States using the theme "Bring 'em back alive." In other words, Buck would journey into the distant homes of the animals he wanted and bring them back alive for people to see. How do you reconnect with those customers who have left your business, to bring them back alive?

Answer: you ask them. "What steps can we take to win back your business?" Then you listen carefully and let your inactive client say what you must do to reearn business.

AmeriSuites Hotel in Irving, Texas, lost and won back an important account. The American Honda account represented roughly $40,000 in annual sales for AmeriSuites. American Honda needed lodging for employees attending a three-week training program. New trainees rotated through the program during the year. The hotel's all-suite concept was ideal for extended-stay accommodations thanks to its refrigerator, microwave, sitting area, and ample space.

The hotel was located close to the Honda offices as well as to the Dallas/Fort Worth airport. Despite these advantages, after approximately a year AmeriSuites lost the account. The director of sales, Rich Gevertz, contacted the decision maker at American Honda and asked, "What can we do to regain your confidence and win back your business?" The American Honda representative outlined the problems that made the company leave AmeriSuites and told Rich not to call back until each and every one of the problems was corrected.

AmeriSuites went to work. The staff focused on the key improvements that American Honda requested. It took two months to get the problems resolved. Once the staff was sure its house was in order, Rich called the company back and arranged a meeting at the hotel for purposes of demonstrating and discussing the changes and improvements. From changing transportation procedures and upgrading amenities offered to Honda guests to streamlining the billing procedures and creating customized hotel check-in information for Honda trainees, AmeriSuites met Honda's requirements. As a result of these actions, AmeriSuites won back the $40,000 American Honda account.

Consider these seven points to win back a lost customer:

1. Ask, "What can we do to win back your business?"
2. Listen closely to what the customer tells you.
3. Meet the customer's requirements; communicate the changes you have made. Ask again for the customer's business.
4. Be patient with the customer. Be open. Remember, some wounds heal slowly.
5. Stay in touch with the lost customer.
6. Make it easy for customers to come back to you. Avoid any "I told you so" stance.
7. When the customer does return, earn his or her business every day.

Never make the mistake of thinking of a lost customer as a lost cause. As we discussed in Chapter Three, untapped revenue from lost customers is an often-overlooked source of incremental profit in any firm. You'll also recall from Chapter Three that research has found a business is twice as likely to successfully sell to a lost customer as to a brand new prospect. Ultimately, an investment in winning back lost customers is good for business.

USING TECHNOLOGY TOOLS TO WIN CUSTOMERS BACK

Leading-edge technology tools are creating exciting new ways to touch inactive customers. Here's a case in point.

In 1998, management of the Toronto Raptors was facing a big dilemma: how to win back fans after a 191-day lockout by the National Basketball Association. At the heart of the issue was how to keep the team's core group of season ticket holders from walking away from a league that many people felt was placing the interest of rich superstar players and team owners ahead of fan interest. As Raptors President Richard Peddie admitted to Toronto sports media, "We've got a job to do to win back fans in Toronto."

Maple Leaf Sports and Entertainment (MLSE), the parent company of the Raptors, went to work to devise a win-back strategy aimed at wooing fans back to the games remaining in that locked-out season. MLSE's director of ticket sales, Chris Overholt, said "there was an urgent need to rebuild our relationship with our four thousand season-ticket holders. We wanted to provide them with updates on ticket pricing, seating, new players, and other benefits as soon as possible." But a quick turnaround was critical; direct mail and other traditional forms of communications alone were deemed too slow or not personal enough.

MLSE built its win-back plan around a CRM technology called Ventriloquist Express, which allows a client's voice, recorded from any touch-tone phone, to reach individual customers as a personal phone message. Ventriloquist, a technology from International Teledata Group (ITG) of Toronto, enabled MLSE to develop five personalized and interactive broadcast messages to season-ticket holders over an eight-week period. The price was right; a message of up to two minutes could be delivered for just forty-five cents each, and a two-to-three-minute message was only fifty-five cents.

MLSE developed a script for the first of five planned messages to Raptor fans. Butch Carter, the new Raptors head coach, delivered the first message, a ninety-second information summary. Carter's strong vocal support of the team during the lockout and his new head coach status made him a natural choice for the initial message.

Concurrent with Carter's recording the message, MLSE forwarded the season-ticket holder list (first and last name and phone number) to ITG. Using its extensive audio database of first names, Ventriloquist matched fans' first names with the corresponding audio files to create a message that sounded as if Carter were calling each fan personally:

> Hi, it's Coach Butch Carter of the Toronto Raptors calling for [first name]. Now that the lockout is over, I wanted to thank you for your continued patience. . . . We are working towards rewarding your commitment with a winning team. . . . I'll have better, younger athletic newcomers and veteran leaders . . . and the new Air Canada Centre. . . . I can tell you that the arena will finally show Toronto the way basketball is really meant to be played. . . ."

At this point in the message, the ticket holder had several options: he could opt to listen for the personal message, request a call back from the Raptors, end the message, repeat the message, or let the answering machine capture the message. Moreover, the Raptor fan also had the option to receive no further messages from Ventriloquist.

Encouraged by the initial response, MLSE decided to use Ventriloquist to contact hundreds of Best-Eight Minipack ticket holders. During the lockout, the fans had been allowed to cash in their tickets for a full refund. MLSE wanted to contact these people to reenlist them as Minipack fans. Within four short hours of the message being delivered, phone lines were lit up with callers confirming Minipack purchase.

Other messaging over the eight-week period included Richard Peddie calling fans about the new six-year collective bargaining agreement and Glen Grunwald, the Raptors general manager, calling fans on the evening of the opening game to update them on the new coach and players and to thank fans again for their support.

Although MLSE's actual Raptor fan win-back numbers are considered proprietary and not for disclosure, management classifies the win-back program a big success.[14]

LOST CUSTOMER STUDIES

No doubt, a lost customer does not have to be a lost cause. As noted, the Toronto Raptors were able to quickly "resuscitate" sports fans after a 191-day strike. Likewise, AmeriSuites was fortunate with the Honda account; the hotel corrected its problems and persuaded the client to return before the car maker formed a strong alliance with another hotel. But many bring-'em-back-alive stories do not end quite so happily.

In the worst case, even after the account is irrevocably lost, there is a prize to be won: the knowledge of why the customer stopped doing business with you.

Customers who leave you can give you a perspective about your business that is not available elsewhere. Though often unpleasant to hear, this information can save you from losing customers under similar circumstances in the future.

Feedback from lost customers can be concrete and specific. They can respond to a direct question such as "What made you leave?" with information that pays a big dividend. Staples, the discount office supply giant, carefully tracks customer purchases, and when it sees a lull or a customer no longer buying certain items, the company calls and gets feedback. The company may discover that the competition has a lower price, information that in turn enables Staples management to explore the issue further. This information is extremely valuable, because it allows Staples to regularly pinpoint noncompetitive products and fine-tune pricing rather than making costly pricing adjustments across all products.

A lost-customer study can also help you decide which value-added services help retention the most. One bank spent a considerable amount of money to improve the accuracy of its customers' monthly statements. Yet when it began to study customer losses, it discovered that fewer than 1 percent of customers left because of statement inaccuracy.

Finally, a lost-customer study helps you determine the kind of customer you do not want. For example, when a health insurance company determined that certain companies bought only on the basis of price and switched insurers every year or so, it decided to eliminate such companies as future prospects. It instructed its brokers not to write policies for a company that had changed carriers two or more times over the preceding five years.*

SUMMARY

- People whose problems and complaints have been handled effectively become your most loyal customers. They will trust and depend on you. You have proven yourself under fire.
- A lost customer is not necessarily a lost cause. Studies find that a business is twice as likely to successfully sell to a lost customer as to a brand new prospect.

---

* For more help on saving customers on the brink of defection and winning back lost customers, refer to *Customer WinBack: How To Recapture Lost Customers and Keep Them Loyal* (Jossey-Bass, 2001), which I cowrote with my colleague, Michael Lowenstein. Our book examines a host of additional win-back topics, including (1) results of our nationwide win-back survey, which profiles what today's firms are (and are not) doing regarding recapturing lost customers; (2) five types of lost customer and which types have the greatest win-back potential; (3) how to use a three-step "CPR" to save at-risk customers; and (4) mobilizing and managing a win-back team. Also, refer to my Website at www.loyaltysolutions.com for more win-back assistance.

- Losing a customer represents more than one lost sale. It is the loss of hundreds of sales in the future.
- Responding immediately to a complaint goes a long way toward retaining a customer.
- Listening to and analyzing complaints can help you keep customers loyal. Make customer complaint monitoring a key tool for executive decision making.
- It is always better to hear complaints than silence. You can fix a complaint, but it is nearly impossible to solve a problem you do not know exists. With the Internet, never has it been easier for unhappy customers to spread the word to many would-be customers about a problem. This makes it critical for your company to search out complaints and facilitate customer complaint.
- Listen, then act. These are the keys to appeasing a troubled customer and keeping the customer loyal.
- When dealing with an irate customer, remember that his anger often masks a different emotion: fear. As you work with him, try picturing him as a scared kid. This may help make the process less intimidating for you.
- The frontline employee is the cornerstone to loyalty building. His or her performance determines and shapes the customer's opinion about your business.
- Responding quickly to customers' needs requires empowered employees.

GETTING STARTED

- Review all customer contact processes and list the current ways in which customers can voice a complaint. Using this list as a starting point, brainstorm with your staff on how to make it easier for customers to complain. Implement the best ideas.
- Review your current customer complaint or feedback system. Establish firm guidelines regarding response time, reporting, trend analysis, and so on. Update all company staff regularly about customer complaint findings.
- Use findings from exit interviews with lost customers to educate staff about why customers leave. Use this learning to modify and improve internal processes and systems to help lessen customer defection.

CHAPTER TEN

How to Develop a Loyalty-Driven Culture in Your Company

When Doug Burgum bought Great Plains Software in Fargo, North Dakota, at the age of twenty-seven, he brought with him a unique perspective that originated from his summers as a kid working for his relatives' grain elevator business: "When you've got a grain elevator, the people you serve are landowners and they move the ownership of that land from father to son. My cousins are serving the grandsons of the people my grandfather served. That was the only business example I grew up with. You served customers for a lifetime. There was no such thing as a quick buck. When we bought Great Plains, [I] figured we had a great opportunity to build something where we'd instill in people that long-term mentality."[1]

Great Plains offers PC-based accounting systems that compete with those produced by the larger companies in Silicon Valley and other high-tech centers. With its North Dakota location, the company is a long way from those cities we associate with computer technology, but its success is generally attributed to Burgum's determination to build a loyal, long-term customer base. "Accounting is not a fad," he reminds us. "Nobody says, 'Gee, business is off; I think I'll stop keeping my books.' It's a fundamental thing you do in good times and bad. Our customers use this stuff for years and years. If you treat them right, you have them as long as they are doing accounting, so long as you listen to their needs and meet them."[2]

To listen to and meet those needs, Burgum began early on to compile a state-of-the-art customer list and turn it into the company's number one marketing weapon. Beginning in the early 1980s, the company designed into each user package a code that, after fifty transactions, blocked work. To unlock the software, customers were required to call Great Plains and get their individual ten-digit number that would serve as a key. When customers called in, the company registered them as users and asked about twenty research questions, including name, location, type of business, and company size. The company explained to the new users that by registering their name, Great Plains could contact them regarding any program changes, problems, or upgrades. The system continues today, and it is credited with enabling the company to have a database of every end user of its software—now numbering in the tens of thousands.

Timely callbacks were vital in offering quality technical support. "We had this policy of returning all calls the same day," said Burgum. "We'd fight to get them all done by 7:00 P.M. Central Time, but you'd end up leaving a lot of messages for people. That wasn't good enough. Given the pressures of accounting, the right answer a day or two late is the wrong answer."[3]

Beginning in 1987, Great Plains took a bold step and began guaranteeing response time to a customer call. The client was guaranteed a return call within one to three hours, depending on the terms of the service contract. A missed deadline meant the customer was given a $25 coupon, good for Great Plains products and services.

Soon after, Great Plains invested in a costly call distribution system that was bridged with the customer database. When users call, they are asked to punch in their ten-digit account number, enabling the system to determine who is calling, which software programs that user owns, and which technical support plan pertains. The call is then routed to a Great Plains technical specialist trained in those programs. Moreover, the specialist can identify how frequently the user has called, who handled past calls, and what advice was given over the past six months.

The new phone system and computer support program cost the company in excess of $1 million, but the results from the investment have been exemplary. The number of calls on a typical day averages eleven hundred, with more than half handled by a support specialist immediately. Since the guaranteed response was created, 99.13 percent have been returned on time; the record for the highest number of successive calls within the guarantee is a whopping 126,400.

Do customers appreciate the service? You bet. Thank-you letters, gifts, and flowers are a routine occurrence. "More than 30 percent of the referrals I get are from existing customers," says Bill Sorensen, a Great Plains dealer in Dallas. "So you know there are lots of satisfied users out there, and support has a lot to do with it."[4]

Great Plains is a company that understood from its inception that it had to find a way to establish an effective relationship with each customer. As its customer list grew from hundreds to thousands, the company was increasingly challenged with developing a system that would evoke loyalty. Sure, Great Plains was ahead of the game by marketing an accounting product that has natural, long-term loyalty-building properties, but Great Plains took these opportunities and leveraged them to the fullest. It began early on to pioneer a system that has evolved into what today is a state-of-the-art loyalty machine.

When you look at companies consistently building a loyal customer base, one common denominator surfaces time and time again: *each company consciously created a system for getting and keeping a customer.*

In this chapter, we examine the steps to building a loyalty system and examine how various businesses have initiated such steps to build a loyalty system in their company. In doing so, we pull together many of the concepts about individual customer stages that we have discussed in prior chapters to illustrate how such a system can work.

PREPARING TO BUILD YOUR LOYALTY SYSTEM

Creating a solid foundation for building loyalty requires some critical first steps.

Loyalty Measurement Factors

The first step in building a client loyalty system is to become familiar with the terminology and variables that define and drive loyalty.

- *Client base.* This is the total number of active customers and clients. You can calculate this number by adding together first-time customers, repeat customers, and clients. It is crucial that you count only customers and clients who are active and have made a purchase or contact with you recently enough to be considered current. Resist the temptation to include inactive customers and clients on this list. Be hard-nosed and brutally honest and include only current names.

- *New customer retention rate.* This represents the percentage of first-time customers who return for a second purchase within a specified period of time. The time period is governed by your typical customer's repeat purchase cycle. For example, in the hair salon industry there is typically no more than ninety days between salon visits; hence, to be classified as retained, a first-time salon customer would have to return for a second visit within a three-month time period.

- *Client retention rate.* This is the percentage of customers who have met a specified number of repurchases over a finite period of time. Continuing with the hair salon example, a person can be considered a client after having made five consecutive visits to the salon, with each visit falling within the average repeat purchase time frame of ninety days or less.

- *Share of customer.* This is the percentage of a customer's total purchases in a particular category of products and services spent with your company. A vendor has captured 100 percent share of a customer when he spends his entire budget for the vendor's products or services on that vendor. A salon whose customer buys all hair care services from the salon but purchases shampoo and styling products (also available at the salon) elsewhere has captured a 70 percent share of customer when 30 percent of his total hair care budget is spent outside the salon. At the highest level of loyalty, a company consistently wins 100 percent share of a customer.

- *Average number of new customers per month.* This is the average of number of first-time customers who buy from your company each month. Use a six-month span of time to calculate this figure.

- *Purchase frequency.* This is the average number of times a customer or client buys from you per year.

- *Average purchase amount.* This is the average amount paid for products and services at each purchase.

- *Attrition rate.* This is the average annual percentage of customers that are lost or go inactive for any reason, including dissatisfaction and relocation.

As a first step in building your loyalty system, calculate these variables and use them to establish goals and monitor the progress of your loyalty program.

Loyalty Program Basics

Your loyalty program should follow these eight steps:

1. Measure and track loyalty using the variables just outlined. Depending on your particular situation, it may be helpful to calculate a variety of rates, for example, total company retention, retention for each individual sales professional, and retention by account team or other group. Using these current rates as a base, set your customer retention objectives for the next five years. The same analysis could be done with share of customer, new customer retention rate, and so forth.

2. Introduce all company employees to the meaning and importance of client loyalty. If you have a small staff, you might choose to introduce this information in a meeting attended by all personnel. If yours is a larger company, consider other communication tools, such as division meetings, corporate newsletters, and training videos, for getting and keeping the word out. A discussion of both current and projected loyalty rates should be an important part of this communication. Begin monthly performance evaluations with employees who have direct customer contact. Use the loyalty measurement factors as a basis for the review.

3. Build customer and client loyalty goals into employee performance and compensation plans. Reward excellent and improving loyalty rates with employee bonuses and raises. Address any substandard or declining rate promptly. Set a time line for improvement and then train and coach employees accordingly. Release employees unable to meet loyalty goals.

4. Evaluate and review loyalty rates monthly. Consider posting rates in the employee break room or other place highly visible to employees. This can help reinforce the company's commitment to loyalty and motivate employees to strive for a superior level of retention.

5. Involve employees in developing and maintaining the loyalty program. Staff member input, recommendations, and ideas can play an important role in the program's success. It is no secret that employees are more likely to support a program they help put together. One way to accomplish this involvement is to set up an employee team to perform specific loyalty "duties," such as retention evaluation and first-time customer program review.

6. Assemble an assortment of marketing, selling, and customer care tools aimed at cultivating loyalty at each customer stage. Develop at least one critical loyalty program for each customer stage. Two examples are a new-customer welcome promotion that motivates the first-time customer to buy again, and a promotion for repeat customers that cross-sells other products and services.

7. Identify the five biggest customer loyalty breakers in your company (the "on hold" delays that callers often get when they call your business, an overly complicated return policy for items purchased, etc.) and develop a plan for eliminating them. Begin implementation immediately.

8. Continue to modify, fine-tune, and course-correct your loyalty system as you go. Time and hands-on experience are great teachers.

ASSEMBLING YOUR MARKETING, SELLING, AND CUSTOMER CARE TOOLS

Every successful loyalty plan is armed with carefully selected tools and techniques that drive results.

Learning from Your Customers, Your Counterparts, and Your Competitors

Harry Truman once said, "The things you don't know are the history you haven't read." The president probably had domestic and foreign policies in mind when he made that comment; he could just as easily have been talking about a company looking for a way to increase sales and loyalty. Answers to "What has worked for you in the past?" "What has brought in new business?" and "What have you found to be the best routes to the market?" are often found in your sales records.

Remember Joan Silver, of Reeves Audio Visual Systems, discussed in Chapter Seven? By analyzing invoices and purchase orders, she better understood the motivation behind her customers' purchases. Armed with these insights, she created effective new strategies for selling to large and small accounts.

Understanding your own sales history is just part of the system planning process. Looking outward to your counterparts and competitors can also be a great source of information. Seek new ideas by asking, "What has been working lately?" and "How are they dealing with the marketing challenges I'm facing?" These are just two of the questions that can help you garner new ways to meet your challenges in developing a loyal customer.

Several years ago, the livelihood of New England car dealers was jeopardized when their markets changed. Gone was the marketplace where buyers traded their car every eighteen to twenty-four months. With sharply increased car prices, the trade-in cycle increased to fifty months. Suddenly, the service department was no longer simply a necessary evil. Instead, it became a key profit component for the dealers' long-term survival.

What did the dealers do next? They looked around the country and discovered that other dealers were successfully offering "planned maintenance" programs of the sort created by John Fisher, a former Chrysler dealer. At the center of the program was a computer-generated coupon booklet for preventive maintenance. Each coupon was redeemable for a prearranged appointment with the dealer's service department.

The coupon booklet was designed around a loyalty-building strategy: encourage new car buyers to bring their cars in for regular check-ups. These regular visits helped a dealer build a long-term customer relationship while also establishing the service department as an important profit center. No significant up-front investment was required by the participating dealer, only a monthly service fee to Fisher, who in turn would process the coupons used and send owners a reminder of upcoming appointments.

By finding out what their competitors and peers were doing to increase business and cope with the changing habits of the market, these New England dealers were able to adjust their longtime practices to the new situation and continue to build a loyal customer base.

Evaluating Your Distribution Channel

When assembling your marketing, selling, and customer care tools for your loyalty system, you must be sensitive to all aspects of your distribution channel. For example, Du Pont turned StainMaster stain-resistant carpeting into the most successful new product introduction in its history by listening to everyone who helps get carpet to market. Early in the product development process, the director of Du Pont's flooring system division, Tom McAndrews, appointed a six-member committee made of representatives of the marketing, R&D, and financial departments. His mandate to the committee was that they constantly ask themselves, "How does what we're doing affect the customer?" Before the product was introduced, the committee spent three years in close coordination with retailers and mill operators, soliciting suggestions about how to price StainMaster and publicize its benefits to consumers.

As a result, Du Pont launched StainMaster with the company's largest advertising budget for a new product ever. In return, the product produced more than $2 billion in revenues and single-handedly revived industrywide carpet sales. McAndrews tells us "the key is, we looked at our customer as the entire distribution chain. You can't simply meet the needs of the end user."[5]

As you plan your loyalty system, start by outlining the distribution path by which your product or service goes to market; consider each member of the distribution path your "customer." For example, the beauty product distribution channel consists of distributors, retailers, and ultimately end users. Hair care and cosmetic manufacturers need to develop a sell-through plan to influence each component of their distribution channel.

To study this example, why, as a manufacturer, should you consider the distributor's customer stages? Or the retailer's customer stages? All the manufacturer really needs to do, you may argue, is sell the product to the distributor. After that, it's the distributor's responsibility. The reason you want to consider the loyalty development stages of others in your distribution channel is this: it is your opportunity to add value and nurture your customer's loyalty.

Holly Farms, a poultry company, found that its fully cooked chicken was a big hit with busy consumers. Not so with grocers who stocked it. Their complaint? The sale expiration date was too short, so they refused to stock it. In response, Holly Farms improved its packaging, thereby extending the expiration date. Sales doubled. With new sensitivity to its distribution channel, the company now makes a point of visiting store meat managers more often and sends them a quarterly newsletter, *Fresh News from Holly Farms*. All along the distribution chain, you have customers. At any point along the chain, a customer may decide to take the business elsewhere. It is wise, therefore, to try to keep all your customers happy and loyal, whether they are the ultimate users of your product or service or those who get the product or service to the final customer.

One of the thorniest issues out there today among channel partners is who owns the customer relationship. The Internet has wrought paranoia among middle men who fear the manufacturer will go direct to the customer. As a result, retailers and distributors are reluctant to share customer information with the manufacturer from concern that they'll be removed from the relationship and the resulting profits. This lack of cooperation among channel partners creates a lackluster customer experience, hobbling loyalty up and down the channel.

Vauxhall Motors, a UK-based division of General Motors, envisioned a better way. When 1998 research showed customers were growing increasingly unhappy receiving disconnected offers from various arms of the company, Vauxhall took action. It revamped a customer relationship management system originally used for direct mail marketing and converted it into a resource to be shared by all the channel partners (GM Card, GMAC financing, SureGuard Warranty, CGU Insurance, telemarketing and direct marketing agencies, and the dealers) that touched Vauxhall customers.

Next, Vauxhall streamlined all its outreach programs so that they addressed such predictable scenarios as warranty expiration, car servicing, insurance renewal, and refinancing. This allowed a customer meeting the scenario qualifications to receive all relevant offers bundled together into one coordinated pitch. For instance, a customer offer might read, "Your warranty is about to expire. Would you be interested in buying the warranty extension? And would you care to take your car in for servicing before the expiration?" Customers responded with gusto. Sales of warranty extension increased from 11 percent to 30 percent and dealers' service business increased an impressive 60 percent.[6]

With such striking success, most manufacturers in Vauxhall's position would have unabashedly charged dealers for using its CRM system and for the outbound calls made on behalf of the dealer. But not Vauxhall. The manufacturer wisely understood two realities: (1) it's the customer, not the vendor, that has the final word on the length and depth of the relationship; and (2) when a customer has a bad experience with a dealer it reflects badly on the manufacturer, and vice versa. This makes hoarding buyer information and attempting to control the customer relationship self-defeating behavior that leads to nothing more than an underserved, uninspired customer looking for the next supplier. Customer relationship guru Patricia Seybold says, "Customers value a blended channel strategy . . . they appreciate it when dealers and the manufacturer work together to provide a seamless customer experience."[7] That's why visionary players like Vauxhall are building loyalty with the end consumer by first working in tandem with their channel partners.

DEVELOPING A LOYALTY PLAN

After identifying all the groups in your distribution path, start to outline a plan for developing their loyalty by using the seven customer stages. It may be helpful to do this in the form of a chart, with channel of distribution down the left-hand side and customer stage across the top. Assuming the Holly Farms distribution channel comprises food broker, food store, and end user, then its loyalty planning chart could be organized as shown in Table 10.1.

Next, examine your current marketing, selling, and customer care tools; chart them beneath the stage or stages they address. This process helps you quickly identify stages you are currently addressing and those you are not. Do not assume that just because you have an existing program addressing a key customer stage, the program is sufficient in its present form. This is your opportunity to question every program that you do or do not have.

As a rule of thumb, a company needs at least one strong program for each distribution component and its corresponding customer stage. Remember that the average U.S. business expends six times more resources on capturing cus-

Table 10.1. Hypothetical Loyalty-Planning Chart for Holly Farms.

	Suspect/ Prospect	First-Time Customer	Repeat Customer	Client	Advocate	Inactive
Food broker						
Food store						
End user						

tomers than on keeping them, yet customer loyalty is worth, on average, ten times the price of a one-time purchase. Look closely at distribution of resources and consider whether you are allocating enough resources to the repeat-customer, client, and advocate stages.

When SuiteMark Hotels created a customer loyalty system for its five Westar hotel properties, the objective was to take various hotel influencers and convert them into loyal business providers. SuiteMark identified five key groups in the distribution channel: corporate travel arrangers, corporate trainers, travel agents, business and government travelers, and personal (nonbusiness) travelers. As with Du Pont's McAndrews, experience had taught SuiteMark to find a way to influence business at each level.

In creating the system, SuiteMark charted a miniature Profit Generator system for each identified market. To take the corporate travel arranger as an example, the challenge was, "What actions can we initiate to identify suspects, qualify prospects, turn prospects into first-time bookers, and turn first-time bookers into repeat bookers and then client bookers?"

In the case of SuiteMark, it was a matter of taking parts of a company's marketing, selling, and customer care programs that were already working and combine them with new programs. SuiteMark had already established an extensive frequent booker program called Westar Select. The Select program was designed to offer assistance and incentives to travel planners making reservations for a Westar property. The program included special promotions and incentives, a Select reservation hotline, Select member luncheon, Select newsletter, and a Select voucher system that regularly informed members of the number of Select Club points they had earned. These points were redeemable for special Westar hospitality and travel privileges. This program was already working well for the company and earned a position in the travel arranger conversion system.

Using the Profit Generator customer stages as a guide, SuiteMark evaluated which among the company's existing tools could be used within the Profit

Exhibit 10.1. Westar Hotels Loyalty Plan for Corporate Travel Arranger Market.

I. Turning suspects into prospects

1. Identify suspects
   Corporatewide sources
   • National reservations systems
   • Corporate telemarketing
   • Corporate sales program to key national accounts

   Property-specific sources
   • Site analysis
   • Visual survey of nearby business centers
   • Visits with property managers of nearby large commercial buildings
   • Chamber of commerce

   • Dunn's direct access "feeder city" list generation

2. Qualify suspects as prospects using qualification criteria
   • Average hotel volume per month
   • Who is traveling? Purpose?
   • Decision maker names and titles
   • Lodging facility/facilities currently used and rate
   • Under current contract? expiration?
   • Criteria used to select hotel
   • Who makes lodging decision?

II. Turning prospects into first-time customers

1. Send introductory direct mail package
2. Make telephone follow-up
3. Make initial sales call (introduce Select program to corporate accounts)
4. Schedule property tour
5. Conduct property tour
6. Send follow-up thank-you letter for taking tour
7. Establish ongoing sales call, frequency based on account volume classification

8. Send Select Club fulfillment package upon request of prospect (including newsletter distribution)
9. Send goodwill:
   Birthday card
   Thanksgiving card
   Westar annual birthday promotion
10. Repeat steps 7–9 until prospect turns into first-time customer

Generator system and what was missing. From that point, a detailed action plan was developed. Prewritten letters, questionnaires, telemarketing scripts, greeting cards, and other communications tools were created so the system user would simply have to insert the booker's name to customize the message.

A sample of the marketing and selling portions of SuiteMark's loyalty-building plan for the corporate travel arranger market segment is outlined in Exhibit 10.1. Notice how the steps for the repeat-customer and client stages are designed so that the communication is frequent, regular, and ongoing.

III. Turning first-time customers into repeat customers, clients, and advocates

1. Send new booker welcome letter
2. Conduct telephone questionnaire ("How'd we do?") after first visit
3. Make regular sales calls and telephone calls
4. Send monthly "Select Newsletter"
5. Send weekly Select points update
6. Send goodwill:
   Birthday card
   Thanksgiving card
   Westar annual birthday promotion
   "You're Our Favorite Client" card
7. Send mail-back questionnaire every six months
8. Repeat steps 3–7

IV. Making lost or inactive customers active again

1. Send "We miss you" card
2. Make follow-up telephone and/or sales call
3. Reevaluate the account based on information received in Step 2
4. Keep account in or remove it from active customer list
5. If active, proceed with steps 3–7 outlined in Part III

This system was designed to be supported by a personal computer or, if a computer is not available, to be tracked manually. The system user had a master schedule template for each account and would use it to track where the customer was in customer stage development. Since this target group was travel arrangers, reservations determined the movement of the account through the system. Letters, questionnaires, and forms were composed and formatted for easy retrieval and use.

SuiteMark's system is built upon one overriding reality. These marketing and selling action steps are meaningful and loyalty inducing only to the extent that they are coupled with excellent, consistent delivery of the customer's basic hotel needs (easy reservation making, prompt front desk check-in of guest, clean rooms, accurate billing, and so on). Without this operational excellence, these loyalty-building actions cannot be effective. With them, loyalty can flourish.

THE STRATEGY BEHIND THE LOYALTY SYSTEM

Benjamin Franklin once said, "Human felicity is produced not so much by great pieces of good fortune that seldom happen as by little advantages that occur every day." The philosophy behind the loyalty system is similar. Rather than depending on a miraculous happening or extraordinary, once-in-a-blue-moon feat, earn the customer's loyalty and goodwill by using a well-conceived, company-wide system that has effective frontline implementation.

In a speech about customer service, Stanley Marcus, the retired president of

Neiman Marcus, described a recent shopping experience to the management group of a major jewelry retailer. Marcus had accompanied a couple in search of jewelry on Fifth Avenue in New York. He later recounted:

> We passed a window, and my friend's wife said, "Gee, that's just what I want! It could have been made to order for me." It was a pair of earrings. We went in for her to try them on. We found the first salesman and said, "We want to see a pair of diamond earrings." And he said . . . "Well, I only sell gold earrings. If you want diamond earrings, go back there." He pointed. We went back and there were diamonds in the case, and my friend said to another salesman, "I want to see a pair of diamond earrings that are in the window." And he said, "Well, I don't sell earrings. I only sell bracelets. Over there."

Marcus continued:

> Finally, after being told that the guard was away at lunch and that the show window could not be unlocked for an hour, the customer left, wandered across the street to Arpel and Van Cleef, and purchased a $92,000 pair of earrings and, still later, a $675,000 necklace.
>
> So I told this story to the [management] group and said, "Are there any questions?" Somebody asked, "Would you mind telling us what store that happened in?" And I said, "Well, hold on to your seats! That happened at your store." Well, of course, you could feel the meeting suddenly disintegrate.[8]

An executive then rose and began reciting reasons the jeweler does not allow salespeople to move from department to department, to which Marcus responded, "You're thinking like a merchant, not a customer. A customer doesn't give a damn about your security. A customer wants to be satisfied. Because you have an antiquated system of locking cases and entrusting a key to one man, you lost maybe six hundred thousand dollars worth of business."

Thinking like a customer and not a merchant is the underlying premise of the customer development system. Outlined in Exhibit 10.2 is a summary of the focus and critical action steps for developing loyalty at each customer stage, explored in previous chapters. The parameters are further summarized in Figure 10.1.

With these foci and action steps as a guide, your challenge is to create marketing, selling, and customer care tools for your business that address each of these stages. Regardless of the product or service you are offering, these customer stages and strategies, modified to meet your particular situation, can help you build a loyalty system.

ADDITIONAL APPLICATIONS FOR THE PROFIT GENERATOR SYSTEM

Creating a customer conversion system for your business requires melding the operations of every department in your company. Accounting, manufacturing,

Exhibit 10.2. Loyalty Building Strategies by Customer Stage.

SUSPECT/PROSPECT
Primary focus: overcome suspect/prospect apprehension
Action steps

1. Project a leadership image.
2. Listen/look for buyer apprehension.
3. Address new buyer apprehension with
   - Empathy/encouragement
   - Client "success stories"
   - Free consultation offer
   - Product/service guarantees

FIRST-TIME CUSTOMER
Primary focus: meet/exceed new customer expectations
Action steps

1. Exceed new customer expectations.
2. Build a vision for return visits.
3. Say thank you for business.
4. Invite customer to return.

REPEAT CUSTOMER
Primary focus: provide value-added benefits with each repurchase
Action steps

1. Uncover/satisfy customer needs, using
   - Value-added visits
   - Cross-selling hooks
2. Sell your loyalty-building products and services.
3. Analyze any competitive purchases for permanent shifts or temporary lapses.
4. Seek regular customer feedback.

CLIENT
Primary focus: tailor service to the needs of the particular client
Action steps

1. Practice customized care. Look for ways to help customers "reinvent" themselves.
2. Don't take the customer's continued business for granted.
3. Let the client know it's smart to do business with you.
4. Seek input and feedback continuously.

Exhibit 10.2. (*continued*)

ADVOCATE

Primary focus: get clients to sell for you

Action steps

1. Encourage advocacy through letters of endorsement from clients, referral acknowledgments, and recommend-a-friend rewards.
2. Develop and regularly communicate with your network of clients and other business influencers.

LOST CUSTOMER OR CLIENT

Primary focus: develop "win back" plan based on inactivity diagnosis

Action steps

1. Detect inactivity as early as possible. Let the customer know that he or she is missed.
2. Activate special communication/purchase offers to woo customer take back.
3. If defection is certain, ask, "What can we do to win back your business?" and listen closely. Meet the customer's requirements, communicate changes, and ask for the business.
4. Be patient with the inactive customer. Stay in touch.

---

delivery, data processing, sales, marketing . . . all these functions must be united by one common denominator: to provide actions that directly or indirectly contribute to the company's ability to attract and keep customers. The importance of attracting and keeping a customer can sometimes seem remote to, say, an accounts payable clerk buried in administration and with no direct customer contact.

The Profit Generator system and its concept of customer stages is an opportunity for demonstrating to all employees where and how their contribution fits in the company's big picture of building customer loyalty. For example, the Profit Generator customer stages could be used

- In an employee handbook, to give all company employees a common language about the cultivation and care of customers
- To illustrate the role(s) each employee and his or her department plays in the company's system for "growing" a loyal customer
- In staff brainstorming sessions (how to get more prospects, how to turn repeat customers into clients, and so on)
- As a problem diagnostic tool; when sales are down, diagnose the problem by determining which customer stages are underperforming and how to improve them

Figure 10.1. The Evolution of Customer Loyalty.

Customer stage	Suspect/ Prospect	First-Time Buyer	Repeat Customer	Client	Advocate
Customer/ account profitability	Little to none		More		Greatest
Marketing/ selling objective	Attraction	Transaction	Develop relationship	Broaden relationship	Leverage relationship
Marketing/ selling strategy	Sell benefits	Deliver on benefits promised	Provide increasing value through service and support	Provide value beyond product or service	Provide value and get clients to sell for you
Cost of marketing/ selling		More		Less	
Knowledge of customer buying preference	Little		More		Greatest

PEOPLE POWER: THE LOYALTY SYSTEM NECESSITY

Employees are the critical ingredient in establishing and sustaining a company's loyalty culture. Here are some key reasons why.

Attitude Is Everything

Having a system to run on is important for building loyalty; procedures, guidelines, tracking systems, and communication materials are important tools that help the employee perform. But that's just part of the equation. The real success of your loyalty system is not just in having the right tools but in having those tools used by employees with a loyalty-driven attitude. Tommaso Zanzotto, American Express travel president, says, "When you want to increase customer satisfaction, technical training—how to write a letter to a card member, for example—is easy. The quantum leap comes from improving employees' attitudes."

If this attitude is not present, even the best-conceived system can break down. Consider Ruth Scherer's experience, as reported in the *New York Times*:

I go into a branch of one of America's leading banks to make a deposit. Hallelujah! No one is there but me and one teller. So I skip the roped aisle and go directly to her window. She lifts her eyes to mine. "Please get in line," she says. I'm bewildered. "Please get in line," she repeats. I look around. "What line? I'm the only one here." "You have to get in line before I can help you." She sighs with impatience.

Do I get nasty or shout? Do I explain that a line has two points or two people, and that I'm the only one there? No. I'm a mature woman.

I look at her. She looks at me. With check and deposit slip in hand, I go to the entrance of the roped aisle, walk between the ropes and turn to the right, then to the left, until I arrive at the front of "the line." I wait a few seconds. I almost don't hear her call, "Next."

The wrong attitude was also the culprit in the experience related by Murray Raphel about a supermarket near his home. The store's management, seeking to promote its friendly cashiers, ran a series of ads saying, "If one of our cashiers ever forgets to say 'Thank you, have a nice day,' we will give you one dollar."

A few weeks went by. Murray and his wife, Ruth, stopped at the store. They shopped for a few items and arrived at the checkout counter. After taking their money, the cashier handed over the change—minus the friendly greeting.

"A-ha!" Murray said. "You owe us a dollar."

"Why?" asked the bewildered cashier.

Murray, smiling, patiently explained the terms of the ad. The cashier smiled back. "I don't have to give you a dollar," she said. "That was last month's campaign."

Harvard Business Review editor Rosabeth Moss Kanter observes, "People at lower rather than higher organizational ranks make or break service strategies. No matter what strategy leaders inside the organization devise, what customers see is at the front line."[9] Effectively implementing strategy at the front lines is the true test of how a system is working.

It is estimated that 90 percent of all customer contact is through an organization's frontline employees. They must understand the company's goals and the role they play in meeting them. Nowhere is that understanding more critical than in implementing loyalty-building programs (frequent buyer program, cross-selling, life cycle promotion). The success of each program is tied directly to the skill with which the frontline employee implements it.

Early in my career, I was the marketing and sales director for AmeriSuites Hotels during its start-up phase. My staff and I had spent substantial resources to identify well-qualified frequent travelers and to mail them a free-night coupon to turn them into first-time customers. We had one hotel in the chain that was a particular challenge to market. It was hard to see from the interstate, and, to add to the problem, access to the hotel off the interstate was difficult. For this hotel, we needed every new guest we could get!

I got a call from the sales director at this location. He reported that a prospective guest had presented the coupon at the front desk but been turned away. It seemed that the coupon had expired the day before and, despite the fact that there were plenty of rooms available, the front desk would not honor it. The customer left angry and disappointed.

The incident taught me a valuable lesson: although I had communicated the mechanics of the promotion to the front line, I failed to successfully build a larger vision to the staff about why the program was in place and why customer loyalty was the result we were after. Had I built the bigger vision, the coupon would have been honored and, by acknowledging the expired date to the new customer, the hotel could even have earned additional points in winning repeat business.

Creating a Vision

No one understands the importance of communicating a vision throughout a company better than Southwest Airlines Chairman of the Board Herb Kelleher. Along with his CEO successor, James Parker, Kelleher oversees the bargain fare airline that is the fourth largest U.S. carrier, providing 90 percent of all discount air travel in America. Year-end results for 2000 marked Southwest's twenty-eighth consecutive year of profitability and ninth year of increased profits. In an industry notorious for lackluster bottom lines, Southwest stands tall. Here are some reasons.

There are twenty states in which the airline (based in Dallas) does not even operate. With a few exceptions, its route map is a constellation of short hops. The airline keeps costs down in a number of ways. For example, no Southwest flights can be booked through the industry's big reservation computers (travel agents must contact the airline directly). Since the mid-1990s, Southwest has moved aggressively to leverage the Internet for online passenger bookings. Approximately 30 percent of its passenger revenue for 2000 was generated by online bookings via Southwest.com (Terra Lycos, the largest global Internet network, found the Southwest Airlines site receives 50 percent more searches than any other airline). Southwest's cost per booking on the Internet is about $1. Compare that to other airlines, which are accustomed to depending on travel agents for bookings and pay $6 to $8 per booking. Would-be flyers keep returning to Southwest.com thanks in part to the 3.3 million people who subscribe to the airline's weekly Click 'n Save e-mails.

Regarding a Southwest flight itself, there is no first-class or preassigned seating. Meal service is not offered, since most flights are ninety minutes or less. Instead, passengers are served snacks and drinks.

Says regular Southwest passenger Richard Spears, vice president of a Tulsa oil research company, "Sure you get herded on the plane and sure you only get peanuts and a drink, but Southwest does everything they can to get you to the right place on time and that's most important."[10] Lots of folks feel that way, and the airline has posted healthy profits while other airlines post losses.

Southwest employees understand Kelleher's philosophy that "those planes aren't making any money while they're sitting on the ground," and they perform accordingly. Consider crew leader Wally Mills. Southwest Airlines Flight 944 from San Diego lands on time in Phoenix. It's 3:15 P.M. Mills and six crew members must have the plane turned around and on its way to El Paso by 3:30. "I think of this as a game," says Mills. "I like to play against the [gate agents] up there working with the people to see if we can beat them."[11]

To win that game, the crew leader needs the cooperation, enthusiasm, and energy of every member of his crew. Workers must unload the bags for Phoenix and reload bags going to El Paso. The drinks and peanuts consumed on the flight have to be replaced and the plane tidied up. Thousands of pounds of fuel have to be pumped into the huge gas tanks. Passengers are boarded and the plane is ready to take off.

Mills and his team have accomplished their task in less than fifteen minutes. Most other airlines take almost three times as long to do the same tasks. Southwest flies approximately twenty-eight hundred flights every day, and 80 percent of them have speedy turnarounds like this one.

Major airlines have suffered dramatic losses in the aftermath of the September 11, 2001, terrorist attacks. But while the rest of the U.S. airline industry was slashing jobs, cutting flights, and threatening bankruptcy, Southwest Airlines kept all its flight capacity, laid off no employees, added a new destination to its flying schedule, and posted a third-quarter profit. At this writing, airline travel remains sluggish. Yet, of the nine major carriers, Southwest is the only one to achieve any profit in first quarter 2002.

But recognition of fine financial performance is not the only kind of recognition Southwest routinely earns. The *Wall Street Journal* reported in spring 2001 that Southwest ranked first among airlines for the highest customer service, according to a survey by the American Customer Satisfaction Index. Moreover, the airline consistently ranks among the highest in the industry for on-time performance and fewest lost bags. It is not surprising that customers are pleased with Southwest's performance, and one of the major reasons the company performs so well is that it has enthusiastic employees.

Employees regularly praise the company and say it is a fun place to work (as well as a good place to work; in 2001, the company ranked number four, and first in the airline industry, in *Fortune*'s annual list of 100 Best Companies to Work for in America). The airline has always included an element of fun in its strategy, whether it be marketing or employee relations. An orientation video for new employees is set to rap music. Flight attendants have costumes for holidays, including turkey suits for Thanksgiving and reindeer antlers for Christmas. Chairman Kelleher himself is known for wearing outlandish outfits to put a laugh in a generally hectic business.

Employees are willing to work hard when they know they are important and appreciated. Legend has it that Kelleher knows every Southwest employee by name. He's not afraid to pitch in and help out either. Flight attendant Raelene Chilcoat reported that on one flight, Kelleher filled the glasses with ice while she took drink orders. The mechanics and cleaners' union head, Tom Burnett, reports that Kelleher has been known to come to the cleaners' break room at 3:00 A.M. to pass out doughnuts and put on overalls to help clean a plane.

The attitude of top management obviously affects everyone in a company. If this management group has a superior, hands-off attitude, it will extend to employees on down the line. If the head of the company is enthusiastic, appreciative, and upbeat, the employees are also likely to share that attitude. As mentioned in an earlier chapter, happy, positive employees are invaluable in growing happy, loyal clients. There is a direct connection between employees' attitude and how they deal with customers. As probably all of us know, a grouchy clerk can turn someone against an entire company.

PUTTING EMPLOYEES FIRST

Winning customer loyalty begins with winning staff loyalty. Here's why.

One Company's Hierarchy of Concerns

When Marcus Rosenbluth founded Rosenbluth Travel in 1892, his main service was helping Europeans immigrate to America. Once they were settled and got jobs, many of those same immigrants gave Rosenbluth five and ten cents at a time until they had saved the fifty dollars required to bring over another family member. From that modest beginning, the company has flourished. Today the Philadelphia-based company generates revenues of $5.5 billion and is one of the largest travel companies in the world.

Marcus Rosenbluth's great-grandson, Hal Rosenbluth, is now at the helm of the business, and he and his staff are busy reinventing the company to meet the customer-driven demands of today. After graduating from the University of Miami in 1974, Hal joined his dad at Rosenbluth. But he didn't start at the top or even in the middle; he started as a gofer, running errands and stamping brochures. A year or so later, he moved to the meetings department, and then gradually, by 1978, worked his way to head of the department.

Rosenbluth describes his observations from his first few years with the company: "What I saw was a tremendous focus on the customer, and it began to bother me that the focus so often created problems for our people. Everyone felt pushed to do heroic deeds for the client, which was fine in its way, except that the competition for hero status sometimes got a little out of hand. Booking agents competed. Vacation consultants fought over who got to sit at the desk nearest the entrance. People played up to the receptionist who directed calls. There was a lot of politics, a lot of scorekeeping, and a lot of stress.[12]

It was when Hal became involved in the business travel market that he truly learned what teamwork was all about. In contrast to the petty backbiting he had seen in other departments, the corporate travel agents worked with one another.

Airline deregulation brought opportunity to the travel market, and Rosenbluth Travel found ways to capitalize on it. Business travel expanded rapidly, and everyone at the company was working long hours, many spending ten to twelve hours a day at work. "I understood—for the first time during that period of rapid expansion—that the people in a company have to come first, even ahead of the customers," says Rosenbluth. "If your people aren't happy with their jobs, the customer will never be uppermost in their minds. When they ought to be focusing on the customer, they'll be thinking about their own frustrations."[13]

The true front liners in any travel agency are the agents. Commenting on the enormous day-to-day demands on these staff members, Rosenbluth explained, "They needed the nerves of an air traffic controller and the brains of a magna cum laude, but we'd been paying them as if they planted flowers." As a way to compensate agents more fairly, the company instituted a "pay for quality" program. The program is based 60 percent on accuracy, 20 percent on professionalism (going the extra mile for colleagues), and 20 percent on productivity (but only if the other two criteria are satisfied).

The pay-for-quality program increased individual agent take-home pay by 32 percent (while reducing the total payroll by 4 percent). Since people began doing things right the first time, the position defined as reworking mistakes was eliminated. Internal competition between coworkers was reduced. Moreover, the company experienced a decrease in turnover, training costs, and human resource expenses, while seeing an increase in productivity.

Rosenbluth concludes, "What we have is a hierarchy of concerns: people, service, profits. We focus on our people, our people focus on service, and profits result—a by-product, you might say, of putting our associates ahead of our customers. I know it sounds simplistic, but I know it works."[14]

Staff Feedback Can Point the Way

Look at any firm that successfully builds customer loyalty, and you'll likely find a firm that successfully builds employee loyalty as well. Generally speaking, a firm can never reach the pinnacle of customer loyalty without first building staff loyalty. Why? Because customers want to buy from people who know them and their preferences. Quite simply, staff turnover impedes customer loyalty.

So, how can a firm strengthen staff loyalty? Staff feedback surveys help. Progressive companies are finding real benefit to having employees give anonymous feedback on the company's (and manager's) performance as an employer. Just ask Marc Brownstein, the president of the family owned Brownstein Group, a small advertising and public relations firm in Philadelphia. For seven years, Marc led the twenty-plus-person agency founded by his father, Berny, who is still its chief executive. Business was flourishing, with the firm attracting new clients and boosting billings.

The only apparent fly in the ointment was a perplexingly high staff turnover rate that seemed stuck at around 30 percent. But that problem was about to grow clearer. In preparation for attending a four-day management seminar, Marc asked his department managers to complete anonymous surveys evaluating his performance as boss. When he opened the sealed surveys at the start of the class, the verdict was clear: managers rated him rather poorly. Problems cited were varied, but the root cause of many of the issues could be traced to poor communication and feedback between Marc and the agency's managers and staff.

So he went to work to improve communications. Within six weeks of his return from the seminar, he was conducting biweekly sessions with department heads and monthly meetings for the entire staff. These feedback sessions were productive and helped uncover another pressing need: staff wanted more say-so about decisions affecting their work. Ultimately, the Brownsteins conceded a big decision: the authority to decide which new accounts the firm should pursue and take on would be put to a managerial vote.

This change has greatly pleased employees and, at times, frustrated the son-and-father team. Take, for example, a marketing and research company looking for a firm to create a film profiling the business, an assignment that would have generated $1.5 million in revenue. Throughout the Brownstein Group, everyone agreed that a film wasn't the best use of the prospect's funds. What the company desperately needed was a marketing plan. But Berny Brownstein believed it was prudent to take the account and then try to "talk them into doing something more rational." The employees' vote, however, overruled Berny, and the agency passed. To this day, Berny still feels the account had merit, but he's delighted with Brownstein Group's overall results. Billings are at $24 million, the highest ever, and staff turnover, once a worrisome 30 percent, has been cut by half.[15]

KEEPING CUSTOMERS LOYAL:
THE ONLY CONSTANT IS CHANGE

Just like the world we live in, your loyalty system must be ever-changing. The particular methods you employ to earn loyalty today may need a major overhaul twelve months from now. You must keep modifying, upgrading, and changing your system to meet the changing demands of your marketplace and your customer.

As we have seen, there are no guarantees of loyalty. Unless you continue to provide value, as your customers define it, even the customers and clients who seem most loyal will eventually go elsewhere. Consider, for example, Stouffer's Lean Cuisine line (now owned by Nestlé), which celebrated its twentieth birthday in 2001. In the 1980s, Stouffer took bold steps to change the frozen food market, as it was known at the time. Through its Lean Cuisine brand, Stouffer offered products available from no other source: low-calorie, ready-to-cook dinners that actually tasted good. The success of the line was immediate and dramatic. Stouffer grabbed an 18.6 percent market share in a $3 million market, and the company expanded to twice its original size. Pleased and proud, Stouffer sat back to rest on its laurels.

But as we pointed out, everything changes. Profits and revenues began to drop, and before Stouffer realized what was happening, sales had fallen 27 percent. Executive Vice President Edward Marra attributed the loss to complacency. The company assumed that its loyal customers would stay loyal, but they did not. As Lean Cuisine succeeded, other companies came along to compete. Competitors offered equally delicious low-calorie meals, at better prices.

Marra understood the message that consumers were sending: "We were no longer a good value, and value had become increasingly important to consumers."[16] The company took steps to respond to the message. Prices came down, the product line was updated and reformulated, and profits began to rise again. In 1990, Stouffer again claimed the number one market share with its Lean Cuisine line, and profits increased fivefold.

Where is the brand today in response to the frozen food customer's definition of value? No longer are consumers simply interested in low calories and grams of fat. Now, nutrition is also important. Paul Bakus, Lean Cuisine's marketing director, says, "A lot of people still think of Lean Cuisine as a brand where you have to 'give up' something." Bakus reports that the brand's marketing and product development face-lift, begun in 2000, was aimed at getting consumers to "see us as a partner in efforts to lead a more healthy life."

Lean Cuisine's skillet meals extension, for example, was developed to bridge the brand with families. Bakus explains: "Lean Cuisine was pretty much a single-serve brand. We've been really successful at bridging the [family] gap with Lean Skillets." From recipe enhancements for most of the line to more meatless dishes and a packaging makeover featuring the new tag line "Do something for yourself," the brand is placing its marketing and product development emphasis on the second half of the brand name. Says Bakus, "We want to leverage the strong history of 'cuisine' to bring new products into the category. . . . We're still used as a 'diet' product. We will always play a role in that. [But] consumers continue to get better educated [about nutrition] and will continue to take more ownership of their own health. We have to stay on top of where [the consumer's] head's at."[17]

This staying on top of how consumers define value is also keeping brand revenues on top. For the fifty-two weeks ended mid-2001, Lean Cuisine sales were up an impressive 18.8 percent, the third consecutive year of double-digit growth for the brand.

Perhaps former Stouffer Chairman Stanley Gault has the best prescription of all for maintaining a loyalty clientele: "There's no magic formula for staying close to your customer. It's basic consideration, time, effort, commitment, and follow-up." Others have learned the same lesson; Doug Burgum of Great Plains Software, Joan Silver of Reeves Audio Visual Systems, Du Pont's Guy Anderson, and Hal Rosenbluth of Rosenbluth Travel have all discovered that the real solution to loyalty lies in creating an ever-changing system that develops and nurtures the loyal customer. Start right now to devise new ways to attract and keep customers. You can always find new solutions in the concept of customer stages and in the fact that loyalty is developed and earned one step at a time.

SUMMARY

- Measurement and tracking are crucial to every successful loyalty program.
- Incorporating customer and client retention goals into employee compensation is an important component of a loyalty system.
- Channel partners that share customer information typically create a better overall customer experience and in turn produce stronger customer loyalty throughout the channel.
- Businesses can learn how to keep customers loyal from their own past experience, from the customers themselves, and from the competition.
- Implementing a companywide loyalty system in phases is important in establishing a workable program.
- Before a company can engender loyal customers, it must have loyal employees who understand their role in the company's success.
- A successful strategy for building loyalty is not static. It must constantly be updated, improved, and adjusted as conditions and people change.

GETTING STARTED

- Ponder this: Which customer service vision is your staff truly acting upon? Don't just guess; find out. Use customer surveys, secret shopper services, 800-line call monitoring, customer e-mail reviews, and so on to get ongoing feedback about how customers are truly being served.
- Evaluate your customer relationship spending habits in relation to the customer loyalty stages. Most companies spend far more on the suspect, prospect, and first-time customer stages and substantially less on repeat customer, client,

advocate, and lost-customer stages. Avoid this trap by spreading your spending more evenly across the stages.

- Using the specific guidelines outlined in this chapter's section "Developing a Loyalty Plan," create a chart with distribution partners down the left side and customer stages across the top. Next, write in your current marketing, selling, and customer care programs that correspond to each distribution partner or customer stage. Question every program you do or do not have.

- Put this philosophy into practice: a company must first serve its staff if the staff is to serve customers. Think about how you can apply the stages of customer loyalty to staff loyalty: prospect, new-hire, one-to-three-year tenure, three-years-plus, and so on. Using these stages, consider your biggest staff defection points and how to improve staff retention.

The Twelve Laws of Loyalty

1. Build staff loyalty.

It's a fact: any firm with a high level of customer loyalty has also earned a high level of staff loyalty. It's darn near impossible to build strong customer loyalty with a staff that is in constant turnover. Why? Because customers buy relationships and familiarity. They want to buy from people who know them and their preferences. The key rule of loyalty: serve your employees first so they, in turn, can serve your customer.

Action step: Hold regular meetings with staff and ask these questions: What makes our company a good place to work? What can be done to make it an even better place to work? Take action on what you learn.

2. Practice the 80/20 rule.

In building customer loyalty, the 80/20 rule is alive and well. Roughly speaking, 80 percent of your revenue is being generated by 20 percent of your customers. All customers are not created equal. Some represent more long-term value to your firm than others. A smart company segments customers by value and monitors activities closely to ensure high value customers get their fair share of special offers and promotions. Unlike many firms that simply measure overall redemption, these savvy loyalty builders pay close attention to *who* redeems.

Action step: Rank your customers according to actual revenue generation, with your highest-ranking customer contributing the most revenue over the past year (or some other relevant time period). Next, rank your customers regarding lifetime value. If your company is like most, you must develop a lifetime value formula by which to calculate this value. Compare the two lists and make sure you are adequately investing in customer appreciation programs that provide for high-ranking customers on both lists.

3. Know your loyalty stages, and ensure your customers are moving through them.

A customer becomes loyal to a company and its products and service one step at a time. By understanding the customer's current loyalty stage, you can better determine what's necessary to move that customer to the next level of loyalty. Our Profit Generator loyalty system comprises six stages: suspect, prospect, first-time customer, repeat customer, client, and advocate. If your customer relationship processes and programs aren't moving customers forward, rethink them.

Action step: Using the customer loyalty stages outlined in this book as a guide, define loyalty for your customers (what distinguishes a repeat customer from a client in your particular business?). Using the customer lists you prepared with rule two, beginning with your highest-ranking customers identify which loyalty stage each customer is in. Next, create a customer action plan for moving that customer to the next higher level of loyalty.

4. Serve first; sell second.

Today's customers are smarter, better informed, and more intolerant of being "sold" than ever before. They expect doing business with you to be as hassle-free and gratifying for them as possible. When they experience good service elsewhere, they bring an if-they-can-do-it-why-can't-you? attitude to their next transaction with you. They believe you earn their business with service that is pleasant, productive, and personalized; if you don't deliver, they'll leave.

Action step: Using your customer list, identify those high-value customers that are most demanding. Next, isolate the needs, expectations, and requests that make these customers more demanding than others. Ask yourself: *What can we do to upgrade our systems and processes to better provide this high level of performance? Which of our other customers would likely benefit from these upgrades?* Let this thinking help guide your development priorities.

5. Aggressively seek out customer complaints.

For most companies, only 10 percent of complaints are ever articulated by customers. The other 90 percent are unarticulated and manifest themselves in many negative ways: unpaid invoices; lack of courtesy to your frontline service reps; and, above all, negative word of mouth. With the Internet, an unhappy customer can now reach thousands of your would-be customers in a few keystrokes. Head off bad press before it happens. Make it easy for customers to complain, and treat complaints seriously. Establish firm guidelines regarding customer response time, reporting, and trend analysis. Make employee complaint monitoring a key tool for executive decision making.

Action step: Review every customer touch point within your company. Brainstorm with staff on how to turn each customer touch point into an opportunity to capture customer complaints and other feedback. Experiment with how to make the feedback mechanism as easy for customers as possible.

6. Get responsive, and stay that way.

Research shows that responsiveness is closely tied to a customer's perception of good service. The advent of the Internet has changed the customer's perception of responsiveness. More and more, customers are coming to expect round-the-clock customer service. Additionally, customers now arrive at a Website time-starved and eager to locate answers. Technology tools such as customer self-service, e-mail management, and live chat and Web callback are proving increasingly critical in addressing the demanding customer's responsiveness needs.

Action step: Review all customer touch points and identify any area that produces a responsiveness bottleneck. Prioritize these areas, with highest priority given to those affecting the most customers. Put ongoing improvement processes in place to raise response standards.

7. Know your customer's definition of value.

The loyalty password is *value*. Knowing how your customer experiences value and then delivering on those terms is critical to building strong customer loyalty. But knowing your customer's true definition of value is not easy because value definitions are constantly changing. Invest in customer loyalty research that enables you to understand, through the eyes of the customer, how well you deliver value.

Action step: Review your company's current knowledge base regarding what your customers value. Look for these insights: (1) What is it about your products or services that drives loyalty today? (2) Which product or service areas most need improvement? (3) Where are you currently overinvesting? (4) Which areas deserve more study for potential future investment? Does this four-point review uncover knowledge gaps? Value-based loyalty research can help.

8. Win back lost customers.

Research shows that a business is twice as likely to successfully sell to a lost customer as to a brand new prospect. Yet winning back lost customers is frequently the most overlooked source for incremental revenue in many firms. Why? Because most firms consider a lost customer a lost cause. With the average company losing 20–40 percent of customers every year, it's imperative that a firm create a hard-working strategy, not only for acquisition and retention but also for winback. Since no customer retention program can be 100 percent foolproof, it follows that every company needs a process for recapturing those high-value customers who depart. Think of it as loyalty insurance.

Action step: Review your company processes and identify which programs, if any, are in place for winning back lost customers. If a program exists, carefully monitor results and look for a way to consistently increase the number of lost customers regained. If no program exists, begin immediately to identify lost customers and use this book's seven-step process to win them back.

9. Use multiple channels to serve the same customers well.

Research suggests customers who engage with a firm through multiple channels exhibit deeper loyalty than single-channel customers. But take note: this finding assumes the customer gets the same consistent service whether coming into the store, logging onto the Website, or calling the service center. To accomplish this, your firm must internally coordinate sales and service across multiple channels so that customer preferences are accessible no matter how the customer chooses to interact. Today's customers expect to hop from channel to channel, and they expect good service to follow.

Action step: Using customer feedback as well as formal customer research processes, monitor customer performance levels for every channel. Isolate a sample of customers who have experience with two or more of your channels and carefully measure their perception of your cross-channel value delivery. Things to watch for: in your customer's eyes, are you providing equal service in each channel? Is one channel preferred over another? Why?

10. Give your front line the skills to perform.

Increasingly, the employee front line is a call center where agents interact with customers. These agents are the loyalty warriors of the future. Converged call centers that bring together multichannel access points (phone, fax, e-mail, Web) are on the rise. Gartner Group estimates that 70 percent of North America's call centers will migrate to multichannel contact centers by 2005. This means these agents need to be equipped as much to produce a well-written e-mail reply and navigate the company Website as to be helpful and friendly on a phone call.

Action step: Review your hiring policies for frontline workers to ensure candidates are being screened for adequate communication skills, especially oft-missing writing skills. Consider making a writing test part of your screening tool.

11. Collaborate with your channel partners.

In today's complex marketplace, a firm is often dependent on many suppliers to help serve its customers. Embracing these supply chain relationships for the greater good of the ultimate customer creates customer value that is hard for competitors to match. For example, a European auto manufacturer converted its customer database program into a system that could be shared by all channel partners. By refusing to hoard the information, the manufacturer helped create a blended-channel strategy that built greater customer loyalty throughout the distribution chain.

Action step: Contact your suppliers routinely and ask them, "If you could change one thing about the way we do business together that in turn creates better value for the customer, what would it be?" Use this feedback to steadily improve channel partner collaboration.

12. Store your data in one centralized database.

Most firms lack a 360 degree view of their customers because they have no centralized database. Billing departments, sales divisions, and customer service centers might all have their own database, with no effective means for creating a complete customer information composite. To effectively implement a sound customer loyalty strategy, data from all customer touch points must be combined into a centralized customer database. Without it, the firm is greatly handicapped in its efforts to serve the customer.

Action step: Review your company's current database situation. How many customer databases exist? For example, does each sales rep keep her own customer database? Does each department keep its own? Brainstorm with staff on how to start consolidating the databases, with the ambitious goal of moving to one centralized database over time.

Next Step: Check Your Loyalty I.Q.

Log on to www.loyaltysolutions.com. Click on "Test Your Customer Loyalty I.Q." and answer some quick questions that measure your *current* loyalty implementation effectiveness. You'll learn how you rate on putting the Laws of Loyalty to work and where to focus to start improving—fast!

References

Chapter One

1. Patton, S. "The Truth About CRM: What You Need to Fight the Hype." *CIO*, May 1, 2001, pp. 77–85.

2. Rosenspan, A. "Delusions of Loyalty: Where Loyalty Programs Go Wrong." *Direct Marketing*, Feb. 1998, p. 24.

3. Stum, D., and Thiry, A. "Building Customer Loyalty." *Training and Development Journal*, Apr. 1991, p. 34.

4. Reichheld, F. F. "Loyalty-Based Management." *Harvard Business Review*, Mar.–Apr. 1993, p. 71.

5. Fay, C. "Can't Get No Satisfaction? Perhaps You Should Stop Trying." (White paper.) Wilton, Conn.: Juran Institute, n.d.

6. Fay (n.d.).

7. Peterson, R. A., and Wilson, W. R. "Measuring Customer Satisfaction: Fact and Artifact." *Journal of the Academy of Marketing Sciences*, Winter 1992, p. 6.

8. Peterson and Wilson (1992), pp. 65–67.

9. Fay (n.d.), p. 5.

10. Fay (n.d.).

11. Brown, P. B. "Return Engagements." *Inc.*, July 1990, pp. 99–100.

12. Brown (1990), p. 99.

13. Skip King, telephone interview, Sept. 27, 2001; "Leslie B. Otten Resigns; William J. Fair Named CEO of American Skiing Company." Mar. 28, 2001. (www.peaks.com/html11/pressreleastemplate.html?prnum = 43).

14. Reichheld, F. F., and Sasser, W. E., Jr. "Zero Defections: Quality Comes to Services." *Harvard Business Review,* Sept.-Oct. 1990, p. 110.

15. Fornell, C. "A National Customer Satisfaction Barometer: The Swedish Experience." *Journal of Marketing,* Jan. 1992, p. 12.

16. Brown (1990), pp. 99–100.

17. Reichheld and Sasser (1990), p. 65.

18. Reichheld and Sasser (1990).

19. MBNA Company Profile. (www.mbna.com/about_company.html)

Chapter Two

1. "Consumer Wariness May Spark Recession". *Austin American Statesman,* Sept. 10, 2001, pp. A1–A2.

2. "Fed Up with Airlines, Business Travelers Start to Fight Back." *Wall Street Journal,* Aug. 28, 2001, p. 1A.

3. Brown (1990), pp. 99–100.

4. Dick, A. S., and Basen, K. "Customer Loyalty: Toward an Integrated Conceptual Framework." (White paper.) *Journal of the Academy of Marketing Science,* Spring 1994, *22*(2), 99.

5. Case, J. "A Business Transformed." *Inc.,* June 1993, pp. 84–91.

6. Case (1993).

7. "Relationship Management Report: Going Multi-Channel: What's the Business Impact?" Accessed Aug. 17, 2001. (www3.ncr.com/product/publications/crm14/article1.html)

8. "Fast Talk." *Fast Company,* Sept. 2001, p. 84.

9. Robinson, B. "A Tradition of Service at Nordstrom." July–Aug. 2001. (http://resources.cisco.com/app/tree.taf?asset_id = 57618)

10. Robinson (2001).

11. Mount, I. "Marketing." *Business 2.0,* Aug.–Sept. 2001, p. 84.

Chapter Three

1. Larson, E. "Strange Fruits." *Inc.,* Nov. 1989, pp. 80–88.

2. Stum and Thiry (1991).

3. "The Ride's the Thing." *Newsday* (Nassau and Suffolk edition), Dec. 7, 1992.

4. Khan, M. A. "Harley: Site Won't Leave Dealers in Dust." *iMarketing News,* Feb. 7, 2000, p. 1.

5. Pruden, D. "How to Win Back Lost Customers." *Direct Marketing to Business Report,* Oct. 1995, p. 7.

6. Reichheld and Sasser (1990), p. 105.

7. Richman, T. "Come Again." *Inc.,* Apr. 1989, pp. 177–178.

8. Richman (1989).

9. Brown, P. "A Bird in the Hand." *Inc.,* Aug. 1989, pp. 114–115.

10. Rapp, S., and Collins, T. *MaxiMarketing.* New York: McGraw-Hill, p. 213.

11. Kaneshige, T. "Who's Buying My Stuff?" Line56.com, Feb. 15, 2001. (www.line56.com/articles)

12. Clancy, K. J., and Shulman, R. S. *The Marketing Revolution.* New York: HarperBusiness, p. 136.

Chapter Four

1. Advertisement reproduced in McCarthy, J. *Basic Marketing.* Homewood, Ill.: Irwin, 1975, p. 396.

2. Swanson, E. "Permission Marketing: The New Campaign Tactic." *Journal of Marketing Research,* 2000, *21*(9), 50.

3. "What a Sales Call Costs." *Sales and Marketing Management,* 1998, *15*(13), **42.**

4. Gupta, U. "Costly Marketing Research Pays Off for Biotech Start-Up." *Wall Street Journal,* Aug. 2, 1993, p. B2.

5. Jeff Hoogendam, interview, Oct. 2001.

6. Steve Tran, interview, June 27, 1990.

7. Tran (1990).

8. Schrage, M. "Fire Your Customers." *Wall Street Journal,* Mar. 16, 1992, B2.

9. Greco, S. "Choose or Lose." Inc., Dec. 1, 1998. (www2.inc.com/search/1039-print.html)

10. Tierney, M. "Marketers Push the Envelope Aside." *Austin American Statesman,* Feb. 10, 2002, pp. J-1, J-8.

11. Clark, M. "Putting the Heart Back in Retailing." *Retailing Issues Letter* (Center for Retailing Studies, Texas A&M University), Jan. 2001, p. 2.

12. Lindeman, T. "Former Payless Chief Hits Pay Dirt with Build-A-Bear." Post-gazette.com, Aug. 3, 2001. (www.post gazette.com/businessnews/20010803bears080bnp1.asp)

13. Clark (2001), p. 2.

14. "Putting the Heart Back in Retailing." Arthur Andersen, Center for Retailing Studies, Jan. 2001, *13*(1).

15. Gaffney, J. "How Do You Feel About a $44 Tooth-Bleaching Kit?" *Business 2.0,* Oct. 2001, p. 126. Copyright 2001 Time Inc. All rights reserved.

16. Gaffney (2001), p. 127.

17. Gaffney (2001), p. 127.

18. Hilliker, K. "Hair Is Big in Dallas and That Troubles Roger Thompson." *Wall Street Journal,* Dec. 29, 1991, p. A8.

19. Hilliker (1991).

20. Laundy, P. "Image Trouble." *Inc.,* Sept. 1993, p. 81.

21. Laundy (1993), p. 80.

22. Laundy (1993), p. 82.

23. "Social Performance Report." Oct. 10, 2001. (www.benjerry.com/socialmission/00socialaudit/letter00.html)

24. Infusino, D. "Brash and Bold." *Profiles,* May 1993, p. 36.

25. Laundy (1993).

26. Myerson, A. R. "This Man Wants to Bury You." *New York Times,* Aug. 1, 1993, sec. 1, p. 1.

27. *Auto Week,* Aug. 19, 1991, p. 10.

28. Fried, J. "Prospects Are Expensive, So Give a Damn." *Furniture Advantage,* Nov. 1988, p. 1.

29. Drawn from Morgan's selling seminar for real estate agents, Austin (Tex.) School of Real Estate, Sept. 1990.

Chapter Five

1. Graham, J. "Competitive Advantage" (newsletter). Aug. 1991, p. 5.

2. O'Connell, W., and Keenan, W., Jr. "The Shape of Things to Come." *Sales and Marketing Management,* Jan. 1990, p. 37.

3. Lant, J. *Money Making Marketing.* Cambridge, Mass.: JLA, 1987.

4. "Painting a Sales Portrait." *Success,* May 1990, p. 35.

5. Peters, T. "60 Minutes" (audiotape). Chicago: Nightingale-Conant, 1987, side 1.

6. Caroll, P. "Sales Detectives: How to Exploit the Information Edge." *Success,* May 1990, p. 43.

7. Barrera, R. "A Direct Approach to Sales Prospecting." *Small Business Reports,* Oct. 1990, p. 34.

8. "Keeping Customers: Case Studies in Online Permission Marketing." *Seybold Report on Internet Publishing,* 2000, *5*(3), 9.

9. "Go out of Your Way." *Creative Selling Newsletter,* 3.

10. Ann Machado, interview, Sept. 2001.

11. Kringle, P. C. "Training Salespeople to Sell Services." *Sales Training,* May 1989, p. 14.

12. Nichols, R. G., and Stevens, L. *Listening to People.* New York: McGraw-Hill, 1957.

13. "Through the Customer's Eyes." *ANA/The Advertiser,* Fall 1991, p. 59.

14. Ozer, J. "Roadmap to the Sale." *Competitive Advantage,* Mar. 1992, p. 4.

15. Azar, B. "Be a Sales Doctor." *Success,* Dec. 1989, p. 24.

16. Azar (1989).

17. "Learn to Think Like a Sales Doctor." *Competitive Advantage,* Aug. 1992, p. 8.

18. Burck, C. "Launching in a Storm." *Fortune,* Aug. 9, 1993, p. 93.

19. Anderson, G. "Tale of the Sale." *Selling Advantage Newsletter,* 1993, p. 3.

20. "What Are the Shared Qualities of Top Sellers?" *Selling Advantage Newsletter,* 1993, p. 2.

21. Lamers, T. "Lost Job Survey." *Inc.,* Apr, 1992, p. 78.

22. Lamers (1992).

Chapter Six

1. Shapiro, R. "One Step Ahead." *Boardroom Reports,* Sept. 15, 1992a, p. 5.

2. Shapiro, M. "Business Joke of the Week." *Austin American Statesman,* Business section, p. B1.

3. "Complaint posting." Downloaded Nov. 15, 2001. (http://us1.complaints.com/read?2250,502)

4. Shapiro, B. P., Rangan, V. K., and Sviokla, J. J. "Staple Yourself to an Order." *Competitive Advantage Newsletter,* [n.d.] p. 3.

5. Shapiro, Rangan, and Sviokla.

6. Teal, T. "Service Comes First: An Interview with USAA's Robert F. McDermott." *Harvard Business Review,* Sept.–Oct. 1991, p. 119.

7. Teal (1991), p. 126.

8. Teal (1991), p. 120.

9. David Travers, interview, Nov. 16, 2001.

10. Shein, E. "The Knowledge Crunch." *CIO,* May 1, 2001, pp. 128–132.

11. Belk, R. "Situational Variables and Consumer Behavior." *Journal of Consumer Research,* Dec. 1975, p. 157.

12. Walther, G. "Reach out to Accounts." May 1990, p. 24.

13. Goodman, J. "Customer Education." *Boardroom Reports,* Apr. 15, 1992, p. 9.

14. "Doctor's Letters Are Linked to Patient's Satisfaction." *Wall Street Journal,* Oct. 11, 1991, p. B2.

15. Potter-Brotsman, J. "The New Role of Service in Customer Retention." *Forum,* Summer 1993, p. 10.

16. Potter-Brotsman (1993).

17. Honeycomb, J. "Insiders Guide to Key Elements of a Complete Internet Customer Service Solution." (White paper.) Bozeman, Mont.: RightNow Technologies, 2001.

18. "California Chamber of Commerce: Helping Business Help Itself." (White paper.) RightNow Technologies, 2000. (www.rightnow.com/resources/casestudy)

19. Honeycomb (2001).

20. Wallace, B., and Hume, G. "The Modern Call Center". *Information Week,* Apr. 9, 2001.

21. Griffin, J. "Deliver Superior Service: Give Customer-Service Agents the Skills They Need to Succeed in Multi-Channel Contact Centers." *IQ* (Cisco.com), Jan.–Feb. 2002.

22. Griffin (2002).

23. Laurie Garvey, interview, Aug. 20, 2001.

24. Garvey (2001).

25. Raphel, M. *Mind Your Own Business.* Atlantic City, N.J.: Raphel Marketing, 1989, p. 91.

26. "Jet Set Service." smartbusinessmag.com, June 2001.

27. Drawn from letter to customer from Allcounty Plumbing and Heating.

28. Worthen, B. "Rock in a Hard Place." *CIO,* May 1, 2001, pp. 114–124.

29. "A Mail Campaign Helps Saab Find and Keep Its Customers." *Wall Street Journal,* June 21, 1993, p. B1.

30. "Guru Watch." *Inc.,* Mar. 15, 1997. (www2inc.com/search/12107.html)

31. Upton, H. "Do They Understand What You Do?" *Spirit,* Jan. 1992, p. 38.

32. Mandel, M. "Shrewd Thinking." *Boardroom Reports,* May 1, 1993, p. 16.

33. Shapiro, R. "Retaining Profitable Customers: A Targeted Approach." Paper presented at QUIS 3 conference, University of Karlstad, Sweden, June 16, 1992b.

34. Shapiro (1992b).

35. Finegan, J. "Survival of the Smartest." *Inc.,* Dec. 1993, p. 88.

36. Smothermon, R. *Winning Through Enlightenment.* San Francisco: Context, 1980, p. 137.

Chapter Seven

1. LaBarre, P. "Leader—Feargal Quinn." *Fast Company,* Nov. 2001, p. 88. Copyright 2001 by Bus Innovator Group Resources/Inc. Reproduced with permission of Bus Innovator Group Resources/Inc. in the format trade book via Copyright Clearance Center.

2. LaBarre (2001).

3. Treacy, M., and Wiersema, F. "Customer Intimacy and Other Value Disciplines." *Harvard Business Review,* Jan.–Feb. 1993, p. 85.

4. Brown, P. B. "Paper Trail." *Inc.,* Aug. 1990, p. 113.

5. Pitt, L. F., Ewing, M. T., and Berthon, P. "Turning Competitive Advantage into Customer Equity." *Business Horizons,* Sept.–Oct. 2000, p. 14.

6. "Targeting Your Best Customers." *Inc.,* Dec. 1992, p. 25.

7. Hyatt, J. "Ask and You Shall Receive." *Inc.,* Sept. 1989, p. 93.

8. Hyatt (1989).

9. Our "loyalty compass" research process is discussed in greater detail in my book *Customer WinBack: How To Recapture Lost Customers and Keep Them Loyal,* which I cowrote with Michael Lowenstein, my research colleague. (You can also learn more about this process on my Website, www.loyaltysolutions.com.)

10. Greco, S. "The Best Little Grocery Store in America." *Inc.,* June 1, 2001. (www2.inc.com/search/22701-print.html)

11. Greco (2001).

12. "Digital Loyalty Networks: e-Differentiated Supply Chain and Customer Management." Deloitte Research Study. Accessed Sept. 15, 2001. (www.dc.com/obx/pages.php?Name = dln.loyatly&report = dln&App = printable)

13. Levinson, M. "Harrah's Knows What You Did Last Night." *Darwin,* May 2001, pp. 61–78.

    Davis, Lisa E. "It's in the Cards." *Teradata,* Spring 2001, pp. 11–17.

14. Walter Janowski, interview, Jan. 5, 2002.

15. Breda, S. G. "Empowerment." *Travel Counselor,* Mar. 16, 1992, p. 44.

16. Breda (1992).

17. Breda (1992).

18. Armstrong, L. "The Customer as Honored Guest." *Business Week* (annual quality issue), 1991, p. 104.

Chapter Eight

1. Phillips, M., and Rasberry, S. *Marketing Without Advertising.* Berkeley, Calif.: Nolo Press, 1986, p. 1:8.

2. Fenster, B. "The New Auteurs." *Harper's,* June 1991, p. 34.

3. Fenster (1991).

4. Fenster (1991).

5. Weingarten, M. "Get Your Buzz to Breed like Hobbits." *Business 2.0,* Jan. 2002, pp. 96–97.

6. "'Rings' Lords over Box Office." *USA Today,* Dec. 27, 2001, p. 2-D.

7. Weingarten (2002), p. 97.

8. Phillips and Rasberry (1986), 1:6–1:7.

9. Brown, P. Y. "The Real Cost of Customer Service." *Inc.,* Sept. 1990, p. 50.

10. "Making Money out of Mellow." *New York Times,* May 4, 1986, p. B1.

11. "Making Money . . ." (1986).

12. "The Sound of Success." *Washington Post,* Apr. 24, 1983, p. H1.

13. "Making Money . . ." (1986).

14. "The Sound of Success" (1983).

15. Brown (1990).

16. Brown (1990), p. 90.

17. Case, J. "Customer Service: The Last Word." *Inc.*, Apr. 1991, p. 90.

18. Case (1991).

19. Chris Rapetto, telephone interview, Dec. 12, 2001; and www.intuit.com/company/press_room/fast_facts.

20. Case (1991), 92.

21. Mount (2001), p. 84.

22. Agins, T. "Clerking at Stein Mart Is a Society Lady's Dream Come True." *Wall Street Journal,* Dec. 2, 1992, p. Al.

23. Agins (1992).

24. Hawk, Amanda. "Intranet Gives ACE a Winning Hand." *Retail Info Systems News,* Nov. 2000. (http://www.risnews.com/issue/nov_e_internet_gives.htm)

25. Kelly, Joanne. "The Right Tool: Ace Hardware's Online Community Makes Dealers Far More Productive." *Context,* Dec-Jan. 2001. (http://www.contextmag.com/archives/200012/Feature2TheRightTool.asp)

26. Cothrel, Joseph. "Half a Mill: Online 'Sales Community' Seals the Deal." SAM, Nov. 2001. (http://www.sammag.com/articles/printable.cfm?issue_styles_id = 30&item_id = 117)

27. Kelly (2001).

28. Hawk (2000).

29. Neuborne, Ellen. "How Commercial Communities Can Click." *BusinessWeek Online,* May 7, 2001. (http://www.businessweek.com/technology/content/may2001/tc2001057_248htm.)

30. Neuborne (2001).

31. Considine, R., and Raphel, M. *The Great Brain Robbery.* Altadena, Calif.: GBR, 1980.

32. Wernle, B. "Food for Thought: Restaurants Keep in Touch with Diners Via Newsletter." *Data Courier,* Dec. 17, 1990, sec. 1, p. 3.

33. Wernle (1990).

34. Griffin, G. "Dissecting a Successful Newsletter." *Graphics Art Monthly,* Oct. 1992, p. 102.

35. Griffin (1992).

36. Garfinkel, D. "CRM: Online Newsletters." SALES and MARKETING.com, Oct. 10, 2001. (http://209.11.43.223/salesandmarketing/headlines/article_display.jsp?vnu_content _id = 1058444)

Chapter Nine

1. Peters, T. In *Thriving on Chaos.* New York: HarperCollins, 1987, p. 120.

2. Bailey, J. "Why Customers Trash the Garbage Man." *Wall Street Journal,* Mar. 17, 1993, p. B1.

3. Greco, S. "Winning Back a Lost Customer." *Inc.,* Sept. 1993, p. 25.

4. Greco (1993).

5. Goldzimer, L. "Business Through Customer Feedback." *America West,* Sept. 1989, p. 87.

6. Welles, E. O. "How're We Doing?" *Inc.,* May 1991, p. 80.

7. Hanan, M., and Karp, P. *Customer Satisfaction.* New York: AMACOM, 1989, p. 157.

8. Jacqueline S. Gold, "Customer Service," *Financial World,* September 28, 1993, 56.

9. Gold (1993).

10. Greco, S. "Every Employee a Service Rep." *Inc.,* Nov. 1993, p. 123.

11. Technical Assistance Research Programs. "SOCAP 800 Number Study: A 1992 Profile of 800 Numbers for Customer Service." (Reprinted.) *Inc.,* June 1993, p. 30.

12. Brown, P. "For You, Our Valued Customer." *Inc.,* Jan. 1990, p. 109.

13. Judge, P. C. "Customer Service: EMC Corp." *Fast Company,* June 2001, p. 138.

14. Griffin, J. "Develop a Win-Back Strategy." *iMarketing News,* Mar. 26, 2001, p. 13.

Chapter Ten

1. Finegan, J. "Taking Names." *Inc.,* Sept. 1992, p. 122.

2. Finegan (1992).

3. Finegan (1992), p. 125.

4. Finegan (1992), p. 126.

5. "Getting Customers to Love You." *Fortune,* Mar. 13, 1989, p. 48.

6. Seybold, P. "You're Not the Boss of Me." *Darwin,* Sept. 2001, pp. 32–34.

7. Seybold (2001), p. 34.

8. Seal, M. "Life of a Salesman." *Inc.,* Dec. 1992, p. 175.

9. Kanter, R. M. "Service Quality: You Get What You Pay for." *Harvard Business Review,* Sept.–Oct. 1991, p. 8.

10. O'Brian, B. "Southwest Airlines Is a Rare Air Carrier: It Still Makes Money." *Wall Street Journal,* Oct. 26, 1992, p. 1A.

11. O'Brian (1992), p. 11.

12. Rosenbluth, H. "Tales from a Non-Conformist Company." *Harvard Business Review,* July–Aug. 1991, p. 27.

13. Rosenbluth (1991), p. 28.

14. Rosenbluth (1991), p. 33.

15. Stout, H. "Self-Evaluation Brings Change to a Family's Ad Agency." *Wall Street Journal,* Jan. 6, 1998, p. B2.

16. Schlossberg, H. "Markets Changing as Never Before." *Marketing News,* Apr. 12, 1993, p. 7.

17. "Stouffers Lean Cuisine Soaring." *Frozen Food Age,* Feb. 2001, p. 44.

Company Index

Subject Index

JILL GRIFFIN WANTS YOUR STORIES

WHAT ARE YOUR TRIED-AND-TRUE WAYS FOR WINNING CUSTOMER LOYALTY?

The good news about the Profit Generator® System and its customer development stages is that they can serve perpetually as your strategic blueprint for building customer loyalty. But just as this edition of *Customer Loyalty* adds new techniques for each of the customer loyalty stages, there remain many more ideas and experiences to uncover and share. That's where your help will be invaluable.

I'd like to hear about your loyalty-building successes (and headaches). For example, do you have favorite ways for turning suspects into prospects? Prospects into first-time customers? Repeat customers into clients? Clients into advocates? Saving at-risk customers? Returning inactive or lost customers to "active" status? What's the single biggest discovery you have made about earning customer loyalty? Biggest disappointment? Funniest experience?

How about employee loyalty? Do you have a tried-and-true way for turning new hires into committed team members? Saving top performers on the verge of defection? Wooing back a former employee?

Write up your thoughts, please, and send them to me:

Jill Griffin
The Griffin Group
2729 Exposition Blvd.
Austin, TX 78703
Fax: 512–482–0022
E-mail: jill@loyaltysolutions.com
Web: www.loyaltysolutions.com

Please make sure you include a mailing address and a telephone number. If I'm interested in including your example in my next book, I'll contact you for permission. And if you want confidentiality, just say so and I'll work with you to change names, locations, and so on. Also, I'll happily include you in the book's acknowledgments if you would like.

No favorite story or experience to share? Please let me hear from you anyway. I'm always striving to increase the value readers receive from my books, and your feedback is key. Here's wishing you much customer loyalty!

Jill Griffin